SPIRITUAL VERSES

MOWLĀNĀ JALĀLODDIN BALKHI, known to the West as RUMI, was an Iranian poet of a status in Muslim civilization comparable to the greatest poets of European culture. For over 700 years he has been famed throughout the Muslim world as one of the greatest spiritual teachers of all time, and is affectionately known as Mowlānā (Turkish Mevlana) 'Our Master', or Mowlavi 'Learned Divine'. He was born in 1207 in a small town near Balkh, in the north-east of present-day Iran, but his family fled the advancing Mongol hordes of Genghis Khan, who by 1220 had devastated Balkh and Samarqand, the cities of Rumi's childhood. Around 1216 his family took him more than 2,000 miles westwards, settling eventually in Anatolia, a province that was still known as 'Rum' (Rome/Byzantium), as it had only recently been conquered by the Muslim Seljuqs. Rumi's name therefore spans cultures and continents.

Rumi's father, Bahāoddin Valad, established himself as a religious scholar in Konya, the Seljuq capital of Rum. Apart from his years spent studying in Aleppo and Damascus, Rumi remained in Konya for most of the rest of his life. Like his father, he was educated in all the religious sciences and became a scholar of a spiritual, Sufi, leaning. In his late thirties he began a profound transformation as a result of meeting a spiritual master called Shamsoddin of Tabriz, who arrived in Konya in 1244. This powerful and highly enigmatic teacher stimulated a spiritual and poetic development in Rumi until his death in 1273, though Shamsoddin himself disappeared mysteriously some twenty-five years earlier, around 1248. Near the time of their first meeting, Rumi began the composition of a body of sublime lyric poems, totalling 35,000 lines. In his later years he turned to the composition of the six volumes of his mystical masterpiece, the *Masnavi-ye Ma'navi* 'Spiritual Verses', a poem of epic proportions that is also one of the most personal and intimate works of spiritual teaching. Rumi is also loved as a saintly teacher. Following his teachings, his disciples formed the 'Mevlevi' Sufi order, best known in the West for its practice of the *sema*, the ritual practice of 'audition' to music and accompanying whirling dance of the Mevlevi dervishes.

It is in the poetry of the *Masnavi*, however, that we find the living teaching and insight of a prodigious and unrivalled spiritual understanding.

ALAN WILLIAMS was born in 1953 in Windsor, Berkshire, England. He was educated at Dulwich College, London and The Queen's College, Oxford, where he studied Classics, then Persian and Arabic, followed by a doctorate in Old and Middle Iranian Studies and Zoroastrianism at the School of Oriental and African Studies, University of London, where he has also taught. He was Lecturer in Religious Studies at the University of Sussex and is now Senior Lecturer in Comparative Religion at the University of Manchester, specializing in Iranian studies. His research has resulted in several books and articles on Iranian studies, the history of religions, comparative literature and translation studies.

RUMI

Spiritual Verses
The First Book of the
Masnavi-ye Ma'navi

Translated with an Introduction and Notes by
ALAN WILLIAMS

PENGUIN BOOKS

PENGUIN CLASSICS

Published by the Penguin Group
Penguin Books Ltd, 80 Strand, London WC2R 0RL, England
Penguin Group (USA) Inc., 375 Hudson Street, New York, New York 10014, USA
Penguin Group (Canada), 90 Eglinton Avenue East, Suite 700, Toronto, Ontario, Canada M4P 2Y3
(a division of Pearson Penguin Canada Inc.)
Penguin Ireland, 25 St Stephen's Green, Dublin 2, Ireland
(a division of Penguin Books Ltd)
Penguin Group (Australia), 250 Camberwell Road, Camberwell, Victoria 3124, Australia
(a division of Pearson Australia Group Pty Ltd)
Penguin Books India Pvt Ltd, 11 Community Centre, Panchsheel Park, New Delhi – 110 017, India
Penguin Group (NZ), 67 Apollo Drive, Mairangi Bay, Auckland 1310, New Zealand
(a division of Pearson New Zealand Ltd)
Penguin Books (South Africa) (Pty) Ltd, 24 Sturdee Avenue, Rosebank, Johannesburg 2196, South Africa

Penguin Books Ltd, Registered Offices: 80 Strand, London WC2R 0RL, England

www.penguin.com

This translation first published in Penguin Classics 2006

023

Copyright © Alan Williams, 2006
All rights reserved

The moral right of the translator has been asserted

Set in 10.25/12.25 pt PostScript Adobe Sabon
Typeset by Rowland Phototypesetting Ltd, Bury St Edmunds, Suffolk
Printed and bound in Great Britain by Clays Ltd, Elcograf S.p.A.

Except in the United States of America, this book is sold subject
to the condition that it shall not, by way of trade or otherwise, be lent,
re-sold, hired out, or otherwise circulated without the publisher's
prior consent in any form of binding or cover other than that in
which it is published and without a similar condition including this
condition being imposed on the subsequent purchaser

ISBN-13: 978-0-140-44791-0

www.greenpenguin.co.uk

Penguin Books is committed to a sustainable
future for our business, our readers and our planet.
This book is made from Forest Stewardship
Council™ certified paper.

Contents

Acknowledgements

Though Rumi's *Masnavi* is vast in scale, it is one of the most personal poems ever written. It is a revolution against imprisonment in personality and against estrangement from our true selves. I first encountered the *Masnavi* more than thirty-five years ago, in Reynold Alleyne Nicholson's (London, 1923–40) translation. It was an experience of entrancement but also perplexity. What poetry lay in the Persian, behind Nicholson's highly literal, prose, version? I ended up switching from an undergraduate degree in Classics to the study of Persian and Arabic language and literature. Now I could read the *Masnavi* in Persian, I saw just how much of the original is lost in prose translation. It was only later, in the experience of trying to teach students how the poetry of Rumi *works*, that I began to wish to do my own metrical English translations of the *Masnavi*. Initially I was asked by my editor to translate the entire work: I pointed out that that would be a long time in preparation. I resisted the idea of anthologizing: this has been done before, and, more importantly, what is lost in such story-based anthologies is the coherence of the didactic structure. So I translated the first book as faithfully as possible, and at the same time into a poetic form, namely iambic-pentameter couplets of blank verse. I have tried to keep faith both with the Persian language and with the poetic integrity of the couplet form. This first book of the *Masnavi* is the key to understanding the whole work.

Nobody who translates the *Masnavi* can step out of the long shadow cast by Nicholson's monumental work of scholarship. However, readers often find his translation difficult to understand because of its archaic language and difficult phrasing; moreover his literalness in explaining the letter of the text in prose loses the poetic coherence and power that drive the *Masnavi* forward and hold the reader's attention. Though a great deal has been written about Rumi over the last hundred years, and about his ideas in the greater context of 'Sufism', to date there has been little written in European languages about the actual *poetry* of the *Masnavi*. Scholars have laboured to translate this and other Sufi classics, but very little analytical work has been done on the literary and linguistic form of the texts. Such is the reverence many readers have for Rumi that in some cases what are intended as serious academic studies are in fact more celebrations than elucidations. This is not a new phenomenon, as for many centuries a devotional culture has surrounded the figure of Rumi: he has been seen, especially outside Iran, as a saintly sheikh at the centre of the Mevlevi tradition rather than as a poet whose works could be thought about. There are signs that this is about to change.

Rumi is both a poet and a mystic, but he is a teacher first, trying to communicate what he knows to his audience. Like all good teachers, he trusts that ultimately, when the means to go any further fail him and his voice falls silent, his students will have learnt to understand on their own. In reading the text with my students, and in reading my translations out to listeners, I began to engage with the structures of Rumi's method of communication and his poetic voice in a way that went beyond merely studying the original text privately. I was particularly fortunate to benefit from working with a master of the Persian *nay* (flute) and voice, Ostad Hosayn Omoumi, in a recitation of the *Masnavi* and musical performance in London in 2002 – an experience that made me realize that any translation must be worth reading aloud! I am deeply indebted to him, and also to the many students with whom I have read the *Masnavi* at the University of Manchester over the years. I also thank the many students and friends, too numerous to mention by name, who have commented on my draft translations. I am particularly grateful to Narguess Farzad for checking the working transcription and translation. I thank my Manchester colleagues Todd Klutz, Jacqueline Suthren Hirst and Alex Samely for their perceptive reading and discussion of my work; I am indebted to the poets Mimi Khalvati and John McAuliffe, who probably do not know how much they helped and inspired me with their interest. Lastly I thank my editors, Marcella Edwards and Andrea Belloli, for their enthusiasm, expertise and patience. My children Charles, Beatrice and Mary have been with me all through this work, and it is to them and their generation of new readers of Rumi that I dedicate this book.

Chronology

c. 1152 Birth of Rumi's father, Bahāoddin Valad

c. 1200 Bahāoddin teaching in Vakhsh

c. 1207 *30 September* Birth of Rumi in Vakhsh, second son of Mo'mene Khātun and Bahāoddin Valad

c. 1208 Bahāoddin in dispute with Qazi of Vakhsh

c. 1212 Valad family living in Samarqand; Khwārezmshāh lays siege to the city

c. 1216 Valad family leave Khorasan for Baghdad and Mecca (March)

c. 1217 Brief stays in Damascus and Malatya (summer)

c. 1218 Valad family in Aqshahr near Erzincan for four years

c. 1219 Mongols destroy Samarqand

1221 Mongols take Balkh

c. 1222 Valad family in Larende (Karaman) for seven years. Death of Rumi's mother (between 1222 and 1229)

1224 Marriage of Rumi to Gowhar Khātun

1225 Birth of Rumi's son Alāoddin

1226 Birth of Rumi's son Soltān Valad

c. 1229 Family settles permanently in Konya

1231 Death of Rumi's father

c. 1232 Arrival of Borhānoddin Mohaqqeq in Konya. Having been a student in Aleppo and Damascus (*c.* 1233–7), Rumi returns to Konya an accomplished scholar. He remains under the spiritual discipline of Borhānoddin

1241 Death of Borhānoddin

1242 Death of Rumi's wife, Gowhar Khātun

1244 *29 November* Arrival of Shamsoddin of Tabriz in Konya. Rumi takes up *samā* and composes *ghazals* (lyric poems)

1246 Shams leaves Konya for Syria (March)

1247 Shams is persuaded to return to Konya (April)

1247 Shams marries Kimiyā

1247–8 Shams disappears from Konya forever. Rumi makes at least two abortive trips to Syria or Damascus in search of him. Rumi chooses Salāhoddin Zarkub as his successor; a conspiracy to remove Salāhoddin is foiled

1258 Death of Salāhoddin. Abbasid caliphate falls to the Mongols

c. **1262** Death of Rumi's eldest son. Composition of Book I of the *Masnavi* begins

c. **1264** Composition of Book II begins; composition of Books III–VI until shortly before

1273 *17 December* Death of Rumi

Introduction

THE AUTHOR: MOWLĀNĀ JALĀLODDIN
BALKHI/MEVLANA CELALEDDIN RUMI

Just as history is written by the victors, so poets' names are
given by those who claim them. To the Western world he is
Rumi 'Westerner', though this name merely describes where
he lived during his adult life: in Rum, the formerly 'Roman'
Byzantine province of Anatolia in Asia Minor, now part of
Turkey. Turks also know him by this name, but they prefix it
with the religious honorific Mevlana 'Our Lord' and the per-
sonal name Celaleddin. Iranians call him Mowlānā Jalāloddin
or Mowlavi, but they always refer to him as Balkhi, taking into
account that he spoke and wrote in Persian and referred to
himself as coming from Balkh, a province in what Iranians
regard as ethnically part of greater Iran, though it is now on
the national borders of Tajikistan and Afghanistan.

The American scholar Franklin Lewis has published a com-
prehensive study of Rumi[1] which gives a full narrative recon-
struction of his biography to the limit of current scholarly
knowledge and attempts to sort out fact from myth and legend.
Lewis discusses Sufi hagiography and the mythical Rumi of the
past and present. His energetic research in all the available
original sources has allowed him to paint a vivid picture of
Rumi, real and imagined, then and now. The chronology on
pages x–xi sets out the principal events of Rumi's life.

Jalāloddin Rumi was born on 30 September 1207 the second
son of Mo'mene Khātun, wife of Bahāoddin Valad, a learned

religious scholar and preacher in his late fifties. Rumi was born in a small town, Vakhsh,[2] in Tajikistan, 150 miles east of Balkh and 300 miles west of the borders of China. Bahāoddin Valad moved his family north-west to the ancient city of Samarqand when Jalāloddin was a very young child (between 1210 and 1212); the family remained there for four or five years. Samarqand would be completely destroyed by Genghis Khan in 1219; whether out of prescience or because of local political instability, Bahāoddin stayed there only a short time before moving his family westwards, around 1216, on a journey of more than 2,000 miles. They travelled through Nayshapur to Baghdad and Mecca, then on to Damascus and Aleppo in Syria. The family finally settled in the capital of Rum, Konya, around 1229, where Rumi's father, by now in his late seventies, gained a position in a *madrase* (college), having won the favour of the Seljuk sultan Alāoddin Kay Qobād. In 1224, at the age of seventeen, Rumi married Gowhar Khātun, also seventeen and from Samarqand. They had two sons, Alāoddin (b. 1225) and Soltān Valad (b. 1226). At his father's death in 1231, Rumi took over his post at the *madrase*, although he himself was only a young man of twenty-four who had not yet completed his studies. One of his father's most senior and devoted pupils, Borhānoddin Mohaqqeq, soon arrived at the *madrase* and became Rumi's scholarly and spiritual mentor. Borhānoddin despatched Rumi to Syria to complete his education, first in Aleppo, then in Damascus, leaving his young wife and two sons behind in Konya for five years (1233–7), during which time he studied the traditional curriculum of all the religious sciences, including law and jurisprudence. Rumi is thought to have heard lectures by the great mystical philosopher and visionary Muhyiddin Ibn 'Arabi and his pupil Sadroddin Qonavi in Damascus. Rumi's spiritual education began in earnest, however, when he returned to Konya in 1237 and Borhānoddin engaged him in rigorous ascetic practices. Borhānoddin died in 1241, as did Rumi's wife, Gowhar Khātun, in the following year. Soon after, he married a young widow, Kerrā Khātun, with whom he had at least two children.

The most intense period of Rumi's life began in 1244, when

he met Shamsoddin of Tabriz, the great teacher who was to
'cook and burn' Rumi's soul. Shamsoddin was both an im-
passioned mystical adept and a deeply learned scholar of the
Shāfeʻi school of law. He was in his sixties when he arrived in
Konya and remains the most enigmatic and powerful figure
in Rumi's biography. Rumi spent a great deal of time with
Shamsoddin in the four years before the latter mysteriously
disappeared in 1247/8: Shamsoddin's influence helped to trans-
form Rumi from a locally esteemed spiritual scholar and writer
of fine lyric verses into a poet and teacher of world stature. The
hagiographical and devotional tradition down to the present
day has feasted on speculation as to what happened between
the two companions, and only recently, with the publication of
Shamsoddin's *Maqālāt* in Persian and English, have scholars
become able to consider properly the relationship and teaching
shared by the two men.[3] Rumi was, it seems, willing to abandon
his reputation for the sake of the spiritual companionship he
shared with Shamsoddin. Shamsoddin apparently recognized
early on that Rumi was destined to exceed his own spiritual
attainment and arrive at the goal of the Sufi life by becoming a
Perfect Man (*ensān-e kāmel*). In Sufi understanding, a Perfect
Man is one in whom all selfishness has died and who lives in
complete union with God, embodying divine attributes in his
perfected human nature. Shamsoddin disappeared from Konya
twice, briefly in 1246 and, two years later, forever.[4]

Rumi's life after Shamsoddin was spent in spiritual enterprise,
writing and teaching, and working closely with two com-
panions, first Salāhoddin, then Hosāmoddin, to whom, succes-
sively, the practical running of the *madrase* was given over.
Rumi's relationship with both men was intense and reciprocally
respectful. Hosāmoddin is said to have suggested to Rumi that
he compose the *Masnavi*, and it is addressed to him throughout
as he wrote down most, if not all, of it from Rumi's dictation.
This process is thought to have been begun in 1261/2. After the
first book was completed, there was an interval of nearly a year,
occasioned, it seems, by the sudden death of Hosāmoddin's
wife. There is much speculation as to exactly when Rumi
composed each of the remaining five books, but it is generally

agreed that he completed the work before his death on 17
December 1273.[5]

In addition to the six books of the *Masnavi* and the com-
pendious *Divān* of thousands of lyric poems, Rumi left behind
him three works in Persian prose. The work traditionally
known as the *Fihe Mā Fih* 'In It What Is in It' is a collection
of semi-formal talks which were transcribed by others rather
than penned by Rumi himself as a literary text.[6] The *Majāles-e
Sab'e* 'Seven Sermons' survive as examples of Rumi's preaching
style, but to date no complete English translation has been
published.[7] Finally there is the *Maktubāt* 'Letters', written in
a more sophisticated literary style: these also have not been
published in translation.[8]

THE *MASNAVI*

The *Masnavi-ye Ma'navi*, the 'Spiritual Couplets' or 'Inner
Verses', is possibly the longest single-authored 'mystical' poem
ever written. In the most recent Iranian edition of the text[9]
it contains 25,683 couplets. But the 'couplet' (Persian *bayt*,
masnavi) is in fact double the length of most European lines,
so the poem is equivalent to one of well over 50,000 lines:
almost as many as Homer's *Iliad* and *Odyssey* together, twice
as many as Dante's *Divina commedia* and five times as many
as Milton's *Paradise Lost*. There had been *Masnavi*s before
Rumi's – most famously Faridoddin Attār's *Manteqottayr* 'The
Conference of the Birds' and *Elāhināme* 'The Divine Book',
and Sanā'i's *Hadiqe al-Haqiqe* 'The Walled Garden of Truth'
– but none of these is considered to rise to quite the sublime
heights of Rumi's *Masnavi*.

The *Masnavi* is a spiritual masterpiece of the Persian Sufi
tradition. It teaches progress to the ultimate goal of the Sufi
path – that is, union with God. God is known primarily through
love and is therefore approached as the divine beloved. Rumi's
principal theme, and in fact his method of working on the
transformation of the human heart, is announced in the very
first couplet of the work, which commands the listener to hear

the story of separations. Separation is the human predicament: love is both the cause of, and the solution to, this predicament. Human love forms attachment to the object of love, which inevitably results in the experience of separation from it. Then, if this transitory love is lost, occasioned by a failing heart or a failing of health, can love be given and felt anymore? The cure is divine love, which is not to be found in other transitory things, not even in the image of a transcendent beloved – for to do so would be to return to things which can be lost and forgotten. Right from the beginning, in the first story of the king and the slave-girl, Rumi leads the reader into the complexities of human love and separation, and discloses the action of divine love when it is earnestly sought and asked for. As the *Masnavi* progresses, the couplets each convey a *nokte*, or 'point of intelligence', that penetrates and lightens the sense of separation felt by the soul, which is dominated by the *nafs*, the egoistical and illusory condition of 'self-regard'. The goal of Sufi teaching is to die to self-regard and live in consciousness of the divine.

The *Masnavi* is also a work of great poetic art. The two categories, spiritual teaching and poetry, are *not* different but one and the same. As one Iranian critic has put it, discussing Rumi's lyrics, '. . . the poems themselves are the mystical experience and the meaning, not a container holding them.'[10] Rumi's skill as a spiritual teacher is visible in the poetic structure of the *Masnavi*. He layers his writing. He begins a story and then quickly moves into telling another story within that story, and another one within that. Often he creates a speech within a speech, and another one within that. Layering is a feature of the deeper structure of his composition. The *Masnavi* is a didactic poem bound together by the poet's own voice, which is itself composed of many voices moving between the high and low registers of its range, just as the *nay*, with which Rumi begins the work, ranges through its several octaves.

The *Masnavi* has no framing plot. Its many stories are all *a plot*, i.e. a strategy, the device and the means to hook imagination. It takes the multifariousness of life as its raw material: all states of existence, from rocks and plants to insects and animals, and all of humankind, from villains and harlots to men of state, kings, saints, angels and prophets. Characters are drawn from all occupations and situations. The tone ranges from popular stories from the bazaar to fables and timeless moral tales, as well as quotations from the stories of the prophet Mohammed and from Quranic revelation itself. Rumi's art is, however, subversive: he subverts expectation and understanding of experience in order to challenge ordinary ideas of the way things happen, and even the worldly notion of causality itself. Folk and popular culture, politics and manners, tell us about how things work in the world: Rumi takes the strands of life and weaves them together, not in order to make common sense but to make a *new* sense based on an understanding of things as they truly are in their inner or spiritual reality. As the folklorist Margaret M. A. Mills has put it, '. . . his poetry presents a holistic flow, a possibility of reading all experience in an enriched mystical way.'[11] The stories Rumi tells are not for entertainment, nor even for moral improvement. He hints that he does not fully believe in the real substantiality of his own characters: they are fictive – but fictions with a purpose.

Why, then, tell stories? Rumi gives us the answer in *Masnavi* l. 2636:

> *If spiritual explanation were enough,*
> *creation of the world were all in vain.*

Margaret Mills explains this dense couplet:

> Rumi ... offers a wealth of commentary, explanation, and interpretation, so much so that a story can seem overwhelmed in sheer volume of words by its interpretations, yet the narrative examples are nonetheless necessary to the process of mystical enlightenment, just as experience of the fragmented, separated created world is necessary in approaching Union.[12]

She adds, with a touch of Rumi's own turn of phrase: 'The poet narrates for the same purpose as the Deity creates.'

In a conventional story, the narrative sequence followed is:

problem/theme → *complication* → *resolution.*

For Rumi this sequence is illusory, arising from a self-centred view of the world that constructs definite images and fixed stereotypes, just as the *nafs* conceives itself as fixed and permanent in a fixed world. Rumi uses many realistic characters in his stories, but he does not treat them as fixed realities. Personas are masks which are worn, taken off and thrown away. Imagery and symbols are not fixed either. The sea means one thing now, then something altogether different. Image, representation – everything is mutable. The only image that has a constancy is the sun, though Rumi reminds us that he speaks of what is *beyond* the merely physical sun. There is a spiritual purpose in his use of imagery that is possible only in the heightened reality of poetic discourse. As the *Masnavi* progresses, Rumi builds into his audience's imagination a sense of freedom from control by the imagery, paradoxically by flooding their minds with imagery. He insists on the realization of the reality that lies beyond appearances: through his poetry, he discovers the nature of meaning.

To whom is the poetry of the *Masnavi* addressed? One of its most striking features is its psychological immediacy: the whole poem is addressed to the second-person 'you' of the human reader, and to the 'You' of the divine presence – though often the two are implicitly linked. Rumi addresses 'you' from the first line, when he commands 'Listen.' The stories that run through the work are told in the third person (i.e. never in the first person) about characters from folklore, scripture and myth, but then Rumi's gaze returns to 'you', addressed affectionately as 'my son', 'father', 'dear reader', 'lad' etc., as, for example, in the gently chastening line from the beginning of the poem (l. 19):

> *Be free, my son, and break your chains asunder!*
> *How long will you be slave to gold and silver?*

As the *Masnavi* progresses, Rumi explores the nature of his audience's identity, as it is his purpose to transform them from being obsessively fascinated by appearances into those who know God. Rumi's voice, directed intensely at 'you/You',[13] is intended to change his audience as they respond to his many voices in this epic journey of enchantment and disenchantment.

THE QUESTION OF DESIGN AND
THE VOICES OF THE AUTHOR

Each of the six books of the *Masnavi* is believed to be focused on one of six themes of progressive development along the Sufi path. Sufism, as the gnostic, mystical interpretation of Islam, teaches that the spiritual path involves embarking on a course of discipline by which one purifies the *ruh* (immortal spirit) of pollution by worldly desires. The purpose of this is to realize union of the spirit with God through surrendering, effacement and, ultimately, dissolution of the concupiscent *nafs*. Indeed this problem of the *nafs* seems to be the main theme addressed in the first book.

The six books are also thought to fall into three groups of two, and each pair is concerned with a major theme.[14] According to this schema:

Books 1 and 2: are principally concerned with the *nafs*, the lower, carnal self, and its self-deception and evil tendencies. The one who follows the Sufi path can resist such evil, but the *nafs* is identical with the devil, i.e. the constant tempter of our true nature.

Books 3 and 4: have as their principal themes Reason and Knowledge. Reason and Knowledge are personified by the figure of the Biblical and Quranic prophet Moses, and are opposed by illusory Imagination, which is personified by Pharaoh. The angelic aspect of our nature replaces the diabolical.

Books 5 and 6: are united by the idea that man must first deny his own existence in order to affirm that of God. Passing away from selfhood, in Arabic and Persian *fanā*, is linked to the heart, the spirit and light.[15]

This schema conforms generally to the overall structure of the Sufi path. There is, however, a dynamic as well as a thematic structure to the poem. Rumi switches his 'point of view'[16] in order to draw the reader under the influence of his imaginative enchantment. This takes the form of a change of voice and shifting of the mode of speaking in a manner that is some-times sudden, at other times so subtle that it goes almost unnoticed.

There is a sevenfold framework of the *Masnavi*'s principal 'voices':

1. *authorial*
2. *story-telling*
3. *analogical*
4. *of speech and dialogue of characters*
5. *of moral reflection*
6. *of spiritual discourse*
7. *of hiatus*

1. *The Authorial Voice*

Rumi begins the *Masnavi* with its most famous passage, known as the *nayname*, or 'Song of the Reed' (ll. 1–35)[17] in his auth-orial voice. This passage resonates with the authority of the *pir* or sheikh, the Sufi teacher: it is majestic, grandfatherly and gently chastising. All Persian poets use this voice occasionally, especially as an aside to the reader in the middle of telling a story. For Rumi, however, the authorial voice is pivotal and frequently used. The person addressed is *You, God*, and *you, all of humankind*. Passages written from this point of view are intensely serious, often wistful and even melancholic and minatory. This is the voice that introduces and ends stories and books, as here when Rumi is just about to begin the first story of the first book (ll. 34–5):

> *Do you know why your mirror tells of nothing?*
>   *The rust has not been taken from its surface.'*
>   *Reflect upon this story, my dear friends;*
>   *its meaning is the essence of our state.*

In the very next line the voice suddenly changes to the story-telling voice.[18]

2. *The Story-telling Voice*

The most obvious indicators of the change of voice or point of view to that of story-telling are (1) change of verb tense from present to past, and (2) introduction of third-person characters in a narrative. The story-telling voice is usually lively and witty, colourful and dramatic. The main story is often interrupted by either a sub-story or various of the other voices described below. Some stories therefore take many hundreds of lines to finish because of Rumi's constant self-interruption. For example, the story of the Bedouin and his wife, which is begun at l. 2255, is not completed until some 700 lines later, having been interrupted by numerous apparent deviations and three separate sub-stories. The story-telling voice is also constantly interrupted by a very characteristic device that is so much a standard feature of Rumi's compositional style that it can be seen as a voice in its own right, namely the analogical voice.

3. *The Analogical Voice*

The analogical voice appears to interrupt the narration of a story: in fact it is a pivotal stage in the poet's development and elucidation of a story. Usually the analogy addresses a point made in the previous line. It instills wit and clarity through an example or examples in a series of 'one-liners' (e.g. the succession of nine analogies in eleven couplets, ll. 2797–807). The following lines, taken from the beginning of the first story, illustrate how Rumi explains the meaning of l. 40 by turning to two analogies, then returning to the story in l. 43.

> *Now when he'd bought her and he had enjoyed her,*
> *by heaven's fate the slave-girl turned to sickness.*
> *A man possessed an ass but had no saddle;*
> *he got a saddle – wolves had got the ass!*
> *Another had a pitcher but no water;*
> *he found the water, but he broke the pitcher!*
> *The king called in the doctors all around,*
> *'The lives of both of us are in your hands.*

The switch to analogy may best be recognized by the change of context from that specified in the story to one of a generalized, proverbial context. The tense may remain the same in the switch, as in the above example, or it may change from past to present, as in the mid-couplet switch, from story to analogy, in l. 107:

> *Her pain was not from black or yellow bile:*
> *the scent of wood is sent up in its smoke.*

From the analogical voice the poet will either return to story-telling or, just as often, move to the fourth or fifth type of voice.

Rumi's use of analogy is fundamental not only to his compositional style but also to his spiritual teaching. According to Sufi teaching, the world is a multitude of reflections of the attributes, or divine names, of God. Phenomena are not real in themselves, only in so far as they constitute finite examples, or likenesses, of their infinite creator. Therefore it is part of Rumi's teaching to coax his readers out of the misapprehension that the world is made up of a multitude of separate selves apart from God and into the knowledge that all reality subsists only in relation to God. The Persian/Arabic word for 'example' and 'likeness' (*mesl*, pl. *amsāl*) is also the word for 'proverbial saying', of which Rumi's analogies are (often freshly minted) coinages. The lively shifting out of conventional narrative into sometimes oblique and challenging analogies therefore has a didactic purpose: constantly to reawaken the reader to the awareness that while meaning may be expressed in story form, and through analogical imagery, these stories and analogies are ultimately interchangeable and disposable, as meaning transcends language.

4. *The Voice of Speech and Dialogue of Characters*

Rumi often tells his stories through speeches and dialogues by and between his characters. It might be thought that these are just part of normal story-telling. In the *Masnavi*, however, they have a voice of their own: a poetic device that makes it impossible for the reader to see when the speech of a character begins and ends, and when the poet moves out of story-telling into other voices. Medieval Persian used no punctuation to indicate speech, and there are no other 'stage directions' to make it clear who is speaking. Having put the reader's imagination into the harness of a story, the voice of speech and dialogue enables the poet to wear and discard multiple personas and, by literary sleight of hand, to leave readers feeling that they are still *in* the story when in fact Rumi has moved into a directly moralistic or spiritually didactic voice.

5. *The Moral Reflection*

Rumi's voice of moral reflection is in some respects similar to his original authorial voice and is identifiable by its prescriptive and proscriptive statements, and by frequent use of the imperative mood. The sentiments are often inspired by quotations from the Quran and from hadith stories of events in the life of the prophet Mohammed. There is a logical, thematic connection between the sequence of verses in this voice: it is 'linear' and 'horizontal' in that it is addressed to the human 'you', the reader, in second-person relation to the poet.

6. *The Spiritual Discourse*

The spiritual discourse of the *Masnavi* is, like the analogical voice, one in which Rumi excels. It almost always follows on from a moral reflection, as a sudden development from it. However, it is addressed not to humankind but to God on a 'vertical' trajectory of flight from this limited world to absorption in the ecstatic state beyond. This voice is characterized by fast-flowing imaginative associations, as if each couplet is no sooner pronounced than it is expendable and replaced. Indeed each couplet has the quality of an impassioned cry or plea rather than a statement, as if the poet is drowning or soaring to express the passion he feels for the divine Beloved. A good example of how Rumi leads the reader from the simplicity of a story and the sobriety of moral reflection to experience the passion of ecstatic flight with him is the famous story of the merchant and the parrot.[19]

7. *Hiatus*

The 'voice' of hiatus signals the limit of spiritual discourse and the return to silence.[20] Hiatus questions the wisdom of continuing to speak, having reached the very brink of incoherence because of the unattainability, or inexpressability, of what the poet is trying to evoke. Sometimes Rumi says that he cannot say more because of the reader's incapacity to understand, as in l. 18 of the very opening of the poem:

> *The raw can't grasp the state of one who's cooked,*
> *so this discussion must be brief – farewell!*

Accordingly, the *Masnavi* should have ended here, 25,000 couplets early, but this is a rhetorical device. Sometimes Rumi wishes for silence to reign, as being more expressive of 'inner' truths than sensual words (a sentiment that is articulated most eloquently in Book I by the wicked vizier in ll. 569–81). Sometimes Rumi says that he does not *wish* to say more (because beyond this, things should remain hidden), as in ll. 142–3 at the conclusion of the passage quoted below; sometimes he is *forbidden* by higher powers to say more. As Fatemeh Keshavarz explains, at times in the lyric poems divine possessiveness 'forbids the poetic discourse from publishing the secrets of love'; she refers to instances when Rumi is told, or even physically forced, to desist from uttering more.[21] Sometimes he desists of

his own free will as his own mind has become distracted or
tired (as at the end of Book I). However, after the hiatus, there
is usually a return to story-telling. In the passage quoted below,
we see the shadow of silence approaching in two pairs of coup-
lets – ll. 112–13 and 130–31 – until it finally reigns at ll. 142–3.

Rumi's writing style is dynamic and polyphonic. As the *Masnavi*
unfolds, there is an increase in the speed and subtlety with
which the different voices change and overlap, and passages
are formed in combinations of several voices. Once the modern
reader has become familiar with the seven principal ones, he
or she will be able to keep up with the faster-flowing, more
complex voicings of the poem as it develops. In order to illus-
trate the whole schema in action, and the process of compli-
cation by the combining of voices, I shall quote one of the most
dynamic passages from Book I (ll. 102–43) and annotate each
couplet with reference to voices 1–7, or to a combination of
voices using the symbol /. The two speakers in the dialogue are
identified as 4a and 4b:

The King Takes the Physician to the Sick Girl to
See Her Condition

He told the tale of illness and the patient,   2
    then seated him beside the sickly girl.

He saw her pallor, checked her pulse and urine,   2
    and listened to her symptoms and her functions.

He said, 'None of the drugs they have prescribed   4
    will build her up – they have destroyed her health.

105   They did not understand her inner state: 4
    I seek God's refuge from what they contrive.'

He saw the pain and opened up the secret   2
    but did not tell the king and kept it hidden.

Her pain was not from black or yellow bile: 2
    the scent of wood is sent up in its smoke.   3

He saw in her distress her broken heart: 2
    her body healthy but her heart in chains.

The sign of being in love's an aching heart;   5
    there is no suffering like the suffering heart.

The lover's suffering's like no other suffering: 6   110
    love is the astrolabe of God's own mysteries.

No matter whether love is of this world   6
    or of the next, it steals us to that world.

Whatever words I say to explain this love,   6/7
    when I arrive at Love, I am ashamed.

Though language gives a clear account of love,   6/7
    yet love beyond all language is the clearer.

The pen had gone at breakneck speed in writing,   6/3
    but when it came to love it split in two.

The explaining mind lies like an ass in mud,   6   115
    for love alone explains love and the lover.

The sun alone is proof of all things solar: 6
    if you need proof, do not avert your face.

Although the shadow gives a hint of it,   6
    the sun bestows the light of life at all times.

The shadow brings you sleep like bedtime stories,   6/3
    and when the sun comes up, 'the moon is cloven.'

There's nothing like this sun in all the world,   6
    the spiritual Sun's eternal – never setting.

Although the outward sun may be unique,   6   120
    still you can contemplate another like it.

And yet the sun from which the aether comes   6
    has no external or internal likeness.

How can imagining contain His essence,   6
    and likeness of Him come into conception?

When news came of the face of Shamsoddin   6/1
    the sun in highest heaven hung its head.

It's necessary, since his name is with us,   6/1
    to give some hint of his munificence.

Upon this breath my soul has scorched my skirt   6/1   125
    and caught the perfume of the shirt of Joseph,

Saying, 'After all our years of comradeship,   6/4a
    explain one of the states of ecstasy,

So that the mind and sight and spirit grow   6/4a
    a hundredfold, and heaven and earth may laugh.'

'Do not impose on me, for I am dead: 6/4b
    my senses dulled, I cannot take things in.

For all that's said by one not yet awake,	6/4b/5
in modesty or boasting, is illicit.	

130
What can I say – no vein of mine is sober –	6/4b/7
to explain that Friend who is beyond a friend?	
But now, leave off until some other time	6/4b/7
talk of this parting and this bleeding heart.'	
He said, 'Give me to eat, for I am hungry,	6/4a
and quick! Time is indeed a cutting sword.	
The Sufi is the son of Time, my friend;	6/4a
tomorrow's no condition of the Way.	
You, are you not indeed yourself a Sufi?	6/4a
Nothing will come from such procrastination.'	

135
I told him, 'Better to conceal God's mysteries	6/4b
and pay attention to what's in the tale!	
It is to be preferred that lovers' secrets	6/4b
are spoken of in tales of other folk.'	
He said, 'Tell it unveiled, the naked truth!	6/4a
The declaration's better than the secret.	
Hold back the veil and speak the naked truth!	6/4a
I don't lie down with clothes on with my lover.'	6/4a/3
I said, 'If He were naked in your sight	6/4b
you'd not survive, nor would your breast nor	
waist.	

140
Ask for your wish, but ask with moderation:	6/4b
a blade of straw cannot support a mountain.	6/4b/3
The Sun, by which this world's illuminated,	6/4b
will burn the lot if it comes any closer!	
Don't seek out trials and griefs and shedding	
blood!	6/4b/7
From now on, no more talk of Shams of Tabriz!'	
There is no end to this. Begin again,	7/1
and go recite the ending of this tale.	

In this passage, all seven voices are used successively and in combination, in a drama that unfolds and becomes so intense that it must be silenced. When T. S. Eliot distinguished between 'dramatic blank verse and blank verse employed for epical, philosophical, meditative and idyllic purposes', he was making a point about how 'the dependence of verse upon speech is much more direct in dramatic poetry than in any other.'[22] In this sense, Rumi's *Masnavi* is written in dramatic verse and resembles a Shakespeare play since, as Eliot puts it, 'in dramatic verse the poet is speaking in one character after another . . . It remains the language not of one person, but of a world of persons.'[23] The *Masnavi* is dramatic, conversational, written in the spoken registers of the day and multivocal/polyphonic, so it sounds like a company of actors or musicians performing on a stage. It represents a culminating stage in Rumi's development as a poet.

Shamsoddin taught Rumi that intellectual knowledge and aesthetic subtlety are not the goals of the Sufi path. The task of the Sufi teacher is to give instruction in how to be free from psychological imprisonment in the self-regarding, carnal self. Rumi takes his readers to the edges of their imaginations, and thence to silence. Metaphor and imagery in the stories, analogies, speeches and discourses are the means of transport from this world in a flight of spiritual ecstasy to the world of *ma'na* – 'inner meaning' or 'spirit' – and back again. Most importantly, Rumi encourages his readers that the *nafs* is to be recognized for what it is, and abandoned.

THE MUSIC AND METRE OF
THE *MASNAVI*

It is thought that Rumi was a great musician and a master of tonality, melody, rhythm and rhyme: the *Masnavi* has a unique musicality, not least because of the metre, or rhythm of the couplet. The constant metre is 'the apocopated six-fold running metre' in which each verse (*bayt* lit. 'house') is a couplet (*masnavi*) of two eleven-syllable half-lines, or hemistiches (*mesrā* lit. 'leaf of a folding door'), each of which breaks up into three rhythmic units ('feet' in classical Western prosody). Hence each couplet has the following pattern of long and short syllables (where the symbol ∪ denotes a short and – denotes a long syllable, reading from left to right):

$$– ∪ – – / – ∪ – – / – ∪ – \quad – ∪ – – / – ∪ – – / – ∪ –$$

In Western musical notation, the rhythm of the basic unit of the *Masnavi*, namely – ∪ – –, is *crotchet, quaver, crotchet, crotchet*, which is an off-beat, syncopated pattern, one quaver short of a regular, walking rhythm, i.e. 4/4. In Persian music, the *masnavi* metre is felt to have a seductive lilt to it when slow, and to be enrapturing when fast, inspiring bodily movement such as dance. The ethnomusicologist Regula Burckhardt Qureshi, writing about the *masnavi* metre in Sufi music, says that this rhythm is considered a hard metre, the most mystical one for *qawwali* (religious singing), in South Asian Islamic culture.[24] It seems not to pause, tending to move the listener out of the rhythms of ordinary consciousness: it is believed to induce ecstasy in performer and listener alike, similar to the complex rhythms set up in performances of the Sufi rite of *zekr-e allāh* (collective remembrance of God).

RHYME AND RHYTHM IN
THE TRANSLATION

In this translation I have tried to translate the couplets into pairs of blank (unrhymed) iambic pentameters, i.e. a metre of five feet of light and heavy stress ∪ –:

$$∪ – / ∪ – / ∪ – / ∪ – / ∪ – / (∪) \quad ∪ – / ∪ – / ∪ – / ∪ – / ∪ – / (∪)$$

The half-line may have an eleventh (light) syllable, i.e. the couplet can have twenty, twenty-one, or twenty-two syllables. As this metre is most familiar to the English ear from Shakespeare's tragedies, I found it to be the best equivalent of the *ramal* (running) metre of the Persian *Masnavi*. As an accentual-stress metre, it lacks the syncopation of the quantitative syllabic

Persian metre, but it has the advantages of being approximately the same syllabic length as the Persian and of being the proven metre of English dramatic verse.

John Milton thought rhyme to be 'the Invention of a barbarous Age, to set off wretched matter and lame Meeter' and thus freed his *Paradise Lost* from what he called 'the troublesom and modern bondage of Riming'.[25] In the past, many translators of Persian poetry have been tempted to have a go at rhyming their translations because classical Persian poetry always uses rhyme. However, rhyme – namely the use of parallel sound patterns between lines, or parts of lines, of poetry – varies greatly in its nature and function from language to language. In the English heroic couplet[26] rhyme usually occurs only in the last one or two syllables. The rhyme scheme of the *Masnavi* is commonly perceived by Western translators to consist primarily in the end-rhyme of each *mesrā'* of the couplet, in the scheme *a a, b b, c c* . . . In fact, Rumi's use of rhyme is a great deal more complex than this. He frequently uses rhyme between the two hemistiches at the beginning, middle and end. Rumi rhymes anything from one to all eleven syllables of each *mesrā'*, or he rhymes groups of two, three, four and more syllables. In Persian this kind of rhyming is a much more flexible and powerful poetic device than the end-rhyme of the English heroic couplet. Rumi uses simple and complex sequences to intensify the power of what he is saying; some of his more definitive and sonorous utterances are given the treatment of 'total rhyme', i.e. where there is a parallelism of form and meaning through use of sound patterns. One example (l. 603) can illustrate this (and also how the translator has to resort to devices other than rhyme in order to convey the intensity of the point – here by chiasmus):

> mā chu nāyim o navā dar mā ze tust
> mā chu kuhim o sadā dar mā ze tust

> We're like the reed-flute and our sound is from You;
> our echoes are from You – we are like mountains.

This was reason enough *not* to rhyme the English translation, but there are two equally important considerations for the translator: first, translating with end-rhymes invariably requires a sacrifice of meaning where the Persian sense must be distorted into a rhyming English word, and hence all too often mistranslated; second, for a modern audience, English end-rhyming generally infantilizes (the nursery rhyme) or ridicules (as in eighteenth-century satirical rhyming) except in the hands of an accomplished poet. These effects are quite the opposite of what Rumi's use of rhyme achieves.

NOTES

1. Franklin D. Lewis, *Rumi Past and Present East and West: The Life, Teachings and Poetry of Jalal al-Din Rumi* (Oxford: Oneworld, 2000).
2. *Ibid.*, pp. 47ff.
3. The text is edited by Mohammed 'Ali Movahhed (*Maqālāt-e Shams-e Tabrizi* (Tehran: Entesharat-e Khwarazmi, 1990)) and translated by William C. Chittick (*Me and Rumi The Autobiography of Shams-i Tabriz* (Louisville: Fons Vitae, 2004)).
4. See further Lewis, *Rumi Past and Present*, chap. 4. Lewis and others are now sceptical about the traditional theory, which developed in the century after Rumi, that Shamsoddin was murdered by the poet's jealous disciples. Rumi never mentions any such murder plot. It is just as likely that Shamsoddin had finished what he had to do with Rumi, the latter having now reached forty, the age of spiritual maturity, and so removed himself from the scene to enable Rumi to continue to develop.
5. See further Lewis, *Rumi Past and Present*, chap. 5.
6. Translated by A. J. Arberry (*The Discourses of Rumi* (New York: Samuel Weiser, 1972)), and also by Wheeler Thackston (*Signs of the Unseen* (Putney, VT: Threshold Books, 1994)).
7. One of these is introduced and translated in Lewis, *Rumi Past and Present*, pp. 130–33; there are excerpts from various sermons in William C. Chittick, *The Sufi Path of Knowledge* (Albany: State University of New York Press, 1989).
8. These letters prove that, as Lewis says, '. . . Rumi kept very busy helping family members and administering a community of disciples that had grown up around him. It should dispel the notion . . . that he lived a reclusive life withdrawn from the affairs of

the world after the disappearance of Shams' (*Rumi Past and Present*, p. 295).

9. *Masnavi*, ed. Mohammad Este'lami, 7 vols., 2nd edn (Tehran: Zavvar, 2000–2001).

10. Fatemeh Keshavarz, *Reading Mystical Lyric: The Case of Jalal al-Din Rumi* (Columbia, SC: University of South Carolina Press, 1998), p. 19.

11. Margaret M. A. Mills, 'Folk Tradition in the *Masnavi* and the *Masnavi* in Folk Tradition', in A. Banani, R. Hovannisian and G. Sabagh, *Poetry and Mysticism in Islam: The Heritage of Rumi* (Cambridge: Cambridge University Press, 1994), pp. 136–77.

12. *Ibid.*, p. 141.

13. The twentieth-century philosopher Martin Buber famously explored the philosophical and spiritual potential of the relationship 'I-You' (*Ich-Du*) in his *I and Thou*. Buber saw human beings as having two 'I's, defined by two 'basic words' (German *Grundwort*): 'I-It', and the other, 'I-You'. Two brief, somewhat aphoristic, quotations from the early part of Buber's work express his sense of the all-important difference between these two aspects of the human self: 'The basic word I-You can only be spoken with one's whole being. The basic word I-It can never be spoken with one's whole being.' 'The world as experience belongs to the basic word I-It. The basic word I-You establishes the world of relation.' (*I and Thou* (Edinburgh: T & T Clarke, 1970), pp. 54, 56); *Ich und Du* (Heidelberg: Verlag Lambert Schneider, 1979), pp. 9, 12.)

14. Julian Baldick has observed that the plan of the *Masnavi* is similar to that of the *Elāhināme* 'Book of the Divine' of Faridoddin Attār. There the Spirit (*ruh*) is invoked as God's caliph, or representative, who has six sons: the lower soul, the devil, the intellect, knowledge, poverty and the realization of God's uniqueness. See J. Baldick, 'Persian Sufi Poetry up to the Fifteenth Century', in *Handbuch der Orientalistik*, vol. 4/2/2 (Leiden: E. J. Brill, 1981), pp. 112–32.

15. Recently Simon Weightman and Seyed Ghahreman Safavi-Homani have been working on a theory of the ring-composition of the *Masnavi*'s entire structure. See S. G. Safavi-Homani, 'Love the Whole and Not the Part : An Investigation of the Rhetorical Structure of Book One of the Mathnawī of Jalāl al-Dīn Rūmī', PhD thesis, SOAS, University of London, 2003. In this theory, thematic similarities, or the mentioning of certain names or themes, both in different parts of the individual books and across

all of them, are taken as evidence that the *Masnavi* was composed in a structure of symmetry based upon parallelism and chiasmus. Following Nicholson's edition and translation, Weightman and Safavi-Homani have counted the sections created by the text headings (most likely a later addition) and have found correspondences in which the beginnings and the ends of sections, of all six books and, ultimately, of the entire book fold upon one another. They have concluded that the work's meaning is buried centrally and esoterically in such an enfolded structure. It will be possible to evaluate this theory properly only when it is published.

16. I.e. in the sense used by the Russian Formalist critics, e.g. Boris Uspensky in *A Poetics of Composition: The Structure of the Artistic Text and Typology of a Compositional Form*, trans. Valentina Zavarin and Susan Wittig (Berkeley and Los Angeles: University of California Press, 1973).

17. A similar voice is heard in a comparable passage at a central point of the first book, 1888–922.

18. In this first book of the *Masnavi*, the best examples of a sustained authorial voice are in the opening *naynāme* (1–35) and in a reflective passage of identical length at 1888–922.

19. 1557 onwards. The story begins and leads into a speech by a parrot (1559 b), then into a speech within a speech (1563) as the parrot dictates to the merchant what he should say to the parrots of India. There is a moral reflection in 1569, then a speech within a speech continues in an impassioned melancholy, until, after another reflection in 1574, it seems to change into the voice of Rumi's own spiritual discourse as he meditates for ten couplets on the exquisite oppression of the divine Beloved (1575–84). The first five couplets are addressed in the second person to the divine You, but then the tone changes again as He is addressed in the third person until we reach an ecstatic utterance in 1584.

20. For a thoughtful discussion of Rumi and silence in his lyric poems, see Fatemeh Keshavarz, 'Rumi's Poetics of Silence', in *Reading Mystical Lyric*, chap. 4.

21. Keshavarz, *Reading Mystical Lyric*, p. 58.

22. T. S. Eliot, 'The Music of Poetry', in *Selected Prose* (London: Penguin Books, 1953), pp. 60–61.

23. *Ibid.*, p. 61.

24. Regula Burckhardt Qureshi, *Sufi Music of India and Pakistan* (Cambridge: Cambridge University Press, 1987), p. 29.

25. From Milton's own Edition of *Paradise Lost*, l. 1669.

26. Used to witty effect by Afkham Darbandi and Dick Davis in their translation of Attar's *Conference of the Birds* (London: Penguin Books, 1984) and, recently, by Jawid Mojaddedi in his translation of the first book of the *Masnavi* (Oxford: Oxford World Classics, 2004).

Further Reading

For a more comprehensive bibliography of printed and electronic material on Rumi, see Lewis, *Rumi Past and Present*, pp. 638ff., 651ff.

EDITIONS OF THE *MASNAVI*

Masnavi, ed. Mohammad Este'lami, 7 vols., 2nd edn (Tehran: Zavvar, 2000–2001)

Mathnawi of Jalalu'ddin Rumi, ed. and trans. Reynold A. Nicholson, E. J. W. Gibb Memorial, N. S., 8 vols. (London: Luzac and Co.: vol. I (1923), text of Bks 1 and 2; vol. II (1926), trans. of Bks 1 and 2; vol. III (1929), text of Bks 3 and 4; vol. IV (1930), trans. of Bks 3 and 4; vol. V (1933), text of Bks 5 and 6; vol. VI (1934), trans. of Bks 5 and 6; vol. VII (1937), commentary on Bks 1 and 2; vol. VIII (1940), commentary on Bks 3–6)

SELECT BIBLIOGRAPHY

Arberry, A. J., *Tales from the Masnavi* (London: George Allen & Unwin, 1961)

——, *More Tales from the Masnavi*, UNESCO Collection of Representative Works: Persian Series (London: George Allen & Unwin, 1963)

——, *The Koran Interpreted* (Oxford: Oxford University Press, 1964)

——, *Mystical Poems of Rumi* (Chicago: University of Chicago Press, 1968)

——, *The Discourses of Rumi* (New York: Samuel Weiser, 1972)

——, *Mystical Poems of Rumi, 2: Second Selection* (Chicago: University of Chicago Press, 1979)

Asad, M., *The Message of the Qur'an* (Dar al-Andalus: E. J. Brill, 1980)

Baldick, J., 'Persian Sufi Poetry up to the Fifteenth Century', in *Handbuch der Orientalistik*, vol. 4/2/2 (Leiden: E. J. Brill, 1981), pp. 112–32

Banani, A., R. Hovannisian and G. Sabagh, *Poetry and Mysticism in Islam: The Heritage of Rumi* (Cambridge: Cambridge University Press, 1994). Of particular interest are the following essays: William C. Chittick, 'Rumi and Wahdat al-Wujud,' pp. 70–111; H. Dabashi, 'Rumi and the Problems of Theodicy: Moral Imagination and Narrative Discourse in a Story of the *Masnavi*', pp. 112–35; and Margaret M. A. Mills, 'Folk Tradition in the *Masnavī* and the *Masnavī* in Folk Tradition', pp. 136–77

Burckhardt Qureshi, Regula, *Sufi Music of India and Pakistan* (Cambridge: Cambridge University Press, 1987)

Chittick, William C., *The Sufi Path of Knowledge* (Albany: State University of New York Press, 1989)

——, *Me and Rumi: The Autobiography of Shams-i Tabriz* (Louisville: Fons Vitae, 2004)

Davis, R., 'Narrative and Doctrine in the First Story of Rumi's *Mathnawi*', in Hawting, G. R., J. A. Mojaddedi and A. Samely, eds., *Studies in Islamic and Middle Eastern Texts and Traditions in Memory of Norman Calder* (Oxford: Oxford University Press, 2000)

De Bruijn, J. T. P., *Persian Sufi Poetry: An Introduction to the Mystical Use of Classical Poems* (Richmond: Curzon Press, 1997)

Elias, Jamal, 'Mawlawiyya', in *Oxford Encyclopaedia of the Modern Islamic World*, ed. John L. Esposito (New York: Oxford University Press, 2001)

Encyclopaedia Iranica, ed. E. Yarshater (London: Routledge & Kegan Paul, 1982–)

Encyclopaedia of Islam, 2nd edn. (Leiden: E. J. Brill, 1960–)

Ernst, Carl W., *The Shambhala Guide to Sufism* (Boston: Shambhala, 1997)

Keshavarz, Fatemeh, *Reading Mystical Lyric: The Case of Jalal al-Din Rumi* (Columbia, SC: University of South Carolina Press, 1998)

The Koran with a Parallel Arabic Text, trans. with notes by N. J. Dawood (London: Penguin, 1990)

Lewis, Franklin D., *Rumi Past and Present East and West: The Life, Teachings and Poetry of Jalal al-Din Rumi* (Oxford: Oneworld, 2000)

Lewisohn, L., ed., *Classical Persian Sufism: From Its Origins to Rumi 700–1300* (London and New York: Oneworld, 1993)

Mardin, Şerif, 'Mevlevi', in *Oxford Encyclopaedia of the Modern Islamic World*, ed. John L. Esposito (New York: Oxford University Press, 2001)

Movahhed, Mohammed 'Ali, ed., *Maqālāt-e Shams-e Tabrizi* (Tehran: Entesharat-e Khwarazmi, 1990)

Thackston, Wheeler, *Signs of the Unseen* (Putney, VT: Threshold Books, 1994)

Note on the Translation

I have set out the verses of the text so that the integrity of each *masnavi* is visually represented; this also slows down the pace at which the text is read. Each distich, or half-line, is a 'breath-line', i.e. it is to be read at the speed of one long exhalation. Italic font in the translation indicates Rumi's use of Arabic instead of Persian, especially in metrically adapted quotations from the Quran, from the hadith and from Arabic proverbs and poetry. The Dedication is entirely in Arabic. The inclusion of Arabic – the language of revelation and learning for Muslims – by Rumi is comparable to European authors' quoting of Latin, Greek or Hebrew. References and contexts for these quotations are given in the Notes.

I have prepared this translation from the first volume of Mohammed Este'lami's excellent and complete critical edition (Tehran, 1379/2000–2001). This is the most accurate modern edition and takes account of variants in all the extant early manuscripts, as well as Nicholson's edited text. The line numbers in the margins (every five lines) refer to Este'lami's edition.

SPIRITUAL VERSES

Dedication

IN THE NAME OF GOD THE MERCIFUL, THE COMPASSIONATE

This is the book of the *Masnavi*, and it is the roots of the roots of religion[1] in respect of revealing the secrets of attainment and of certainty, and it is the greatest knowledge of God, and it is the most radiant way of God and the clearest proof of God; the likeness of its light is 'like a niche in which there is a lamp shining'[2] with a radiance brighter than the dawn. It is the paradise of the heart with springs and boughs, among which there is one which the followers of this way call Salsabil,[3] and among the possessors of the stations and graces it is 'best as a station and fairest place of repose'.[4] The virtuous eat and drink there, and the free are gladdened and overjoyed by it. And like the Nile of Egypt it is a drink to the patient and an affliction to the people of Pharaoh and the unbelievers,[5] as He has said, 'In this way He causes many a one to go astray and in this way He guides many a one aright.'[6] It is 'a cure for hearts'[7] and remover of sorrows and uncoverer of the Quran, source of abundance of boons and healer of characters, 'by the hands of messengers, noble and most virtuous'[8] who forbid, saying 'none but the pure can touch it,'[9] a revelation from the Lord of the Worlds; 'falsehood cannot reach it from before or from behind,'[10] and God observes it and watches over it, and 'He is the best of guardians and He is the most merciful of the merciful.'[11] And it has other titles by which God honoured it. And we have constrained ourselves to this little, for the little is a sample of the much, and a mouthful is a sample of the pool, and a handful is a sample of the great threshing floor.

The feeble slave, who is in need of the mercy of God Most High, Mohammed Ibn Mohammed Ibn al-Hosayn of Balkh, may God accept this from him, says, I have exerted myself in the composing of the poem of the *Masnavi* which contains marvels and rarities, the finest treatises and brilliant guidance and the way of the ascetics and the garden of the devotees, brief in expression, copious in meaning, at the request of my master and support and dependable one, the location of the spirit in my body and the treasure of my today and my tomorrow, namely the sheikh, the model of knowers of God, the leader of guidance and certainty, helper of humankind, custodian of their hearts and minds, entrusted by God among His creatures, the quintessence of His creation, and His orders to His Prophet and his secrets to the chosen favourite, the key of the celestial treasuries, custodian of the riches of the earth, the father of virtues, Hosām [Sword] of Truth and religion, Hasan Ibn Mohammed Ibn Hasan, known as Ibn Akhi Tork, the Abu Yazid of the time, Jonayd of the age, *seddiq* son of the *seddiq*, son of the *seddiq*, may God be pleased with him and with them, originally of Urmiya, descended from the sheikh who was endowed with miraculous grace inasmuch as he said, 'In the evening I was a Kurd and in the morning an Arab.' May God sanctify his soul and the soul of his successors, how blessed is the ancestor, how blessed the successor! He has a lineage upon which the sun has cast its mantle and an esteem of ancestry before which the stars have dimmed their radiance. Their court-yard has always been the qibla of good fortune, to whom the sons of sovereign power turn, and the Ka'bah of hopes which those who come for favour circumambulate, and may it always be so long as the star rises and a sun in the east rises resplendent over the horizon, so that it may be a refuge for those possessors of insight, godly, spiritual, heavenly, celestial, enlightened ones, those who are silent in their contemplation, the absent ones who are present, those who are kings beneath their tattered clothes, the nobles of the nations, the masters of virtues, the lights of divine witness. Amen. O Lord of the Worlds!

This is a prayer that will not be refused, for it is a prayer that includes all species of creation. Praise be to God alone, and blessings upon our master Mohammed and his family and progeny. And God is sufficient – how excellent a Protector.

THE SONG OF THE REED

– Listen to this reed as it is grieving;
    it tells the story of our separations.

'Since I was severed from the bed of reeds,
    in my cry men and women have lamented.

I need the breast that's torn to shreds by parting
    to give expression to the pain of heartache.

Whoever finds himself left far from home
    looks forward to the day of his reunion.

I was in grief in every gathering;   5
    I joined with those of sad and happy state.

Each person thought he was my bosom friend,
    but none sought out my secrets from within me.

My secret is not far from my lament,
    but eye and ear have no illumination.

There's no concealment of the soul and body,
    yet no one has the power to see the soul.

The reed-flute's sound is fire, not human breath.
    Whoever does not have this fire, be gone!

The fire of love is burning in the reed;   10
    the turbulence of love is in the wine.

The reed is friend to all who are lovelorn;
    its melodies have torn our veils apart.

Whoever saw a poison and a cure,
  a mate and longing lover like the reed?

The reed tells of the road that runs with blood;
  it tells the tales of Majnun's passionate love.

This sense is closed to all except the senseless,
  and words are all the ear can ever purchase.

15   In all our grief the days turned into nights,
  the days fell into step with searing pains.

If days are gone, say "Go! There is no fear,
  and stay, O You who are uniquely holy."

His flood deluges all except the fish;
  the day is long for him who has no bread.

The raw can't grasp the state of one who's cooked,
  so this discussion must be brief – farewell!

Be free, my son, and break your chains asunder!
  How long will you be slave to gold and silver?

20   If you should pour the sea into a pitcher,
  how much will it contain? At best, a day's worth!

The greedy eye's a pitcher never filled;
  the pearl won't fill the discontented shell.

They will be wholly cleansed of greed and faults
  whose clothes are torn to shreds by lovers' passion.

Rejoice, O Love, that is our sweetest passion,
  physician of our many illnesses!

Relief from our pomposity and boasting,
  O You who are our Plato and our Galen!

For Love the earthly body soared to heaven,   25
    the mountain took to dancing and to skipping.

When Love approached Mount Sinai's soul,
    O lover,
    Sinai was drunk and *"Moses fell aswoon."*

If I were pressed to my companion's lips,
    then like the reed I'd tell what must be told.

A man cut off from fellow native-speakers
    is tongue-tied, though he has a hundred songs.

And when the rose is gone, the garden faded,
    you will no longer hear the nightingale.

The lover is a veil, All is Beloved,   30
    Beloved lives, the lover is a corpse.

When Love no longer has a care for him
    he's like a wingless bird – alas for him!

How can I understand the things around me
    when my companion's light is not around me?

But Love demands that these words shall be spoken;
    how can a mirror be without reflection?

Do you know why your mirror tells of nothing?
    The rust has not been taken from its surface.'

Reflect upon this story, my dear friends;   35
    its meaning is the essence of our state.

THE KING WHO FALLS IN LOVE WITH A
SLAVE-GIRL AND BUYS HER

In former times there was a king who was
    the ruler of this world and of the next.

It happened that one day the king went riding
    with all his retinue in search of game.

The king espied a slave-girl on the highway:
    the king became a slave-boy to that slave-girl.

His fledgling soul aflutter in its cage,
    he paid his money and he bought the slave-girl.

40   Now when he'd bought her and he had enjoyed her,
    by heaven's fate the slave-girl turned to sickness.

A man possessed an ass but had no saddle;
    he got a saddle – wolves had got the ass!

Another had a pitcher but no water;
    he found the water, but he broke the pitcher!

The king called in the doctors all around,
    'The lives of both of us are in your hands.

My life is worthless! She is all my life!
    I'm wounded and in pain. She is my cure.

45   Whoever cures the darling of my life
    shall take away my treasures, pearls and corals.'

Together they replied, 'We'll give our lives,
    and pool our knowledge in collaboration.

Each one of us is saviour of a world,
    the salve for every wound is in our hands.'

They did not say 'God willing' in their boasting,
    and so God showed them mankind's helplessness.

I mean wilful omission of the phrase
    not just the words – for that would be a slip.

How many do not say the phrase 'God willing',   50
    yet in their souls they have the phrase's spirit!

With every drug and remedy they gave her,
    the pain increased and her condition worsened.

The illness shrank the slave-girl to a hair's breadth;
    the king's eyes were a stream of bloody tears.

By fate the oxymel increased her bile,
    and oil of almonds desiccated her.

The myrobalan caused her constipation,
    and water fed her fever like a fuel.

Demonstrating the Incompetence of the Doctors in
Treating the Slave-girl, and the King's Turning to
God and His Seeing a Spiritual Being in a Dream

And when the king perceived the doctors' weakness, 55
    he ran barefoot towards the mosque at once.

He went into the mosque, towards the prayer-niche,
    he soaked the prayer-rug with his royal tears.

When he returned from his transcendent state,
   he spoke with gentleness, in praise and prayer:

'What shall I say to You who know all secrets,
   Whose meanest gift's the kingdom of the world?

O constant haven to us in our need,
   once more we are mistaken on our way.

60   But You have said, "Although I know your secret
   you should declare it openly right now."'

Just as the cry was uttered from his soul,
   the ocean of His grace came to the boil.

And then amidst his tears sleep snatched him off,
   he dreamed he saw a sage appear to him,

Who said, 'Dear king, good news, your needs are met.
   Tomorrow if a stranger comes, he's from Us.

When he arrives he'll be the skilful doctor,
   and be assured he's good and to be trusted.

65   Behold the utter magic of his treatment!
   Behold the power of God in his composure!'

The allotted hour arrived and it was day,
   the sun rose from the East and scorched the stars.

The king was in the watch-tower on the lookout
   to witness what had been disclosed in secret.

He saw a virtuous, substantial man,
   a man who was a sun amidst the shadows,

Approaching from afar, a crescent moon,
   he was and yet was not, like an illusion.

Illusion in the spirit is as nothing: 70
   behold a world that runs upon illusions!

Their war and peace are made upon illusion,
   their glory and their shame are from illusion.

Illusions which ensnare the Friends of God
   reflect the moon-faced ones of God's own garden.

The image which the king saw in his dream
   was now apparent in his visitor's face.

The king pushed past his courtiers to go forward
   himself to greet the guest from the Unseen.

The two of them were seasoned seafarers   75
   whose souls were sewn together seamlessly.

He said, 'In truth you were my love, not she,
   but in this world one thing becomes another.

O You who are Mohammed to my Omar,
   I gird my loins to be of service to you.'

*Asking the Lord, Who Is Our Guidance, for
Guidance in Observance of Politeness in All
Our Affairs, and Explaining the Grievous
Harm of Impoliteness*

We seek from God the gift of courtesy,
   the grace of God is not for the discourteous.

Discourteous men abuse not just themselves;
   indeed they put the whole world to the torch.

A feast of food was coming down from heaven   80
   – no buying, selling, haggling was involved.

In Moses' flock there were discourteous persons
   who clamoured, 'Where's the garlic, where's the
      lentils?'

The feast of food from heaven was cut off;
   the toils of cultivating it were left.

And God, when Jesus interceded for them,
   again sent trays and ample food on dishes.

Again the rude ones left their manners elsewhere
   and made off with the feast of food like beggars.

85   So Jesus pleaded with them, saying thus,
   'This will remain, it will not go from earth.'

To be so disaffected and so greedy
   is plain ingratitude at God's high table!

That door of God's compassion closed on them,
   those surly people blinded by their greed.

The rain-cloud goes when charity is stopped;
   debauchery spreads plague in all directions.

The trouble and affliction that you have
   are all from rudeness and impertinence.

90   Whoever is discourteous on God's path,
   he is a human kidnapper, a scoundrel.

By courtesy this sky was filled with light;
   the angels were impeccable and pure.

The sun became eclipsed by arrogance –
   Azāzil was expelled for insolence.

The King Meets the Friend Who Had Been Revealed to Him in a Dream

With open arms he clasped him to his bosom,
    he took him to his heart and soul like love,

And he began to kiss his hands and forehead,
    began to ask him of his home and journey.

Inquiring thus he led him to the throne   95
    and said, 'I've found a treasure through my
        patience,

O light of God and barrier against sin!
    The meaning of "*the key to joy is patience*"!

O You, whose gaze will answer every question,
    O You who solve our problems peacefully!

Interpreter of all that's in our hearts,
    Who saves us all from sinking in the sands.

So welcome, O Most Chosen, O Approved One,
    "*If You go, Fate will come, the space will
        narrow.*"

Protector of the people! He who spurns You   100
    is damned already. "No, if he does not . . ."'

Now when their session and their feast were over,
    the king escorted him into the harem.

The King Takes the Physician to the Sick Girl to
See Her Condition

He told the tale of illness and the patient,
    then seated him beside the sickly girl.

He saw her pallor, checked her pulse and urine,
    and listened to her symptoms and her functions.

He said, 'None of the drugs they have prescribed
    will build her up – they have destroyed her health.

105   They did not understand her inner state:
    I seek God's refuge from what they contrive.'

He saw the pain and opened up the secret
    but did not tell the king and kept it hidden.

Her pain was not from black or yellow bile:
    the scent of wood is sent up in its smoke.

He saw in her distress her broken heart:
    her body healthy but her heart in chains.

The sign of being in love's an aching heart;
    there is no suffering like the suffering heart.

110   The lover's suffering's like no other suffering:
    love is the astrolabe of God's own mysteries.

No matter whether love is of this world
    or of the next, it steals us to that world.

Whatever words I say to explain this love,
    when I arrive at love, I am ashamed.

Though language gives a clear account of love,
   yet love beyond all language is the clearer.

The pen had gone at breakneck speed in writing,
   but when it came to love it split in two.

The explaining mind sleeps like an ass in mud,   115
   for love alone explains love and the lover.

The sun alone is proof of all things solar:
   if you need proof, do not avert your face.

Although the shadow gives a hint of it,
   the sun bestows the light of life at all times.

The shadow brings you sleep like bedtime stories,
   and when the sun comes up, *'the moon is cloven.'*

There's nothing like this sun in all the world,
   the spiritual Sun's eternal – never setting.

Although the outward sun may be unique,   120
   still you can contemplate another like it.

And yet the sun from which the aether comes
   has no external or internal likeness.

How can imagining contain His essence,
   and likeness of Him come into conception?

When news came of the face of Shamsoddin
   the sun in highest heaven hung its head.

It's necessary, since his name is with us,
   to give some hint of his munificence.

Upon this breath my soul has scorched my skirt   125
   and caught the perfume of the shirt of Joseph,

Saying, 'After all our years of comradeship,
  explain one of the states of ecstasy,

So that the mind and sight and spirit grow
  a hundredfold, and heaven and earth may laugh.'

'Do not impose on me, for I am dead:
  my senses dulled, I cannot take things in.

For all that's said by one not yet awake,
  in modesty or boasting, is illicit.

130   What can I say – no vein of mine is sober –
        to explain that Friend who is beyond a friend?

But now, leave off until some other time
  this talk of parting and this bleeding heart!'

He said, 'Give me to eat, for I am hungry,
  and quick! Time is indeed a cutting sword.

The Sufi is the son of Time, my friend;
  tomorrow's no condition of the Way.

You, are you not indeed yourself a Sufi?
  Nothing will come from such procrastination.'

135   I told him, 'Best to hide God's mysteries,
        and pay attention to what's in the tale!

It is to be preferred that lovers' secrets
  are spoken of in tales of other folk.'

He said, 'Tell it unveiled, the naked truth!
  The declaration's better than the secret.

Hold back the veil and speak the naked truth!
  I don't lie down with clothes on with my lover.'

I said, 'If He were naked in your sight,
    you'd not survive, nor would your breast nor
        waist.

Ask for your wish, but ask with moderation: 140
    a blade of straw cannot support a mountain.

The Sun, by which this world's illuminated,
    will burn the lot if it comes any closer!

Don't seek out trials and griefs and shedding blood!
    From now on, no more talk of Shams of Tabriz!'

There is no end to this. Begin again,
    and go recite the ending of this tale.

The Sage Asks the King if He May Be Alone in Order to Understand the Slave-girl's Illness

He said, 'My Lord, evacuate the house
    and send away both family and guests.

No one shall eavesdrop in the corridors   145
    while I am asking questions of this girl.'

The house was emptied and no staff remained,
    no one except the doctor and the patient.

He gently asked her, 'Where is your home-town?
    For patients' treatments vary with their region.

And in that town, who are your family?
    To whom are you related and connected?'

He laid his hand upon her pulse and asked her
    such questions, one by one, of fate's oppression.

150   As when a thorn has stuck in someone's foot,
            he takes his foot and puts it on his knee,

        And with a needle's point seeks out the tip,
            and if he does not find it, licks the point.

        That thorn is so elusive in the foot,
            tell me, how much more hidden in the heart!

        If any fool could see the thorns in hearts,
            then when indeed would sorrows overwhelm us?

        You stick a thorn beneath an ass's tail,
            the ass can't get it out and writhes in pain,

155   And as it writhes, that thorn is biting harder –
            it takes intelligence to pick out thorns.

        The ass will thrash about with kicks and blows,
            to get rid of the thorn, in burning pain.

        That thorn-removing doctor was an expert;
            he tapped his hand now here, now there to test her.

        He asked the girl to tell him in a story
            about the nature of the friends she had.

        She told her stories freely to the doctor
            of places, masters, towns and all the rest.

160   He listened very closely to her story,
            attending to her pulse and to its rhythm.

        As to whose name would send her heart-beat racing –
            he'd be her soul's desire in all the world.

        He counted up her friends in her home-town
            and then moved on to mention other towns.

He said, 'When you would leave your own home-
        town,
    which other town did you most often visit?'

She named one town and moved on to another –
    her colour and her pulse remained unchanged.

She told of towns and masters one by one,   165
    the places and the kind of life she led.

She spoke about so many towns and houses,
    her pulse did not increase, nor did she blanch.

Her pulse was normal and unfaltering
    until he asked of sweetest Samarqand.

Her heartbeat leapt, her colour blushed and
        blanched –
    she had been parted from a goldsmith there.

The doctor found this secret in his patient
    and found the root of her distress and pain.

He asked, 'What is the street in which he lives?'   170
    She answered, 'Ghātafar in Sar-e Pol.'

He said, 'I know precisely what your pain is.
    I'll work some magic on you for your health.

Be joyful, be relaxed and have no fear,
    I'll do for you what rain does for the meadow.

I shall take care of you – you must be carefree.
    I'll be more tender than a hundred fathers.

But mind that you do not disclose this secret,
    not even if the king himself should press you.

175   The sooner that your heart's your secret's tomb
            the sooner shall your heart's desire come true.

        The Prophet said, "Whoever hides his secret
            will soon become united with his wish."

        As when a seed is hidden in the earth,
            its secret is the garden's lush new growth.

        If gold and silver never were concealed,
            how could they have been nourished in the mine?'

        The doctor's promises and kindnesses
            assured his patient to be free of fear.

180   There are true promises which soothe the heart;
            there are false promises which breed distress.

        While good men's promises are sterling coin,
            the scoundrel's promise is the spirit's pain.

            *The Friend Understands the Illness and
            Reports Her Illness to the King*

        He then got up and set off for the king,
            and told His Majesty of bits and pieces.

        He said, 'My counsel is that we should bring
            that fellow here, because of what she feels.

        So call the goldsmith from that distant town,
            with gifts of gold and finery beguile him!'

185   The sultan, when he heard this from the sage,
            embraced his counsel with his heart and soul.

The King Sends Messengers to Samarqand to
Fetch the Goldsmith

The king sent messengers in that direction,
  astute and capable judicious men.

These gentlemen arrived in Samarqand,
  sent to the goldsmith from the king of kings.

Saying, 'Subtle master, perfect in your wisdom,
  whose qualities are known throughout the land,

Behold, a certain king has chosen you
  for all your expertise in working gold.

So take these robes and all this gold and silver,   190
  and when you come you'll be a special guest.'

The man saw all the riches and the robes;
  he was deceived, abandoned home and children,

And set upon the road a happy fellow,
  oblivious that the king would have his blood.

He rode an Arab horse and galloped gaily,
  mistook the blood price for a royal robe.

Gone on a journey with his full consent!
  He made his way towards an evil fate.

To wealth, and power and greatness – in his   195
            dreams!
  Ezrā'il told him, 'Go ahead and get it!'

Now when that man of foreign parts arrived,
  the saint-physician came before the king.

They brought him with all splendour to the king
   to burn him on the candle of Terāz.

The king saw him and honoured him aplenty;
   he offered him the treasury of gold.

The saint-physician told him, 'Mighty ruler,
   present the slave-girl to this gentleman,

200   So that she will take pleasure in her union.
   The water of their love will quench her fire.'

The king endowed him with the moon-faced one;
   he joined those two who craved each other's
      presence.

They gratified their urges for six months,
   until the girl was fully back to health.

And then a potion was prepared for him
   to drink, that he should fade before the girl.

In sickness now, his beauty was no more;
   the girl's soul would not see him through his
      sufferings.

205   As he turned ugly, grim and pale of face,
   he gradually went cold within her heart.

When love is for the sake of a complexion,
   it is no longer love; it ends in shame.

If only he'd been ugly from the start,
   he'd not have suffered such an evil sentence.

The blood was rolling from his eyes like rivers;
   his face became his mortal enemy.

The peacock's feathers are its enemy.
How many a king is murdered by his glory!

He said, 'I am that deer whose holy blood   210
this hunter sacrificed to get my musk.

Oh, I who am that ambushed country fox,
decapitated just to get my fur.

I am that elephant whose blood was spilled
by hunter's blows, and just to get my tusks!

He who has slain me for mere part of me,
he does not know my blood shall not be
sleeping.

It's me today, tomorrow it is him.
Why is the blood of such as us so squandered?

Although the wall may cast a lengthy shadow,   215
at length the shadow will return to it.

This world's a mountain and our acts are calls:
the echo of our call returns to us.'

He said this, then at once went to his grave.
The slave-girl was released from love and pain.

Because the love of dead men does not last,
because the dead man does not come to us.

A living love in spirit and in sight
is fresher than a rosebud every moment.

Choose love of that Immortal Living One,   220
the bearer of rejuvenating wine.

Choose love of Him from Whom the prophets all
    derived their power and glory from His love.

Don't say, 'We have no access to that King.'
    There is no hardship dealing with the Gracious.

Explanation That the Killing by Poison of the Goldsmith Was Caused Not by Selfish Lust and Vicious Intention but by Divine Intimation

This killing by the saint-physician's hand
    was done not out of hope nor out of fear.

He did not kill him just to suit the king
    but when the inspiration came from God.

225   The people do not understand the secret
    of why it was that Khezr cut that boy's throat.

Whoever has what God reveals and answers,
    whatever he commands, is reason's essence.

He who gives life is right though he take life:
    his hand is God's, he is His deputy.

Lay down your head like Esmā'il before Him
    and, laughing gaily, give His sword your soul

So that your soul will laugh for ever more
    just like Mohammed's pure soul with the One.

230   For lovers drink the soul's wine at that moment
    their lovers slay them with their own bare hands.

The king did not pour out that blood for lust's sake.
    Be free of wicked thoughts, be free of strife!

You thought he'd acted in impurity –
   can cleansing leave a stain in purity?

The purpose of these austere ways is that
   the furnace purges dross out of the silver.

The trial of good and bad takes place so that
   dross rises to the surface when gold boils.

If his affairs were not inspired by God,   235
   he'd be a vicious dog and not the king.

Unstained by lust, cupidity and craving,
   the good he did was good in evil dress.

If Khezr smashed the boat upon the sea,
   he had a hundred reasons so to do.

With all his light and virtue, Moses' mind
   was veiled – do not attempt a wingless flight!

It is a red rose; do not call it blood!
   He's drunk on reason; do not call him mad!

If his desire were for a Muslim's blood,   240
   I'd be the infidel to bring his name up.

God's throne is shaken when a villain's praised;
   such praise infuriates a pious man.

He was the king and a most knowing king.
   He was the chosen intimate of God.

A person who is slain by such a king
   is led to luck and to a higher place.

If he'd not seen the benefit of violence,
    how would this utter grace have wished for
        violence?

245   The infant trembles at the surgeon's knife
    just as its fearful mother is rejoicing.

For half a life He gives a hundred lives:
    what He is giving you, you can't imagine.

You fashion your opinions from yourself;
    you've fallen very far, take utmost care!

THE TALE OF THE GREENGROCER AND
THE PARROT, AND THE PARROT'S
SPILLING OIL ON THE STALL

There was a greengrocer – he had a parrot,
   a sweetly singing bird of verdant voice.

She'd keep the counter for the shopkeeper
   and say some clever thing to all the merchants.

She was adept at human conversation   250
   and quite proficient in the song of parrots.

She sprang up from the counter and flew up
   and knocked the rose-oil bottles everywhere.

And when her master came back from his house
   and sat down in his easy merchant way,

He saw his stall and clothes all soaked in rose-oil;
   he smacked the parrot's head and made her bald.

For many days she did not talk at all;
   the greengrocer was sighing with remorse.

He tore his beard repeating, 'O alas!   255
   My fortune's sun is hidden in the clouds!

I wish my hand had broken at that moment.
   How could I strike that sweetly singing head?'

He offered gifts to every mendicant
   in order to retrieve his dear bird's speech.

Three days and nights passed in a daze and groaning,
   slumped in his shop, he sat all out of hope.

He showed the bird all kinds of mysteries
   that maybe she'd come round and talk again.

260   A shaven-headed mendicant walked by,
   his head as hairless as a chamberpot.

The parrot found her tongue just at that moment
   and hollered like a wise guy at the dervish,

'Hey, baldy, how come you're mixed up with baldies?
   Have you been spilling oil from bottles too?'

The crowd all found her comment very funny
   that she had thought the dervish like herself.

Don't judge the ways of saintly ones by *your* ways,
   though 'lion' and 'milk' are spelled the same in
      Persian!

265   It's why the world has gone astray entirely:
   few know the representatives of God.

They see themselves as equals of the prophets;
   they fantasize the saints are like themselves.

They say, 'Look here, we're human, they are human,
   both they and we are bound to sleep and eat.'

And in their blindness they are unaware;
   between them there's an endless separation.

The wasp and bee feed from the same food source;
   from one there comes the sting, from one comes
      honey.

Both types of deer will feed on plants and water;   270
  from one comes dung, from one the purest musk.

Both types of cane are drinking from one source;
  this one is empty, that one full of sugar.

Observe a hundred thousand semblances
  like this, and how they are a life apart.

This one consumes and out will come defilement;
  this one consumes: divine illumination.

This one consumes and spawns its greed and envy;
  this one consumes and radiates God's light.

This is good earth, and that is poor and brackish;   275
  this holy spirit, that's the beast and demon.

It may well be that both appear the same –
  both sweet and bitter water can be clear.

Who knows except a man of taste? Find one!
  He will distinguish sweet from brackish water.

He who confuses magic with the marvel
  will think that both are based upon deceit.

In Moses' day the quarrelsome magicians
  held up a staff which looked like Moses' staff.

Between these two there is a world of difference;   280
  a mighty distance lies between these actions.

God's curse is consequent on one of them;
  God's mercy is the other action's prize.

The unbelievers' nature is the ape's;
  their nature is a cancer in their side.

Whatever men may do, the ape does too;
   it mimics what men do at every moment.

It thinks, 'I have behaved as he behaves.'
   How can ill-tempered brutes like that know
      better?

285   One acts by God's command, one brutishly.
          Pour dust upon the heads of brutish men!

The faithful stand in prayer with hypocrites
   who come to quarrel, not to offer prayer.

In prayer and fasting, *hajj* and giving alms,
   the faithful play the hypocrites at chess.

And in the end success comes to the faithful;
   the next life for the hypocrites is death.

Though both of them compete in the same game,
   the two of them inhabit different worlds.

290   Each will proceed towards his own abode;
          each goes according to the name he holds.

They call him 'faithful' and his soul rejoices;
   if 'hypocrite', he's furious and fiery.

The one's name is adored for its true essence;
   the other's name is loathed for its affliction.

The 'f' 'a' 'i' 't' 'h' are not just formal;
   the spelling 'faithful' is not information.

If you should call him hypocrite, this curse
   would bite him like a scorpion inside.

If this bad name has not a hellish root,   295
    then why has it a taste of hell about it?

The ugliness of names is not from letters –
    sea-water's saltiness is not from pails.

The word's a pail with meaning like the water,
    'sea' means *with Him the Mother of the Book*.

Between the world's fresh lakes and salty seas
    there is *the barrier which they do not breech*,

And both of these are flowing from one source:
    to reach their source pass on from both and go!

Without the touchstone, with the naked eye,   300
    you'll never know false gold from precious gold.

All those who have God's touchstone in their souls
    can recognize all certain things from doubtful.

If grit should end up in a person's mouth,
    they do not rest until they have expelled it.

Among a thousand morsels if one speck
    gets in, the living senses root it out.

The worldly sense will let you climb this world;
    the spirit's sense will let you climb to heaven.

To keep these senses healthy, see a doctor,   305
    but for those senses' health, see the Beloved.

This sense grows stronger building up the body;
    that sense grows stronger breaking down the body.

The spirit's path demolishes the body,
    then, after demolition, reconstructs it.

The house is ruined for the buried gold,
    and with that gold a better house is built.

The water is cut off, the stream is cleansed,
    and then the stream will flow with drinking water.

310   The skin is cut to draw the arrow out,
    and afterwards new skin begins to grow.

The fort is razed and taken from the heathen;
    a hundred towers and ramparts then go up.

Who can describe the ways of the Sublime One?
    Necessity has prompted what I've said here.

Sometimes it seems like this, sometimes like that.
    Religion's work is all astonishment –

Not such as makes you turn your back to Him
    but rather drunk and drowning in the Friend.

315   While this one has her face towards the Friend,
    the other's face is only in her own face.

Look on the face of every one, be watchful!
    with practice you may come to know their faces.

For many a devil has a human face;
    you should not give your hand to every hand.

The bird-catcher will make the whistling sound
    so that he'll trick the bird, that bird-catcher.

The bird will hear the call of its own species,
    fall from the air, and then be snared and speared.

320   The wicked steal the words of dervishes
    to cast their spells upon the gullible.

The work of real men is light and warmth;
  the work of wicked men is shameless fraud.

They make a woollen lion for their begging;
  they give the Prophet's name to Bu Mosaylem.

The name of 'liar' stuck with Bu Mosaylem;
  Mohammed is of 'those who understand'.

The wine of truth is sealed with purest musk,
  but liquor's sealed with stinking, painful headaches.

THE STORY OF THE JEWISH KING
WHO KILLED CHRISTIANS ON
ACCOUNT OF HIS BIGOTRY

325   There was a cruel king among the Jews,
        a Christian-cleansing enemy of Jesus.

      It was the time of Jesus and his era,
        for he was Moses' soul and Moses his.

      The cross-eyed king divided up those two
        divine companions on the path of God.

      A master told his cross-eyed servant, 'Come,
        go on and get that bottle from the outhouse.'

      The cross-eyed man said, 'Which of those two bottles
        shall I bring you? – Please tell me what you mean.'

330   The master said, 'There aren't two bottles; go,
        leave off your squinting, don't be seeing double!'

      He said, 'O master, don't be so sarcastic!'
        The master said, 'Try breaking one of them!'

      When he broke one, both disappeared from view:
        a man goes cross-eyed from such lust and anger.

      There was one bottle: two appeared to him.
        He broke one and there was no other bottle.

      Desire and anger make men go cross-eyed,
        for they distort the spirit from uprightness.

When craving comes, then virtue is concealed;   335
   a hundred veils divide the heart and sight.

A judge allows corruption in his heart –
   how can he tell the victim from oppressor?

The king was so cross-eyed from Jewish hatred
   that we cry out, 'O mercy, Lord have mercy!'

He killed a hundred thousand innocents,
   saying, 'I'm the bastion of Moses' faith.'

The Vizier Teaches the King Trickery

He had a vizier, infidel intriguer,
   who could tie knots in water with his tricks.

He said, 'The Christians try to save their lives   340
   by hiding their religion from the king.

Stop killing them, for killing them is useless;
   faith has no smell – it is not musk or aloes.

The secret's hidden in a hundred sheaths –
   outside they're for you, inside they're against you.'

The king asked him, 'Then tell me, what's your
      counsel?
   What is the answer to their tricks and lies?

So that no Christians in the world remain,
   none to declare their faith or keep it secret.'

He said, 'O king, cut off my hands and ears,   345
   and slice my nose off in a harsh decree.

And after that despatch me to the gallows,
   so that some rescuer will plead for me.

You must perform this in a public place,
   upon the royal highway at a crossroads.

Then drive me from you to a distant city
   to sow among them evil insurrection.

The Vizier's Knavery among the Christians

'Then I shall tell them, "Secretly I'm Christian!
   O God who knows all hidden things, You know
     me.

350   The king became suspicious of my faith,
   attacked my life with persecuting zeal.

I tried to keep it hidden from the king
   and practised his religion outwardly.

The king got wind of what I was concealing;
   the things I told the king were now in doubt.

He said, 'Your words are needles in my bread;
   there is a window from my heart to yours,

And from this window I have seen your mind.
   I do not swallow any of your words.'

355   If Jesus' soul had not come to my rescue,
   the king would have made Jewish mincemeat of
     me.

For Jesus' sake I'd give my life, my head;
   to Him I owe a hundred thousand debts.

I don't refuse to give my life to Jesus,
  but I am so well versed in his religion!

How much it grieves me that the Holy Faith
  is being destroyed among the ignorant!

Thank God and Jesus that we have become
  the guide to the religion of the truth.

From Jew and Jewry we have found our freedom   360
  to bind ourselves within the Christian girdle.

This is the age of Jesus, O my people!
  your hearts must hear the mysteries of his
      faith."'

The king performed on him what he had told him;
  the people were astonished by his actions.

He drove him out and sent him to the Christians,
  and after that the vizier started preaching.

The Christians Accept the Vizier's Trickery

A hundred thousand men of Christian faith
  began to flock around him where he lived.

He intimated to them explanations   365
  of secrets of the Gospel, prayer and girdle.

He seemed to be the preacher of the law;
  in truth he was the trap and decoy whistle.

It was for this that some Companions asked
  the Prophet of the ghoulish soul's deception,

And said, 'What hidden motives does it mix
    with pious acts and purity of soul?'

They were not asking him about true service
    but looking where the outward fault might lie.

370   But hair by hair and bit by bit they sensed,
    like roses among herbs, the soul's deception.

The most assiduous of these Companions
    were dazzled in their souls by all this teaching.

The Christians Follow the Vizier

The Christians opened all their hearts to him –
    how habit rules the unreflecting herd!

They sowed their love for him within their breasts;
    they took him as the deputy of Jesus.

He was the accursed one-eyed Antichrist
    in secret! God, the True Defender, help us!

375   There are a hundred thousand baits and traps,
    O God, and we're like greedy, helpless birds!

Each moment we are stuck in a new trap,
    though we become a falcon or Simorgh.

Each moment You are liberating us,
    we fall back in a trap, O God of freedom!

While we are storing wheat inside this grain-store,
    we're losing wheat which has been harvested.

And finally we have no sense to see
    that loss of wheat is from the mouse's tricks.

The mouse has burrowed in to raid our grain-store   380
    and wrecked our grain-store with his craftiness.

My soul, first stop the mayhem caused by mice,
    and then get busy harvesting the wheat.

Pay heed to a tradition of the Most High:
    'No *prayer is done without the heart's attention*.'

If there's no thieving mouse inside our grain-store,
    then where's the wheat of forty years' hard work?

Why is it that each day's sincerity
    is not amassing slowly in our grain-store?

How many a star of fire jumped from the iron   385
    and then that flaming heart received and sowed it!

But in the darkness there's a hidden thief:
    it's he who puts his finger on the stars.

Then one by one he puts out all the stars
    so not a single light will shine from heaven.

Though there may be a thousand snares before us,
    when You are with us there is no distress.

How, when Your favour's with us constantly,
    could there be any fear of that low thief?

Each night You liberate the spirits from   390
    the body's trap and wipe the records clean.

The spirits can escape this cage each night;
    when free, there's no commander or commanded.

At night-time, prisoners forget the prison,
    at night, guards disregard the discipline.

No sadness and no thought of gain or loss,
  no fancies about anyone at all.

This is the gnostic's state while wide awake.
  God said, '*they were asleep*' – don't flee from this!

395   Asleep to worldly matters night and day,
  led like the pen held in God's guiding hand.

Whoever does not see the hand in writing
  assumes the pen is doing all the moving.

He gives some inkling of the sage's state
  when sensual sleep transports the intellect.

Their souls have gone into the matchless desert;
  their spirits and their bodies are at peace.

Back to the snare You draw them with a whistle;
  You draw them all to justice and the Judge.

400   And when the light of dawn lifts up its head,
  and when the golden eagle soars to heaven,

Like Esrāfil, '*the kindler of the dawn*',
  He brings them all to form out of those regions.

He re-embodies the exultant spirits;
  He makes each body pregnant once again.

He strips the saddle from the souls' own steeds –
  this is the secret of '*Sleep is death's brother.*'

But so they will come back again by day,
  He ties a lengthy tether to their legs,

405   To bring them from that meadow in the day
  and from the pasture bring them back to burden.

If only He kept watch over this spirit,
　　like Noah's ark or like the Cave Companions,

So that this mind and eye and ear could go
　　free from this flood of waking and of sense.

There are so many 'of the Cave' in this world,
　　beside you and before you in these times.

The Friend and Cave are with them as they sing.
　　Your eyes and ears are sealed – to what advantage?

The Tale of the Caliph's Seeing Layli

The caliph said to Layli, 'Are you that one   410
　　for whom Majnun became distraught and wild?

You are not better than the other beauties.'
　　She said, 'Be silent! You are no Majnun!'

Whoever is awake is more asleep,
　　his being awake's much worse than all his sleep.

For when our souls are not awake to truth,
　　awakening's as if we've slammed the door.

All day under imagination's kicking,
　　and fear of loss and gain and its extinction,

The soul retains no purity, nor grace,   415
　　nor glory, nor the journey's path to heaven.

He is asleep who cherishes a hope
　　in all his dreams and who converses with them.

He sees the demon as a girl while dreaming;
　　in lust he spills his fluid with the demon,

He spills his semen on the barren earth,
   comes to himself as fantasy escapes him;

He sees his stupor and his body stained,
   ah, by that seen yet unseen apparition.

420   The bird is up above; below, its shadow
   is flying bird-like, running on the ground.

A fool goes after it to chase that shadow;
   he runs so much that he becomes exhausted:

He's ignorant of where the shadow's source is,
   that it's the shadow of the bird on high.

This man will shoot an arrow at the shadow;
   his quiver will be emptied by his efforts,

His own life's quiver emptied, and his life
   run out from chasing hot-foot after shadows.

When God's own shadow has become his
425   nursemaid,
   it frees him from his shadow and illusion.

God's shadow is the servant of the Lord;
   he's dead to this world and alive to God.

Now quickly grasp his hem decisively,
   escape upon the hem of time's last days.

'*Draws out the shadows*' is a saintly form,
   a witness to the light of God's own sun.

Without this guide do not enter this valley.
   Say like Khalil, '*I love not those who set.*'

Go on and grab a sun out of the shadow   430
    and scorch the royal hem of Shams of Tabriz.

And if you cannot find this wedding feast,
    then ask Hosāmoddin, 'God's Radiance'.

If envy grabs your throat upon the way,
    remember Eblis is extreme in envy.

For he looks down on Adam out of envy;
    he wages war with joy all out of envy.

So blessed is he who travels without envy,
    there is no greater hurdle on the Way.

This body can become the house of envy: 435
    beware, whose household will be stained with
        envy.

The body may become the house of envy,
    yet God once made that body very pure.

For 'purity' see 'Purify my temple';
    it is the store of light, though charm of earth.

When you deceive and envy someone good,
    that envy brings a darkness to your heart.

Be dust beneath the feet of men of God;
    pour dust on envy's head just as we do.

Explanation of the Vizier's Envy

440   That paltry vizier was of envy's stock;
          he gave the wind his ears and nose for nothing.

         All in the hope that from the sting of envy
            his poison would seep into wretched souls.

         So all who turn their noses up in envy
            cut off their nose and ears to spite themselves.

         The nose is that which can detect a scent;
            the scent takes him to the beloved's quarter.

         All those who have no scents are without gnosis;
            this scent's the scent that is the sacred fragrance.

445   When he had caught a scent and gave no thanks,
            ingratitude for kindness nipped his nose.

         Give thanks and be the servant of the grateful;
            before them be as one who's dead. Be constant.

         Do not, like this vizier, subsist on crime;
            do not hold people up and steal their prayers!

         That infidel vizier took holy orders;
            he spiked the cake with garlic by a trick.

The Astute among the Christians Understand
the Vizier's Tricks

All men of taste could see in what he said
    delight and malice joined as one in him.

He made his subtle points, and he would mix   450
    the poison poured into the sweet rose-water.

Appearance said, 'Be active on the path!'
    But in effect he told the soul, 'Be idle!'

While silver has a surface new and shiny,
    the hands and clothes are blackened by it still.

Though fire may have a red face from the sparks,
    you'll see the effects of what it does to you.

Though lightning shines a light into the eyes,
    it has the power to rob you of your sight.

For all except discriminating knowers,   455
    his words were like a chain around their necks.

For six long years in exile from the king,
    that vizier took his refuge with the Christians.

The people gave their faith and hearts to him;
    the people would have died at his command.

The King's Secret Messages to the Vizier

Between the king and him went messages
    of secret consolations for the king,

That in the end according to his wishes
    he'd scatter them like dust upon the wind.

460   To him the king wrote, 'O my favourite,
    the time has come, now quickly free my heart!'

He said, 'Your Majesty, I am about
    to launch revolt within the faith of Jesus.'

Explanation of the Twelve Tribes of Christians

The Christian congregation was in conflict,
    there were twelve leaders as their ministers.

Each sect was dedicated to its leader,
    enslaved to him by their own expectations.

These dozen leaders and their congregation
    became enslaved to that malicious vizier.

465   They all had confidence in what he said,
    all followed the example of his conduct.

Were he to tell them 'Die!', each of the leaders
    would give their lives up there and then for him.

The Vizier's Confounding of the Gospel's Injunctions

He made a manuscript in each one's name,
  each manuscript designed a different way.

Each one had doctrines of a different kind,
  this one opposed to that right to the end.

In one the path of hardship and of hunger
  was vital for repentance and return.

In one he said, 'Austerity is useless;   470
  on this path generosity is all.'

In one he said, 'To fast or to be generous
  makes partners of yourselves with your Adored
  One.

Except for trust and utter self-surrender,
  in sorrow or repose, all is deception.'

In one he said, 'Your service is required,
  or else all thoughts of trust are mere suspicion.'

In one he said, 'Commands and prohibitions
  are warnings of our weakness, not for practice,

So we may see our weakness signalled in them,   475
  and at that moment we shall know His power.'

In one he said, 'Do not look at your weakness;
  such weakness is ingratitude for blessings.

See that your power is power gained from Him;
  know that your power's His grace, the grace of
  Hu.'

In one he said, 'Pass far beyond these two;
    all that which sight contains is but an idol.'

In one he said, 'Do not put out this lamp;
    this vision is the lamp that gives you focus.

480   When you leave vision and imagination,
    you have snuffed out the lamp of midnight union.'

In one he said, 'Snuff out them all. Fear not!
    And you shall see a hundred thousand visions.

From snuffing out, the lamp of soul increases;
    your Layli will become Majnun with patience.

Whoever leaves the world by his own striving,
    the world will come the more to him again.'

In one he said, 'All that which God has given you
    God made it sweet for you in His creating.

485   He made it easy for you, take it gladly!
    Do not subject yourself to suffering.'

In one he said, 'Abandon what you are;
    acceptance of your nature is appalling!

The different paths have all become convenient,
    and each one's creed as dear as life to them.

If making God seem easy were the way,
    then every Jew and infidel would know Him.'

In one he said, 'That would be easiness,
    if inner life could be the spirit's food.

490   When all your nature's tastes are given up,
    it yields no growth and fruit, like barren soil.

And there will be no fruit except repentance,
and selling it will bring forth only loss.

And that will not be "easy" in the end,
for in the end its name is "difficult".

Make sure you can tell "difficult" from "easy"
and see that both have beauty in the end.'

In one he said, 'Go find yourself a master;
you'll not find vision in your ancestry.

The diverse forms of faith could see the end;   495
they could not but be prisoners of sin.

To see the end is not like spinning yarn
– if so, could there be differences in faiths?'

In one he said, 'Indeed you are the master!
Because indeed you're knower of the master.

Be bold, and do not be the butt of jokes;
go use your head and do not have it turned!'

In one he said, 'The whole of this is one –
he who sees two is but a cross-eyed pup.'

In one, 'How can a hundred be just one?   500
He certainly is mad, whoever thinks that!'

Each statement contradicted all the others.
How can a poison be the same as sugar?

Until you quit the poison and the sugar,
how can you smell the flowers of unity?

Like this, twelve manuscripts were written down
by that opponent of the faith of Jesus.

Explanation That These Dissensions Are in the Form of the Procedure, Not in the Truth of the Path

He had no scent of Jesus' purity
    nor nature dyed in Jesus' dying vat.

505   In that pure vat, clothes of a hundred colours
    turned pure and single-hued as little children.

It's not the monochrome that brings fatigue,
    more like a fish in water crystal clear.

A thousand colours there may be on land,
    but for the fishes there is war on dryness.

What is a fish and sea in my example
    to which the great and glorious King is likened?

In fact a hundred thousand seas and fishes
    bow down to that munificence and kindness.

510   How many showers of favour were rained down
    so as to make the ocean strew its pearls!

How many a noble sun has blazed to teach
    the clouds and oceans generosity!

The ray of knowledge struck the earth and clay
    that earth become accepting of the seed.

The faithful earth is all you've ever sown;
    you've reaped its product, never disappointed.

This faithfulness comes from that Faithful One,
    the Sun of Justice has shone down upon it.

Until God's sign is brought by spring anew,   515
   the earth does not reveal its mysteries.

That Generous One who gave the mineral state
   these intimations, faithfulness and truths,

To minerals His favour is enlightening,
   yet prudent men are blinded by His wrath.

This ardour is too much for heart and soul.
   Whom can I tell? There's no ear in the world.

Where there was ear, He turned it into eye;
   where there was stone, He turned it into jasper.

He is an alchemist, and what is alchemy?   520
   He is the source of miracles – what's magic?

For me to praise is interrupting praise
   – it's proof of 'being'. 'Being' is an error.

You must not be when you are in His presence,
   and what is being with Him? Blind and blue.

For He would melt you if you were not blind;
   you would have known the scorching of the sun.

And if they were not blue in consolation,
   how could these shores have stayed congealed like
     ice?

Explanation of the Vizier's Downfall
in This Deception

525 The vizier, like his king, was dull and stupid,
   he fought against Necessity Eternal,

A God so powerful that out of nothing
  He instantly creates a hundred worlds.

He makes a hundred worlds like this appear
  the instant that He makes you see through
   selfhood.

Look, if this world seems vast to you and endless,
  before His might it's no more than a speck.

This world is just the prison of your souls.
  Be gone from here towards your open plains!

530 This world is finite, that one infinite;
   reality is blocked by form and image.

The hundred thousand lances of the Pharaoh
  were broken by a Moses with one rod.

The hundred thousand medicines of Galen
  were laughable compared to Jesus' breath.

There were a hundred thousand books of poems
  all shamed by words of the unlettered Prophet.

With such an overwhelming Lord to face,
  would anyone not die, except a scoundrel?

535 How many a mountain-heart did He uproot!
   He hung the crafty bird by its two feet!

To hone the mind and wits is not the way;
 the broken man alone gets royal favour.

How many treasure-hunters digging holes
 disgraced themselves before that fantasist?

Who is the ox that you should be its beard?
 What is the earth that you should be its weed?

When woman was ashamed of her wrong-doing,
 God changed her form and made her into Venus.

If it was change to make a woman Venus,   540
 is not becoming clay a change, O rebel?

The Spirit brought you to the highest orbit,
 you fell down to the depths in mud and water.

You did transform yourself by this descending
 from that existence envied by the angels.

Then look at what this alteration is –
 compared with that, it's infinitely worse.

You raced ambition's stallion to the stars,
 you did not know how Adam was adored.

You're Adam's offspring, O unworthy one,   545
 how long will you think villainy distinguished?

How often will you say, 'I'll take a world,
 I'll keep on filling up this world with me!'

If all the world were snowed up end to end,
 the sun's ray would dissolve it with a glance.

So in a single flash God can destroy
 a hundred thousand viziers and their crimes.

He turns the essence of those lies to wisdom,
    the essence of that poison into nectar.

550   He turns the seeds of doubt into assurance,
    makes loving kindness grow from roots of hatred.

He nurtures Abraham within the fire,
    makes strength of spirit out of fearfulness.

Perplexed to see the burning up of causes,
    I'm like a sophist wondering about Him.

The Vizier's Stirring Up of More Deception in the Misleading of the People

That vizier hit upon another trick:
    he went into retreat and gave up preaching.

He lit the fire of yearning in his students;
    for five and forty days he was secluded.

555   His flock were going mad with yearning for him,
    without his states and talks and his experience.

They cried, lamenting without ceasing, for him,
    bent double in the pains of his retreat.

They said, 'We have no light without yourself.
    What is the blind man's fate without the guide?

For kindness' sake and for the sake of God,
    don't keep us parted from you anymore!

We are like infants, and you are our nursemaid.
    Spread out your shadow over all our heads.'

He said, 'My soul's not far from my adorers,   560
    but I am not allowed to venture out.'

The leaders came to him with their entreaties,
    and devotees arrived full of rebuke.

'O how unfortunate this is for us, sir,
    in heart and faith without you we are orphans.

You make excuses, we in all our pain
    heave out cold sighs from burning in our hearts.

We have grown used to your delightful words;
    we have been suckled on your wisdom's milk.

For God's sake, do not be so cruel to us.   565
    Be kind to us today; don't say "Tomorrow".

Does your heart let you leave these lovesick souls
    to end up with the desperate men without you?

All flap about like fish upon dry land.
    Unblock the stream and let the waters flow.

Incomparable one in all the world,
    for God's sake, be the saviour of your people.'

The Vizier's Refusal to the Disciples

He said, 'Look here, you slaves of speech and talk,
    who seek advice in words of tongue and ear.

Stuff cotton-wool into the sensual ear;   570
    strip off the sensual blindfold from your eyes.

The sensual ear blocks up the ear of mystery –
    till it goes deaf, the inward ear is deaf.

Be sense-less and be ear-less and be thought-less
   so that you hear the call that says, "Return!"

While you're caught up in wakeful conversation
   how can you catch the fragrance of dream-talk?

Our speech and action are an outer journey;
   the inner journey is above the sky.

575   Born out of drought, sense always looks at dryness,
   the Jesus of the soul steps out to sea.

Dry body's journey takes it over dry earth,
   the soul's goes on into the heart of oceans.

Since life is passed upon the road of dryness,
   now over mountain, over sea and plain,

Where will you take the living water from?
   Where will you break the wave upon the sea?

The earthly wave is fancy, thought and reason;
   the watery wave is death, effacement, stupor.

580   While you're drunk here, you're far from that drunk
      state.
   Blind drunk on this, you're blinded to that cup.

Your worldly speech and talk have turned to dust.
   Be silent for a while and understand!'

The Disciples Repeat 'Break Your Retreat!'

The crowd were saying, 'Loophole-finding sage,
    don't ply us with these tricks and cruelty!

Load on the beast a burden it can bear;
    impose upon the weak what they can do.

The bait for every bird should fit its size –
    how could a fig be food for every bird?

You give a baby bread instead of milk –   585
    you'll see the poor thing die of that same
    bread.

But after that, when teeth are coming through,
    then of itself its heart will seek for bread.

When any wingless chick takes off to fly,
    it is the meal of every vicious cat.

When it grows wings, it flies all by itself
    without complaint, without a call or cry.

Your utterance will make the Demon silent;
    your speech is edifying to our ears.

Our ears are edified when you are speaking;   590
    our dryness is the sea when you're the ocean.

With you, earth treats us better than does heaven,
    illuminator of the constellations!

Without you we have darkness over heaven;
    with you, dear moon, who is this heaven at all?

The heavens appear to have great elevation.
   True elevation is the pure in spirit,

And bodies seem to have great elevation,
   but bodies are mere names before the spirit.'

The Vizier's Answering, 'I Shall Not Break My Retreat!'

595   He said, 'Just put a stop to all your pleas!
      Make way for counsel in your hearts and souls.

If I am true, my trust should not be doubted,
   though I should say to you that heaven is earth.

If I am perfect, why deny I'm perfect?
   If not, then what's this trouble and distress?

I do not wish to leave this solitude,
   for I am busy with my inward states.'

The Opposition of the Disciples to the Vizier's Retreat

All said, 'O vizier, this is not denial;
   our words are nothing like an enemy's.

600   The tears run from our eyes from missing you;
      the sighs come up from deep inside the soul.

The infant does not quarrel with its nurse
   but cries although it knows no good or bad.

We're like the harp, and you are striking it.
   We do not make the cry – you make us cry.'

We're like the reed-flute and our sound is from You;
    our echoes are from You – we are like mountains.

We are like chessmen caught in check and mate;
    our check and mate are Yours, Whose moves are
       lovely.

Who are we, You Who are our soul of souls,   605
    that we exist at all when in your presence?

We and our being are nonentities,
    You, Being Absolute, who shows us death.

We are all lions but lions upon a flag
    whose onrush from the wind is every moment.

Their onrush can be seen, the wind is unseen.
    May that which is unseen be never lost!

Our breath and our existence are Your gift;
    all our existence is of Your invention.

You showed the joy of being to nothingness;   610
    You'd made this nothingness Your paramour.

Don't take away the pleasure of Your grace;
    don't take away Your sweets, Your wine and
       wine-cup.

And if You do remove them, who protests?
    How can the image struggle with the artist?

Do not regard us, do not gaze on us;
    look on Your grace and liberality.

Both we and our demands were never here.
    Your grace has heard what we have never said.

615   Before the artist and the brush, the picture
           is like the foetus, weak and limited.

       Before His power, all creatures of the court
           are powerless like the thread under the needle.

       He paints the demon's form, or sometimes Adam's.
           He will paint joy sometimes, or sometimes sadness.

       No one can ever raise a hand to stop Him;
           no tongue can say a word in help or loss.

       You should explain the verse of the Quran:
           God said, 'You did not smite when you were
               smiting.'

620   If we shoot arrows they are not from us;
           we are the bow, the one who shoots is God.

       It is not fate, it's His almighty spirit;
           'almightiness' is said for lowliness.

       Our lowliness confirms necessity;
           our shamefulness confirms our own free-will.

       If there is no free-will, what is this shame?
           What is regret, or shame or modesty?

       Why tension between masters and their pupils?
           Why does the mind make changes to its plans?

625   You say they take no note of His compulsion,
           and God's moon hides its face behind the cloud.

       A good response to this, if you will listen,
           is: Turn from unbelief and turn to faith.

It's sighs and sorriness when you are sick;
　the time of sickness is a time to waken.

Just at the time when you are falling sick,
　you beg forgiveness for your trespasses.

The hatefulness of sin is shown to you,
　and you resolve, 'I'll come back to the path.'

You promise and you pledge that 'After this,　　630
　I'll only choose obedience for my deeds.'

So this becomes a certainty, that sickness
　will bring good sense to you, and wakefulness.

So know this for a fact, fact-finding one:
　whoever is in pain has got the scent.

She who is more awake is in more pain;
　she who is more aware is paler-faced.

You know His power? Where's your humility?
　Where is your sense of His Almighty chain?

How can you be content bound up in chains?　　635
　When can the prisoner be free in gaol?

And if you see that your two feet are bound,
　and soldiers of the king are guarding you,

Don't treat the helpless as if you're a soldier!
　That's not the way the helpless should behave.

If you can't see His power, don't say you do,
　and if you can see it, how shall we know?

In all the actions of which you approve,
　you clearly see the power that is yours.

640 But in those actions you don't like or want,
    you make yourself a fatalist: 'God did it!'

The prophets are the fatalists of this world,
    and infidels the next world's fatalists.

There's free-will for the prophets in the next world;
    the ignorant have free-will in this world.

For every bird will follow its own species;
    it flies behind the soul which takes the lead.

The infidels were like the race of hell;
    they have become well used to this world's hell.

645 The prophets were all like the race of heaven;
    they went towards the heaven of heart and soul.

These words go on forever, but we shall
    go back to tell the ending of the tale.

The Vizier's Making the Disciples Lose Hope of His Leaving His Retreat

That vizier shouted out from his retreat,
    'Disciples! Be informed by me of this,

That Jesus sent this message down to me:
    "Withdraw yourself from all your friends and
    kinfolk.

Sit all alone, your face turned to the wall,
    and choose seclusion from your very being."

650 Henceforth I am prohibited to speak,
    no more have I a use for words and speech.

Farewell to you, my friends, for I am dead,
    departed to the fourth estate of heaven.

So I'll not burn beneath this fiery dome
    like kindling wood, in sorrow and affliction.

From now on I am seated next to Jesus,
    right at the top of heaven's fourth estate.'

The Vizier's Separate Appointment of Each
One as Successor

And there and then he called upon those leaders,
    and one by one instructed each alone.

He said to each, 'You are God's deputy   655
    and my successor in the faith of Jesus.

Those other leaders are your followers;
    Lord Jesus made them all your underlings.

Seize any leader struggling in resistance,
    and kill him or arrest him as a prisoner.

But while I live do not reproach them thus;
    until I die do not claim this command.

Until I die you must not make this known;
    do not pretend to rulership and power.

You have here the Messiah's scroll and precepts;   660
    read each one clearly to the congregation.'

Each leader was addressed by him in private:
    'God's faith has no vicegerent except you.'

Each one he honoured individually,
and what he said to each he said to all.

He gave a different scroll to every leader,
each one designed to contradict the rest.

The content of those scrolls was all contrary,
as different as the letters 'A' to 'Z'.

665   The rule of one was flouted by another –
we have described this state of strife before.

The Vizier's Suicide in Retreat

He shut himself away for forty days,
then killed himself and fled from his existence.

When people were informed about his death,
it was the Day of Judgement round his grave.

So many people gathered at his grave,
all tearing hair and ripping clothes in grief,

That God alone can estimate their number,
of Arabs, and of Turks and Greeks and Kurds.

670   They heaped the dust upon their heads for him;
they saw their pain for him as their own cure.

A month long those poor creatures at his grave
were streaming paths of blood from both their eyes.

The Church of Jesus, on Whom Be Peace, Asks the Leaders, 'Which of You Is the Successor?'

A month passed and the people said, 'O sirs,
    which leaders are appointed in his place?

Instead of him we'll take him as our leader,
    and put our hands and skirts into his hand.

And since the sun has set and left us scorched,
    there's nothing in his place except a lamp.

Now union with the Friend is lost from sight;   675
    an heir is needed to remind us of him.'

Now that the rose is gone, the garden ruined,
    where shall we find the rose's scent? Rose-water.

When God does not come clearly into view,
    these prophets are the deputies of God.

No, my mistake; if you should count them two
    this deputy and chief – it's wrong not right.

They're two while you're a worshipper of form.
    For anyone beyond form they're united.

When you are seeing forms, your eyes are double.   680
    Look at the light from which the eye has grown.

The light of two eyes can't be separated
    when people turn their gaze upon their light.

If ten lamps are together in one place,
    each one is different from the next in form.

You cannot tell apart the light of each
   when you are looking at them, there's no doubt.

If you should count a hundred quince and apples,
   they won't remain a hundred when you crush them.

685   There are no parts or numbers in the spirit,
   no persons or partitions in the spirit.

The oneness of the Friend delights the friends –
   catch hold of spirit's foot, for form is stubborn.

Dissolve the stubborn form with acts of hardship
   till you see oneness under it like treasure.

And if you don't dissolve it, then His favours
   themselves dissolve it, O my heart, His slave.

He even manifests Himself to hearts
   and He will mend the ragged dervish robe.

690   We were all open-hearted, all one essence;
   we were all headless, we were footless there.

And of one essence were we, like the sun;
   we had no knots and we were pure like water.

When that pure light began to take on form,
   it multiplied like battlements in shadows.

Destroy the battlements with catapults,
   so that division leaves this company.

I would explain this quite contentiously,
   and yet I fear that some minds may be shaken.

695   The points are sharp as swords of steel are sharp –
   if you have not a shield, then run away!

Do not approach this diamond steel unshielded,
   because this sword is not ashamed to cut.

It's for this reason I have sheathed my sword,
   that one who reads askew will not read wrongly.

We're coming to the ending of the tale
   about the righteous flock's fidelity.

That once this demagogue had gone, they rose up
   demanding in his place a deputy.

The Leaders' Struggle over Succession

One of those leaders of the church stepped
         forward   700
   and went before that flock of faithful hearts.

He said, 'See, I am that man's deputy,
   the deputy of Jesus for this time.

Behold! This manuscript is how I demonstrate
   that after him your deputy is me.'

Another leader came out from the shadows;
   his claim to be successor was the same.

His arms also displayed a manuscript,
   and Jewish anger rose in both the men.

Those other leaders one by one in order   705
   had taken up their swords of tempered steel,

And each a sword and scroll to hand, they fell
   on one another like wild elephants.

A hundred thousand Christians went to slaughter,
　　till there was heaped a hill of severed heads,

Blood rushing in a torrent left and right,
　　the dust thrown up by them as high as
　　　　mountains.

The seeds of disagreement he had sown
　　turned into this calamity for them.

710　　The walnuts cracked and those which had a kernel
　　would keep a spirit pure and clear in death.

The death and dying of the body's form
　　are like the opening of pomegranates.

That which is sweet is pomegranate juice;
　　the rotten one is nothing but hot air.

That which has spirit will indeed be seen;
　　that which is rotten will be in disgrace.

Go seek the spirit, worshipper of form;
　　the body of this form has wings of spirit.

715　　Be close to those of spiritual nature
　　that you acquire that gift and be humane.

A soul that lacks in spirit in this body
　　is like a wooden sabre in your scabbard.

So long as it is sheathed, it looks the part;
　　when it is drawn, it's firewood to be burned.

Don't take a wooden sabre into battle.
　　Check first, so things do not go all awry!

If it is wooden, go and find another;
   if adamantine steel, go happily.

This sword is in the storehouse of the saints;   720
   to see them is a transmutation for you.

The wise have all agreed on this exactly;
   the wise one is '*a mercy to all creatures*'.

A pomegranate should be bought when laughing
   so that its laugh will tell you of its seeds.

How lucky is its laugh, for from its mouth
   its heart is shown like pearls in soulful caskets.

But inauspicious was the tulip's laughter
   whose mouth displayed the blackness of its heart.

The pomegranate's laugh delights the garden   725
   and human company will make you human.

You may be stone, or you may be of marble,
   but when you meet the heart-strong you're a jewel.

Implant the pure ones' love within your soul,
   and keep your heart for love of the sweet-hearted.

Do not go down the hopeless track – there's hope.
   Do not go to the darkness – there are suns.

The heart will lead you to the heart-strong way,
   the body to the gaol of earth and water.

Go on and feed your heart from friendly hearts;   730
   go find your fortune with the fortunate.

The Praise of the Description of Mohammed (Peace and Blessings Be Upon Him), Which Was Mentioned in the Gospel

Mohammed's name was in the Christian Gospel,
  the paragon of prophets, purest ocean.

It spoke about his qualities and looks;
  it spoke about his wars and food and fasting.

One sect of Christians used to come upon
  his name and those remarks and, for some
  favour,

Would offer kisses to that noble name
  and bow their faces at that fine description.

735   In that dispute we just described, that group
  were safe from dispute and from fearfulness,

Safe from the wicked vizier and his leaders,
  protected by Mohammed's name, in refuge.

And their descendants multiplied as well.
  Mohammed's light befriended them and helped
  them.

Those other groups among the Christian folk
  would hold the name 'Mohammed' in contempt.

They were despised and ruined by the plot
  of that vile-thinking, vile-behaving vizier.

740   And their faith and their laws were overthrown
  by those perversely worded manuscripts.

Mohammed's name is such a friend as this,
  so then, how does his light afford protection?

And if Mohammed's name was such a bastion,
  what is the essence of that faithful spirit?

THE STORY OF ANOTHER JEWISH KING WHO MADE AN ATTEMPT TO DESTROY THE RELIGION OF JESUS

Now after this incurable mass-murderer
who fell under the spell of that vizier,

There was another king of that Jew's line
who was intent on killing Jesus' flock.

745   If you would know about this other outrage,
recite 'By heaven of the constellations'.

This second king began to take a step
upon the evil way the first had opened.

Whoever sets out on a wicked path,
a curse befalls him each and every hour.

Good men proceeded and their paths remained,
but base men left injustices and curses.

Till Resurrection Day all evil types
who come into existence face that fact.

750   In every vein these sweet and bitter waters
flow in our natures till the last trump sounds.

Sweet water is the inheritance of the good.
What is that gift? 'We have bequeathed the Book.'

You'll notice that the prayers of those who seek
are flashes from the jewel of prophecy.

The flashes are revolving round the jewels;
   the flash goes everywhere the jewel turns.

The skylight's beam is running round the house
   because the sun goes through the zodiac.

For each man has a kinship with a star;   755
   he is a fellow-traveller with his star.

With Venus his ascendant, his whole cast
   of mind and love and quest will be for joy.

And if his birth is under murderous Mars,
   he will seek war and calumny and hatred.

And way beyond the stars are other stars
   with nothing burning or unlucky in them.

They are the travellers of other heavens,
   not of these seven heavens that we know.

Established in the brilliance of God's lights,   760
   not joined with, nor apart from, all the rest.

He whose ascendant is among these stars,
   his self strikes unbelievers with a stoning.

His anger's not that of the Mars-born man,
   with face upset in triumph and defeat.

The winning light is safe from fault and gloom
   between the fingers of the light of God.

When God diffused that light upon all souls,
   all those who would receive it held their skirts
      out.

765   And she who gained that offering of light
           has turned her face from all except the Lord.

       Whoever did not have the skirts of love
           has not partaken of that gift of light.

       Particulars are facing towards the whole;
           the nightingales adore the rose's face.

       The ox's colours are outside, and man's
           are red and yellow to be found within.

       Fair hues are from the vat of purity;
           the hideous stains are from the murk of crime.

770   'God's dye' is what we call that subtle colour,
           'the curse of God' that dirty colour's smell.

       And what is from the sea is going back,
           returning to the place from which it came,

       The torrents rushing down from mountain peaks,
           and from our bodies souls mixed up with love.

The Jewish King Made a Fire and Placed an Idol by the Fire so That Whoever Adored the Idol Would Escape from the Fire

       Now see what plot the Jewish dog contrived:
           he placed an idol just beside the fire,

       'All who adore the idol shall escape,
           but if you won't, you'll sit upon the fire.'

775   He did not smash the idol of his self,
           and his self's idol spawned another idol.

Self's idol is the mother of all idols.
   That idol is a snake, this one's a dragon.

The self is iron and stone, the idol sparks,
   those sparks have their extinguishing from water.

But how can water calm the iron and stone?
   How can a man with these two be secure?

The idol is black water in a pitcher.
   Know that the self's the source of this black water.

That sculpted idol's like the blackening tide,   780
   the idol-self's the fountain of the channel.

One piece of stone will smash a hundred pitchers,
   and all the while the fountain gushes forth.

To smash the idol's simple, very simple;
   to see the self as simply smashed is stupid.

To get an image of your self, my boy,
   go read the story of hell's seven gates.

Each moment some contrivance! And in each
   a hundred Pharaohs and Egyptians drowned.

Flee to the God of Moses, and to Moses;   785
   don't pour away faith's water like the Pharaoh.

Join hands with God the One and with Mohammed,
   escape the Bu Jahl of the body, brother!

The Child Began to Speak from within the Fire and Encouraged the People to Throw Themselves into It

The Jew then brought a woman with her child
  before the fire – the fire was all aflame.

He seized her child and threw it in the fire;
  she was afraid and rid her heart of faith.

But as she went to bow before the fire,
  her child cried out, 'I am not going to die.

790   Come in, dear mother. I am well in here,
         though in appearance I am in the fire.

The fire's a blindfold on the eye – a veil;
  this is a mercy that has reared its head.

Come in, dear mother. See the proof of God,
  and see the rapture of God's favourites.

Come in. See how this water looks like fire;
  come from a world of fire which looks like water.

Come, see the mysteries, how Abraham
  found cypress and found jasmine in the fire.

795   I looked at death when I was born from you;
         I had great fear of falling from your loins.

When I was born, I broke out of the gaol
  into a world of fragrant air and lovely hues.

Now I have seen the world's a womb once more,
  for in this fire I've seen tranquillity.

Within this fire I've seen a universe
  where every atom has the breath of Jesus.

Behold the world of no-form which has essence,
  the world of form which has no constancy.

Come in, by your maternal right, dear mother.   800
  See how this fire is free of fieriness.

Come in, dear mother. Happiness has come.
  Come in, dear mother. Don't let go of triumph.

You saw the power which that dog possessed;
  come in and see the power and grace of God.

I pull you by your feet for mercy's sake,
  for in my joy I'm not beholden to you.

Come in, and call the others in as well,
  for in the fire the king has spread a table.

Will you come in, dear Muslims, all of you!   805
  For all is pain except for faith's fresh water.

Will you come in, like moths upon the wing
  into this hundred-springtime happiness!'

The child called out before the multitude;
  the people's souls were filled with reverence.

And then the people were beside themselves;
  the men and women leapt into the fire,

Unforced, unpulled, but in their love for Him,
  the Friend who sweetens every bitter thing.

So much that it transpired his mercenaries   810
  were holding back the crowd: 'Keep off the fire!'

That Jewish king turned black of face with shame;
    he turned regretful, sick at heart at this,

That people grew more ardent in their faith,
    more earnest in transcendence of the body.

The devil's tricks backfired on him, thank heaven!
    The devil saw himself black-faced, thank heaven!

What he was rubbing on to people's faces
    was heaped upon that worthless fellow's face.

815   He who was tearing all the people's clothes
    was all torn up while they remained intact.

How the Mouth of the Man Who Mocked the Name of Mohammed (Peace Be Upon Him) Remained Screwed Up

A man screwed up his mouth and shouted rudely
    to mock Mohammed, and his face stayed twisted.

Returning, he said, 'Pardon me, Mohammed,
    O you who have the gift of higher knowledge.

For I poured scorn on you from foolishness.
    It's I who should be scorned and do deserve it.'

When God desires to show somebody up,
    He turns their minds to vilify the holy.

820   And if God should desire to hide their faults,
    He does not criticize the ones at fault.

When God desires to give us his assistance,
    He moves our tendency to lamentation.

O happy are the eyes lamenting Him!
    How blessed are the hearts that burn for Him!

When weeping ends there is a smile at last.
    How happy is the man who is far-sighted!

Wherever water's flowing, flowers grow,
    and mercy flows wherever tears are flowing,

Groan like the water-wheel and be moist-eyed   825
    that green may grow the meadows of your soul.

If you want tears, show mercy to the tearful;
    if you want mercy, show the weak your mercy.

The Fire Rebukes the Jewish King

The king reproached the fire, 'O hasty one!
    Where has your world-consuming nature gone?

Why aren't you burning? Where's your nature gone?
    Or has our fortune altered your intent?

You do not spare the worshipper of fire.
    How do non-worshippers of fire escape you?

You're never the long-suffering one, O fire!   830
    If you're not burning, why? Are you not able?

Is this some marvel blinding eyes and mind?
    Why is not such a high fire incandescent?

Are you bewitched by someone, or some magic?
    Does your unnaturalness come from our fortune?'

The fire said, 'I'm the same, idolater!
    Come in, so that you may perceive my heat.

My element and nature are unchanged.
  I am Truth's sword – and by His leave I cut.'

835 The Turcomans have dogs at their tent doors
  which fawn and cringe before the visitor.

But if a strange face passes by the tent,
  he sees the dogs attack him just like lions.

In service I am no less than a lapdog;
  in life God is no less than Turcomans.

And if your nature's fire should cause you pain,
  it burns by order of the Lord of Judgement.

And if your nature's fire should cause you joy,
  the Lord of Judgement puts the joy in it.

840 When you are feeling pain, then ask forgiveness:
  the pain that the Creator wills is useful.

He wills, and pain itself is turned to joy.
  His very manacles will make you free.

Wind, earth and fire and water are his slaves;
  dead things with us, they are alive with God.

The fire is always upright before God,
  and writhing like a lover day and night.

You strike a stone on iron and out it leaps;
  it is by God's command that it comes forth.

845 Do not strike cruelty's iron and stone together
  for these two multiply like man and woman.

Indeed the stone and iron are causes, yet
  consider what's above them, my good man,

That Cause has given rise to all these causes.
    Were causes ever of themselves, and causeless?

Those Causes which give guidance to the prophets
    are higher Causes than these causes are.

That Cause will implement these causes here,
    or then sometimes It makes them ineffective.

Our minds became familiar with these causes;   850
    the prophets are familiar with those Causes.

What is this 'cause' in Arabic? It's 'rope'.
    This 'rope' has come into this 'well' by scheming.

The purpose of the rope's to turn the wheel,
    but not to see the turner is a sin.

These ropes of causes that are in the world,
    do not suppose they're from this giddy wheel!

Don't end up blank and giddy like the wheel,
    and do not burn without a brain, like wood.

The wind consumes the fire at God's command;   855
    both are intoxicated by God's wine.

The streams of mercy and the fires of wrath
    are both from God, you'll see, when you are
        looking.

Had God not told the spirit of the wind,
    how could it have distinguished all Ād's people?

Around the faithful, Hud had drawn a line;
    the wind subsided when it reached that place,

And everyone who stood outside that line
   it blew up into pieces in the air.

860 Just in the way the shepherd Shaybān drew
   a clear line round and round his flock of sheep,

Whenever he would go to Friday prayers
   so that the wolf did not come raiding them.

There was no wolf could go into that circle,
   nor any sheep could stray across that line.

The winds of greed of both the wolf and sheep
   were fastened by the circle of God's man.

The wind of death is like this for the sages,
   so soft and pleasant like the breeze of Joseph.

865 Fire could not bite the prophet Abraham,
   a chosen one of God – how could it bite him?

The pious are not burning in lust's fire,
   which swept the rest down to the earth's abyss.

The ocean wave could rush at God's command
   and know all Moses' people from the Egyptians.

As, when the order came, the earth could drag
   Qārun, his gold and throne to its abyss.

The clay and water, fed on Jesus' breath,
   could spread out wings, become a bird, and fly.

870 Your praise is breathing out of clay and water,
   become the heavenly bird of heart's truth-breath.

Mount Sinai danced to see the light of Moses,
  became a perfect Sufi, freed from fault.

What wonder if the mountain was a Sufi,
  for Moses' body too was made of clay.

*The Scoffing and Denial of the Jewish
King and Refusal of the Advice of
His Own Counsellors*

That Jewish king saw all these miracles
  but only ridiculed and disbelieved them.

His counsellors said, 'Don't exceed the limit;
  don't ride the charger of your spite so hard.'

He tied the counsellors' hands and chained them   875
      up;
  he joined one chain of terror to another.

When things had got this far, a cry came up:
  'Stand still, you dog! Our vengeance has arrived!'

The fire flared up a hundred feet in height –
  it formed a ring around those Jews and burned
      them.

Their origin was fire from the beginning,
  and in the end they went back to their source.

The members of that sect were born of fire;
  the way of all the parts is to the whole.

They were a fire set up to burn the faithful   880
  – no more – their fire had burnt them up like
      straw.

And he whose Mother is the abyss of hell
   will find his refuge in the abyss of hell.

The mother of the child is seeking it;
   the origin is in pursuit of offspring.

If waters are entrapped within a pool,
   the wind absorbs it – like an element.

It sets it free and takes it to its source,
   but slowly – you don't see it being taken.

885   And this breath steals away our souls like this,
   but slowly, from the prison of this world.

The perfumes of our words ascend to Him,
   ascending from us up to where He knows
      them.

Our breaths go upwards in the chosen words
   as gifts from us to the eternal palace.

Then in reward for words there comes to us
   a double mercy from the Lord Almighty.

Then He will make us say the words like those,
   so that his slave may keep what he possesses.

890   *Thus they are going up and it comes down,*
   and may you never cease to keep that up!

Let's speak in Persian: I mean, this attraction
   comes from that quarter whence that tasting came.

The eyes of all the people turn towards
   that place where once a taste was gratified.

One kind will like its own kind's taste for certain;
   see how the parts are partial to the whole.

Or if one does accept another kind,
   as it is joined it turns into that kind.

So bread and water which were not our kind   895
   became our kind and multiplied in us.

These two do not appear to share our nature;
   from hindsight know that they are of our kind.

And if our taste is for another kind,
   it probably resembles our own kind.

That which resembles us is loaned to us –
   a loan is not forever, in the end.

And though the bird may have a taste for whistles,
   yet when it cannot find its own, it squawks!

Although the thirsty man may like the mirage,   900
   he'll get to it and flee in search of water.

The down and out are very pleased with false gold,
   but in the bank it will give rise to shame.

Beware lest false gold throw you off the path,
   lest crooked thinking throw you in the well.

Look at that fable now from Kalila
   and in that fable seek what you can find.

EXPLANATION OF TRUST IN GOD, AND THE HUNTED ANIMALS TELLING THE LION TO CEASE FROM STRIVING

Some animals lived in a lovely valley;
    forever they were harrassed by a lion.

And since that lion would ambush them and snatch
905   them,
    their grass had taken on a bitter taste.

They made a plan – they came to meet the lion
    and said, 'We'll keep you full with an allowance.

From now on don't come here in search of prey
    so that this grass may lose its bitter taste.'

The Lion Answers the Hunted Animals and Tells Them of the Excellence of Effort

'If I see faith, not trickery, then yes,
    but many a trick I've seen of Zayd and Bakr.

The shams and tricks of men are killing me;
    I have been stung by snake and scorpion bite.

910 The man of selfhood hiding in myself
    is worse than anyone in tricks and spite.

I heard "*The faithful are not bitten twice . . .*"
    the Prophet's saying gnawed my heart and soul.'

The Hunted Animals Insist on the Superiority of Trust over Effort and Striving

They all replied, 'O Knowledgeable Sage,
  "Let caution go, it's no use against fate."

In caution there is stirring up of turmoil.
  Go trust in God, for trust is so much better.

Don't shake your fist at fate, impetuous one,
  lest fate should also pick a fight with you.

You must be dead when faced with God's decree   915
  and be not struck down by the Lord of
    Daybreak.'

The Lion Insists on the Superiority of Effort and Striving over Trust and Surrender

'All right,' he said, 'if trust in God's the guide,
  the Prophet's Sunna is the means as well.

The Prophet said once in a great loud voice,
  "With trust in God, tie up your camel's leg."

Hear how *"the worker is beloved of God."*
  In trusting God do not ignore the means.'

The Hunted Animals Insist on the Superiority of Trust in God over Effort

They all told him, 'To gain from others' weakness
    is all a pack of lies to swallow whole!

920   There is no gain surpassing trust in God.
    What is indeed more precious than surrender?

How many flee one trial for another
    and run away from snakes and into dragons?

Man worked things out and his devices trapped him,
    and what he took for life would suck his blood.

He shut the door with enemies in the house –
    the Pharaoh's trick was such a tale as this.

He killed a hundred thousand sons in malice,
    and yet the child he sought was in his house!

925   There is so much defective in our sight.
    Give up your vision for the sight of God.

His vision for our vision – fair exchange –
    and in His vision gain all that you crave.

The baby cannot grasp and cannot walk;
    her only carrier is her daddy's neck;

But when she's busy on her own two feet,
    she's in all kinds of trouble and disaster.

Before their hands and feet, the human souls
    were flying on their faith in purity.

When they were bound by God's command "Go
  down!" 930
   their apathy and lust and anger gaoled them.

We are God's family and need His milk,
   "*Creation is a family in God.*"

The One who gives the rain that comes from heaven
   can also out of mercy give us bread.'

The Lion Asserts the Superiority of
Effort over Trust in God

The lion said, 'Yes, and yet the Lord of Slaves
   has put a scaling-ladder at our feet.

And step by step we must ascend the roof.
   It's vain desire to be a fatalist.

You have two feet so why make out you're lame? 935
   You have two hands so why conceal your grip?

A master gave his slave a spade to dig with;
   he made his purpose known without a word.

His intimations are the hand and spade;
   His meanings are reflection on the ending.

When your soul understands His intimations,
   you'll give your soul up to be faithful to them.

He gives you intimations of the secrets;
   He lifts your burden, giving you control.

He makes you who are burdened lifted up; 940
   He makes you well-received when you're
      receptive.

Receiving His commands, you are His mouthpiece.
  Seek union and you'll later be united.

Your striving thanks Him for His power's favour;
  your resignation questions all His favour.

Thanks for His power will increase your power;
  your resignation makes His favour leave you.

It is like sleeping in the road – don't sleep!
  Don't sleep until you see the gate and entrance.

945   Look out! Don't sleep, you lazy good-for-nothing,
  except beneath that tree laden with fruit,

So all the while the wind will cause the branches
  to shed sweet things upon the sleeper's head.

Your resignation and your sleeping rough!
  How can you trust the cock who can't keep time?

And if you should despise His intimations,
  you'll think you are a man when you're a woman,

And all that you possess of mind is lost –
  the head becomes a tail when mind has left it.

950   For thanklessness is niggardly and shameful;
  it takes the thankless to the depths of hell.

If you put trust in God, put trust in action,
  and sow the seed, then lean on the Almighty.'

The Hunted Animals Insist on the Superiority
of Trust in God over Effort

In unison they shouted out to him,
   'Those greedy ones who sowed the seeds of
     "causes"

– so many hundred thousand men and women –
   then why did they remain deprived of fortune?

A hundred thousand ages since creation
   have opened up a hundred mouths like dragons.

Such ruses that ingenious group contrived   955
   that mountains were uprooted by their ruses.

The Glorious One described their ruses thus:
   "That thereby might the mountain tops be moved".

Except what happened in eternity,
   their exploits and their ventures came to nothing.

They all fell short in planning and in action;
   the Lord Creator's acts and laws endured.

Don't think that gain is anything but name,
   and striving's anything but vanity!'

Ezrā'il Looks at a Man and That Man Flees to
the Palace of Solomon (Peace Be Upon Him)
Stating the Superiority of Trust in God over
Effort and the Pointlessness of Effort

960   One morning there arrived a nobleman
               who ran into the court of Solomon.

           His face was pale with grief, his lips were blue.
               Said Solomon, 'What is the matter, sir?'

           'Ezrā'il threw me such a look,' he answered,
               'so full of anger and of enmity.'

           He said, 'Come, tell me now what you desire.'
               'O saviour of my soul, instruct the wind

           To carry me from here to Hindustan
               that maybe there your slave's soul will be saved.'

965   Mankind is taking flight from poverty;
               mankind's a morsel for desire and greed.

           The fear of poverty is like that fellow;
               desire and greed are like his Hindustan.

           He ordered that the wind should quickly take him
               by river into inmost Hindustan.

           Next day it was the time of court and council
               when Solomon remarked to Ezrā'il,

           'So, did you cast that look upon that Muslim
               so angrily to drive him from his home?'

'When did I cast a glance at him in anger?   970
   I was astonished when I saw him passing,

For God had so instructed me, "Today
   you'll snatch his soul away in Hindustan!"

Surprised, I said, "Had he a hundred wings
   it would be far for him to go to Hindustan."'

You must judge all the world's affairs like this!
   Be shrewd and open up your eyes and see!

Who are we fleeing? Us. Impossible!
   Who are we robbing? God. It is a sin!

Again the Lion Insists on the Superiority of Effort over Trust in God and Explains the Benefits of Effort

The lion said, 'Oh yes, but now examine   975
   the struggles of the prophets and believers.

For God Most High supported their exertions,
   the cruelty and heat and cold they suffered.

Their strategies were all in fine condition;
   "all things are clever from a clever man."

Their traps have captured the celestial bird;
   all their shortcomings took a better turn.

Strive on, sir, for as long as you are able
   upon the prophets' and the saints' highway.

Our striving's not a wrestling match with fate,   980
   for fate itself imposed the struggle on us.

I'm damned if anyone was ever lost
    upon the path of faith and of obedience.

Don't bandage up your head if it's not broken!
    Make efforts for a while and then you're laughing!

He sought bad company who sought this world;
    he sought a happy state who sought the next.

Plans for the gaining of this world go cold;
    plans for the leaving of this world succeed.

985   The plan is that he burrows out of prison;
    the plan's gone wrong if he has blocked the tunnel.

This world's a prison: we are prisoners,
    so burrow out of prison and escape!

What is the world? Obliviousness of God,
    not goods and money, weighing-scales and
      women.

As for the riches that religion brings,
    the Prophet said, "*How good is righteous wealth!*"

The water *in* the boat will sink the boat,
    which floats upon the water *underneath* it.

990   Since Solomon had cleansed his heart of wealth
    and power, he'd only call himself "the poor".

A stoppered jar, in troubled waters even,
    can float on water, with its air-filled heart.

So when the air of poverty's within us,
    there's peace upon the waters of the world.

Although this whole world is His sovereign
   kingdom,
   this kingdom is as nothing to his heart's eye.

So close and seal the entrance of the heart
   and fill it with the air of majesty.

Effort's a fact, like cures and sicknesses.   995
   The sceptic makes his effort against effort.'

The Agreement That Effort Is Superior
to Trust in God

The lion offered many proofs like this;
   the fatalists got tired of answering him.

The fox and antelope and hare and jackal
   gave up their sophistry and resignation.

They made agreements with the raging lion
   that he should not lose out in this arrangement.

He must receive his portion without worry;
   there'd be no need for him to ask again.

Whoever drew the shortest straw each day   1000
   would run towards the lion like a cheetah.

But when this bitter cup came to the hare,
   the hare exclaimed, 'O how much more
      injustice?'

The Hunted Animals' Rejection of the Hare's Delaying Its Going to the Lion

The animals all told him, 'All this time
    we've sacrificed our lives to keep our promise.

Don't bring disgrace upon us, troublemaker!
    In case the lion gets upset, go quickly!'

The Hare Answers Them

'My friends,' he said, 'give me a little respite
    and by my trick you'll get out of this strife,

1005   And by my trickery you'll save your lives,
    and this will be your children's legacy;

For every prophet in the world has called
    his people to asylum in this way.

From heaven he has seen the way of freedom,
    contracted like the pupil of the eye.

For like the pupil he was seen as small.
    None understood the greatness of the pupil.'

The Hunted Animals' Criticism of the Words of the Hare

They all replied to him, 'You ass, you listen!
    Don't be an ass, remember you're a hare!

1010   Ha! What conceit is this that would not come
    into the minds of better men than you?

You are so smug! Will something fateful happen,
or else who's worthy of you at this moment?'

The Hare's Answer to the Animals

'My friends,' he said, 'God gave me inspiration;
a strength of mind possessed a feeble one.

What God has given as teaching to the bees
is not the teaching for the lion and zebra.

They make their houses full of liquid sweetness;
the door of such a craft God opened for them.

The teaching that God gave the little silkworms,   1015
no elephant can know those kinds of skills.

From God did clay-born Adam get his knowledge;
his knowledge shone up to the seventh heaven.

He broke the angel's name and reputation,
in spite of him who is in doubt of God.

For that six-hundred-thousand-year ascetic
God made a muzzle for that calf to wear,

So he'd not drink the milk of sacred knowledge
and so he'd not frequent that lofty palace.

The sciences of sensual men's the muzzle   1020
preventing them from milk of higher
knowledge.

A pearl fell in the droplet of the heart,
which He gave neither to the seas nor skies.

O worshipper of form, how much more form?
  Cannot your empty soul escape from form?

If man is human only through his form,
  Mohammed and Bu Jahl would be the same.

The painting on the wall resembles Adam –
  see what of him is missing from the image.

1025 The soul is lacking in that brilliant image.
  Go, find that pearl which is so seldom found.

The lions of all the world hung down their heads
  when God assisted the Companions' dog.

What loss is there from that repugnant shape?
  His soul was drowning in the sea of light.

In pens there is no true account or image;
  'the learned' and 'the just' are only names.

The learned and the just exist in spirit;
  they are not found in space, before or after.

1030 The spirit's sun beats down upon the body
  from no-place – not preserved within the heavens.'

The Account of the Hare's Knowledge and the Description of the Perfection and Profit of Knowledge

These words go on forever – quiet please!
  Do pay attention to the story of the hare!

Go sell your hare-brained ear and buy another!
  Your hare-brained ear will never hear these words.

Go see the foxy games the hare will play,
    the stunts and lion-taming of the hare.

The seal of Solomon's realm is purely knowledge,
    and all the world is form: its soul is knowledge.

The seas, the plains and mountains of creation   1035
    became subject to mankind from this virtue.

The lion and leopard fear him like a mouse;
    the river crocodile is in blind panic.

The demons and the sprites were grounded by him,
    and each one hid to get away from him.

Since man has many hidden enemies,
    the cautious man indeed is one who's wary.

The hidden creatures that are good and evil
    strike at the heart with blows at every moment.

If you should go to bathe yourself in streams,   1040
    a thorn may prick you while you're in the water.

Although the thorn is hidden in the water,
    you know it's there immediately it pricks you.

The wounds of inspirations and temptations
    come from a thousand sources, not from one.

Be still so that your senses are transformed,
    that you may see them and the pain is cured.

So that you see whose words you have refused
    and who it is you've made your sovereign lord.

The Animals Ask the Hare the Secret
of His Thought

1045   So then they said, 'Hey, you! You speedy hare!
        Set out before us what you have in mind.

        O you who've got yourself wrapped round a lion,
        announce the plan you think you will rely on.

        Consulting gives perspective and good sense,
        for, as they say, two heads are far superior.

        The Prophet said, "*O counsellor take counsel*"
        for "*He who is consulted will be trusted.*"'

How the Hare Kept the Secret from Them

        He said, 'Not every secret should be told,
        for things can turn out other than expected.

1050   Breathe on a mirror accidentally and
        the mirror straightaway becomes opaque.

        Don't breathe a word to tell of these three things:
        not of your going, nor your gold nor god.

        For many enemies and foes will wait
        in ambush when they know one of these three.

        And if you give it out to one or two – *Good-bye*,
        '*for every secret shared is known to all.*'

        For if you tie together several birds,
        they stay upon the ground caught in distress.

They have their consultation all in private,   1055
    in metaphor mixed with misleading things.

The Prophet took his counsel privately;
    they answered him while yet they did not know.

He'd speak his point of view in metaphors
    such that his rivals could not fathom him.

He'd get his answer from the other person
    who would detect no scent of his real question.

The Account of the Hare's Trickery

The hare delayed a little while in going,
    and then he visited the sharp-clawed lion.

Because he'd left it very late in going,   1060
    the lion was tearing up the earth and roaring.

He roared, 'I said the promise of those wretches
    would be in vain, in vain and weak and hopeless!

Their prattle threw me headlong from my donkey.
    How long will I be fooled by circumstances?'

The feeble prince is stuck when, like a fool,
    he does not look at what is all around him.

The road is level – under it are traps –
    there is a lack of meaning in the names.

The words and all the names resemble snares;   1065
    the sweetened word's the sand of our life's
        water.

The one sand from which water gushes out
　　is very seldom found – go seek it out!

The Man of God is just that sand, my son,
　　for he is one with God, devoid of selfhood.

Sweet waters of the faith gush out from him.
　　For those who seek there's life and growth from
　　　　him.

You know the man of God's not like the dust,
　　which always drinks your living water dry.

1070　So go in search of wisdom from the wise,
　　and with them you become both seer and sage.

The wisdom seeker is the source of wisdom,
　　for he is freed from gain and from resource.

The guarding stone becomes the guarded stone;
　　his mind becomes contented by the spirit.

To start with his instructor was his mind,
　　then later on his mind became his pupil.

Like Gabriel, the mind says, 'O Mohammed,
　　if I take one more step I shall be burned.

1075　Leave me behind, press further on than this;
　　this was my limit, sultan of the soul.'

Ungrateful and impatient lazy people
　　all know 'compulsion' has them by the foot.

Whoever gets compulsion will fall sick
　　until that sickness puts them in the grave.

The Prophet said that illness which is feigned
    brings sickness till you're snuffed out like a light.

So what is *jabr*? To bind up what is broken,
    to try to mend a vein that has been severed.

But since your leg's not broken on this path,   1080
    whom do you mock? Why wear a plaster cast?

He broke his leg upon exertion's path:
    Borāq arrived for him and on he got.

Faith's bearer, he became the one borne up.
    He was commanded and became commander.

Till now he took his orders from the king;
    henceforth he gives the orders to the troops.

Till now the stars have made impressions on him;
    henceforth he is the emperor of stars.

If difficulties now occlude your sight,   1085
    then you will doubt '*the moon was split
       asunder.*'

Renew your faith but not by speech of tongues,
    O you who have renewed your lust in secret.

As long as lust is new, your faith is not;
    this lust's indeed a lock upon that door.

You have interpreted the virgin word –
    interpret your own self, not holy scripture!

You lustfully interpret the Quran;
    you lowered and distorted its high meaning.

The Worthlessness of the Fly's
Filthy Explanation

1090   Aboard a straw on a pool of donkey piss,
             a fly would raise its head, a proud ship's skipper.

         It said, 'I speak of them as "sea" and "ship" –
             for quite a while I've been considering this.

         See! Here's the sea, and here's the ship – and me.
             I am the skipper, masterful and trusty.'

         He'd sail his little 'ship' upon his 'sea' –
             to him that little puddle seemed immense.

         And boundless to his size was that wee drop.
             Where is the eyesight that could really see it?

1095   His world is just as much as he can see;
             with this much eye his 'sea' is just as much.

         The useless exegete is like the fly:
             his mind is donkey piss, his concepts straw.

         And if the fly would quit his explanation,
             fortune would make the fly a bearded vulture.

         He who might think like that is not a fly;
             his spirit is not what his form belies.

The Lion's Roaring at the Late Arrival of the Hare

Just like that hare who struck against the lion,
　how could you match his spirit with his size?

The lion was saying in fury and in anger,　　　　1100
　'My enemy has blinded me with words!

The fatalists have stuffed my ears with tricks
　and pricked my body with their wooden swords.

From now on I'll not listen to their noise;
　it's all the sound of devils and of ghouls.

O heart, do not desist from rending them.
　Tear at their skin, for skin is all they are.

For what is skin? Just words of different hues,
　like waves on water with no permanence.'

These words are skin-like; meaning is the core.　　1105
　These words are surface; meaning's like the
　　soul.

Skin hides the faults inside the rotten kernel,
　with zeal it hides the healthy inner kernel.

For when the pen is wind, the book is water.
　Then all you write will quickly pass away.

It's water drawn – if you seek faith from it,
　you'll come back gnawing at your very hands.

The wind in man is vanity and lust.
　When you leave vanity, His message comes.

1110   How sweet are the Creator's messages;
            they stay from the beginning to the end.

        The sermons of the kings and realms will change,
            but not the realms of prophets and their sermons,

        Because the pomp of kings is from desire,
            but prophets' glory is from majesty.

        Though they efface the names of kings from coins,
            they stamp the Prophet's name on them forever.

        The Prophet's name is that of all the prophets,
            for with the hundredth we have ninety-nine.

            More on the Trickery of the Hare

1115   The hare made much delay in going forth
            as he recited to himself his plot.

        He reached the road after this long delay
            to whisper secrets in the lion's ear.

        So see, what worlds are in the core of reason!
            And how capacious is this sea of mind!

        Our forms are flitting on this limpid ocean
            like goblets bobbing on the water's surface.

        Until they're full like cups upon the sea –
            when they are full, the cups are drowned in it.

1120   The mind is hidden and a world appears;
            our form becomes the wave or spray from it.

        The form will use whatever means to reach it;
            the ocean casts away those means afar.

So long as hearts don't see the secret's giver,
   the arrow does not see the long-range archer.

A man thinks he has lost his horse and yet
   perversely speeds his horse upon the road.

That fine one thinks that he has lost his horse,
   and off his horse has swept him like the wind.

That silly man, in panic and in seeking,   1125
   goes searching on all sides from door to door:

'Who is the one who stole my horse, where is he?'
   'Sir, what's this one you have between your legs?'

'Indeed it is this horse, but where's this horse?'
   Come to yourself, O horseless cavalier!

The soul's so visible and near, it's lost,
   lips dry as dust and belly full of water.

How can you see the red and green and brown
   unless you see the light before these three?

But since your mind has gone astray in colours,   1130
   the colours formed a veil before the light.

And when at night those colours disappeared,
   you saw your seeing colour was from light.

No colour's seen without the outward light;
   the colours of the inward sight are like this.

This outward light is from the sun and Sohā,
   the inward light's reflection of sublime light.

Your own eye's light's light is the light of hearts;
   the eye's light is the outcome of the heart's light.

1135   Your own heart's light's light is the light of God;
           it's pure and far from mental, sensual light.

       At night there was no light; you saw no colours.
           Then it appeared to you through light's opponent.

       There is the sight of light and then of colour;
           you know this instantly from light's opponent.

       For God created pain and grief for this,
           that by these opposites contentment comes.

       So hidden things appear through opposites.
           God has no opposite; He stays concealed.

1140   For vision falls on light and then on colour.
           Extremes reveal extremes like black and white.

       So you know light by its own opposite –
           they show up one another coming forth.

       But God's light has no opposite in being,
           that you might make Him known through
               opposites.

       Undoubtedly our eyes 'Do not see Him,
           though He sees us' – see Moses and the mountain.

       – Like lions from the bush, form springs from spirit,
           or as the voice and words emerge from thought.

1145   This voice and all these words arise from thought;
           you do not know where this thought-sea resides.

       But since you've seen the wave of words is graceful,
           you know the sea they're from is noble too.

When knowledge sped the wave of thought along,
    it made the form of words and of the voice.

The form was born of words and died once more;
    the wave withdrew itself into the sea.

And form emerged from that which had no form,
    and it returned '. . . *to Him do we return.*'

Each moment you have death and the return –   1150
    the Prophet said the world is for an hour.

Our thought's an arrow in the air from Him.
    How could it stay aloft? – it goes to God.

Each instant is the world renewed and we
    are blind to its eternal renovation.

Life comes anew, afresh just like a stream;
    it seems to be perpetual in its form.

Its speed has made it seem continuous
    just as you whirl a firework in your hand.

You skilfully revolve the flaming torch;   1155
    to onlookers the fire appears so long.

This length of time is from the speed of action;
    it's manifested in the launch of action.

The seeker of this secret may be learned.
    Behold Hosāmoddin, who is a book sublime!

The Hare Comes to the Lion

The lion, on fire with anger and in frenzy,
  could see the hare approaching from afar.

Quite unperturbed and swaggering, he runs
  in fury, fierce and cruel and sour-faced,

1160 Because a meek approach would raise suspicion
  whereas his impudence would staunch all doubt.

When he arrived there and was at his doorstep,
  the lion yelled at him, 'Aha! you scoundrel!

I've ripped apart not one but many elephants!
  I've seen off many a rogue of my own species.

What is this half-wit hare who seems to wish
  to cast upon the ground what we've imposed?'

Renounce the sleep of hare-brained ignorance,
  you ass! And hearken to the roaring of this lion.

The Hare Apologizes

1165 The hare said, 'Mercy! There's a reason, if
  Your Lordship will extend the hand of pardon.'

'What reason? Oh, the uselessness of fools!
  This is the time they come before the king!

Late-crowing cock! Your head must be cut off.
  The fool's excuse should not be entertained.

The fool's excuse is worse than his offence;
  the stupid one's insults intelligence!

Ass-ears! your "reason" is devoid of wisdom.
 I'm not so hare-brained as to fall for this.'

'O king, regard a nobody as someone,   1170
 and hear the excuse of one who's been
  oppressed.

Especially for the alms of your high rank,
 do not repel someone who's lost his way.

The sea which opens up to every stream
 bears all the driftwood on its head and face.

It's not diminished by its bounteousness;
 the sea is neither lessened nor increased.'

'I give of bounty in its proper place;
 I cut the cloth to fit each person's size.'

'Look here, if I'm not fit for your indulgence, 1175
 I'll lay my head before your cruelty's dragon.

I set off on the road at breakfast time;
 I set off with my friend towards the king.

There was another hare with me for you,
 one chosen by my group as my companion.

Upon the road a lion attacked your servant,
 assailed the two companions going to you.

"We are the servants of the king of kings,"
 I said. "We're humble servants of his court."

He said, "What king of kings? Show some
  respect!   1180
 don't mention every nobody to me!

I'll tear you and your so-called king apart
    if you and your companion try to leave."

I told him, "Please allow me one more time
    to see the king, and take him news of you."

He said, "Deposit with me your companion,
    or else you'll be my sacrificial victim."

We begged and begged – it did no good at all,
    He took my friend and let me go alone.

1185   My friend was twice the hare I am in size,
    in grace, in beauty and in body too.

And as of now that lion has blocked this road –
    that was what happened to me – now I've told you.

From now on you cannot expect a ration.
    I'm telling you the truth *"and truth is bitter"*.

So clear the road if you require the ration,
    and hurry! Come and stop that fearless one.'

The Lion Answers the Hare and
Sets Off with Him

He said, 'In God's name come, find where he is,
    you go ahead if all you say is true.

1190   And I shall punish him and hundreds like him
    – if it's a lie I'll punish you instead.'

He went ahead as if he were a guide,
    so as to lure him straight into his snare.

Towards a well where he had made his mark,
a deep well which he'd made into a death-trap.

This pair were going in the well's direction –
behold a hare like water under straw!

The water steals the straw down to the plain.
Surprise! How does the water steal a mountain?

His tricky snare became the lion's noose –   1195
a most surprising hare, who bags a lion.

A Moses and the river Nile will take
the Pharaoh and his army and his host.

A gnat with half a wing will ruthlessly
be splitting into two the skull of Nimrod.

The state of him who listened to his foe!
The lot of him a jealous one befriends!

The Pharaoh's state who listened to Hāmān!
And Nimrod's state when he gave ear to Satan!

Though enemies address you as a friend,   1200
beware the trap, although they talk of bait.

If he should give you sweetness, it is poison;
if he is good to you, there will be violence.

When judgement comes, you'll only see the skin;
you'll not distinguish enemies from friends.

So there! Begin to say your tearful prayers;
prepare to weep and glorify and fast.

Weep on, 'O You who know the unseen world,
don't grind us with the stone of evil tricks.'

1205   If we have been a dog, O lion creator,
           don't let the lion get us in this ambush.

       Don't give the form of fire to pleasant water;
           don't give the form of water to the fire.

       You make us drunk on wine of violence;
           you make non-being take the form of being.

       What's drunkenness? The blindfold of the eyesight,
           when rocks resemble jewels, and wool is jasper.

       What's drunkenness? To alter all your senses,
           and tamarisk shall turn to sandalwood.

The Tale of the Hoopoe and Solomon (Peace Be Upon Him), Which Explains That When Destiny Comes, Clear Eyes Are Closed

1210   When Solomon's royal pavilion was erected,
           the birds all came to pay him their respects.

       He talked their language and they found him friendly;
           they flocked to him devotedly, each one.

       With Solomon the birds all gave up warbling
           and learned to speak more clearly than your brother.

       A common language is a bond and blood-tie;
           with strangers one is like a prisoner.

       O many a Turk and Hindu share a language,
           while many a pair of Turks are total strangers.

1215   For intimacy's language is quite different;
           it's better sharing hearts than sharing language.

With neither speech nor sign nor scribe to help,
    the heart gives out a hundred thousand meanings.

The mysteries of every single bird –
    its skills and knowledge and experience –

Were shown one at a time to Solomon.
    They praised themselves to try to win his favour.

Not for the sake of pride or self-regard,
    but so that he would give them access to him,

As when a captive needs to have a master   1220
    he gives an introduction to his skills.

But when he is not keen on being bought,
    he makes himself look sick, deaf, lame and
        palsied.

It was the hoopoe's turn to show his skills
    and explanation of his work and thought.

'Your Majesty, there is one little skill
    which I shall tell you – best to keep it short.'

'Then tell it so I know what skill that is.'
    'When I am at the highest point of heaven,

And look from heaven's height with perfect sight,   1225
    I see the water deep within the earth,

And where it is, how deep, what sort of colour,
    from where it flows, from out of soil or rock.

O Solomon, to help your troops' encampment,
    retain this clever one for your campaigns.'

Then Solomon said, 'O what a good companion
    to have in far-flung deserts with no water.

So you'll find water for the troops, and on
    campaigns you'll be the soldiers' water source.'

The Crow Derides the Hoopoe's Claim

1230   The crow came forth and, hearing this, grew jealous
    and said to Solomon, 'It's lies and nonsense!

Such speech is impolite before the king,
    especially false and ludicrous self-praise.

If he had always been so sharp of sight,
    could he not see the snare under the surface?

Why would he have been captured in the snare
    and gone into the cage against his will?'

So Solomon said, 'Hoopoe, is it right
    there are these dregs left in your first full cup?

1235   Why feign inebriation, yoghurt-drinker?
    You're boasting to me even as you lie!'

The Hoopoe's Answer to the Crow's Attack

'O king, don't listen to my enemy's slanders
    on me, a naked beggar. Heaven's sake!

For if I'm claiming something meaningless,
    I'll hold my neck out while you cut my head off.

The crow, who's in denial of fate's decree,
    had he a thousand wits would not believe.

So long as there's a *k* of *kāfer* in you,
   you harbour stench and lust just like your arse.

I see the trap when I am in the air,   1240
   if destiny does not obscure my mind's eye.

When destiny comes, wisdom goes to sleep.
   The moon turns black; the sun stops in its tracks.

Why is this show of destiny so rare?
   It's destiny that makes us deny destiny.'

The Story of Adam (Peace Be Upon Him)
and How Destiny Prevented His Vision
from Seeing the Prohibition Clearly and
from Refraining from Interpretation

The first man, master of '*He taught the names*', has
   a hundred thousand skills in every vein.

Until the end of things, his soul has power
   of all the names of things as they exist.

Each name he gave became unchangeable,   1245
   and no one he called 'swift' was ever 'slothful'.

And from the first he saw the last believer
   and knew who'd be the infidel at last.

So hear the name of all from one who knows,
   and hear the secret of 'He taught the names'.

To us the name of every thing is outward;
   for Him who is Creator it's the secret.

As Moses' staff was called by him 'the rod',
   its name to the Creator was 'the dragon'.

1250   Here Omar's name was 'idol-worshipper',
           but in *eternity* he was 'believer'.

       The one who had the name of 'seed' for us,
           for God this was the form 'he who has selfhood'.

       In pre-eternity, this seed was form;
           to God this was no more nor less than being.

       What is to come is truthfully our name,
           for it will be our ending before God.

       He names man in accordance with the ending
           and not with what He designates as 'borrowed'.

1255   As Adam's eye was seeing by pure light,
           he knew the secret and the soul of names.

       And when the angels caught God's light in him,
           they fell in praise and hurried to his service.

       If I praise Adam till the resurrection,
           I'm failing him whose name I am pronouncing.

       He knew all this and at the fateful time,
           he failed to know just one forbidden thing.

       He thought, 'Is it forbidden by a stricture,
           or just conjecture and interpretation?'

1260   And when his heart preferred interpretation,
           his nature ran astounded to the fruit.

       As when the thorn had pierced the gardener's foot,
           the thief had seized the chance and got the goods.

When panic passed, he came back to his senses;
  he saw the thief had stolen from his shed.

He said, 'O Lord, *we have done wrong!* Alas!'
  That is, the darkness came; the road was lost!

So destiny's a cloud that hides the sun.
  It makes a mouse of lions and of dragons.

If I don't see a trap at judgement time,   1265
  I'm not alone not knowing judgement's paths.

O happy one who took to doing goodness,
  his strength departed as he took to groaning.

If fate should veil you darkly like the night,
  so one day fate will also take your hand.

If fate attempts your life a hundred times,
  so also fate revives you and will heal you.

Though fate should hold you up a hundred times,
  it will pitch tent for you on heaven's summit.

It is from kindness that he frightens you,   1270
  then seats you in the kingdom of good faith.

These words go on forever – it is late
  Now hear the story of the hare and lion.

The Hare Steps Back from the Lion When
He Gets Close to the Well

Now when he neared the well, the lion saw
    the hare still on the road and stepping back.

He said, 'Why do you drag your feet along;
    don't drag your feet behind you – hurry up!'

He said, 'My legs, my hands and feet have gone;
    my soul is trembling and my heart has failed.

1275   And don't you see my face is sallow gold?
    My colour shows what's going on inside me.

Since God has called the look "informative",
    the sage's eye is fixed upon the look.

The scent and colour, like the bell, announces;
    the horse's neigh informs us of its state.

The sound of all things tells us so we know
    the donkey's braying from the creaking gate.

The Prophet said on understanding people,
    "A man is hidden when his tongue is folded."

1280   The face's colour shows the heart's condition.
    Have mercy on me, love me in your heart.

The face's ruddy colour speaks of thanks,
    the sallow face, endurance and denial.

The palsy of the arms and legs has got me;
    it drains my facial colour, strength and looks.

It's that which shatters everything it reaches;
   it tears up every tree from root and base.

I'm overcome by that which has checkmated
   the human, animal and plant and mineral.

Indeed these things are parts, but whole things too   1285
   are yellowing and putrefied by it.

Sometimes the world is patient, sometimes grateful.
   Sometimes the garden's dressed, sometimes it's
      bare.

The sun is fiery hot when it comes up;
   in a few hours' time it hangs its head and sinks.

The stars that glitter in the four directions
   are liable to burn out any time.

The moon, which now outshines the stars in beauty,
   becomes just like a ghost from wasting illness.

This earth, so tranquil and so civilized,   1290
   is hurled by earthquakes into trembling fever.

How many a mountain in this world is blown
   to smithereens and dust by this bequest!

This atmosphere became infused with spirit –
   when fate arrived, it turned to plague and foulness.

The lovely water, sister to the spirit,
   turned yellow, bitter, muddy in a ditch.

The fire that is puffed up in its own whiskers
   is put out by a single breath of wind.

1295   From turbulence and boiling of the seascape,
     you'll understand the changes of its mind.

The giddy heavens, which are ever-searching –
     their inward state is like the state of children.

There are both lucky and unlucky stars,
     at times in nadir, medial or zenith.

From your own self, a part composed of wholes,
     you'll understand the elemental states.

For just as wholes have pain and suffering,
     so why should not their parts be pale of face?

1300   Particularly parts which are composed
     of opposites: fire, water, earth and air.

It's no surprise the sheep leaps from the wolf,
     for sheep to long for wolves *would* be surprising.

Life is the harmony of opposites;
     death is the fact that war broke out between them.

The grace of God has given companionship
     to lions and asses, wildly opposite.

And since the world is ailing and in prison,
     what wonder if the patient fades away?'

1305   And thus the hare regaled the lion with counsels:
     'I've lagged behind because of these constraints.'

The Lion Asks the Reason for the Hare's Stepping Back

The lion said, 'What's the particular
    that causes you distress? I want to know!'

He said, 'That lion is living in this well;
    he is secure from troubles in this bunker.

The clever choose the bottom of the well;
    the heart's delights are found in solitude.

The gloom of wells is better than the world's.
    Those fettered to the world do not survive.'

He said, 'Come on, my blow will overwhelm
       him,   1310
    see if that lion is sitting in the well.'

He answered, 'I am burning with a fever.
    Would you perhaps take me alongside you?

And then with your support, O mine of kindness,
    I'll use my eyes to peep inside the well.'

The Lion Looks into the Well and Sees His Own Reflection and That of the Hare

And when the lion took him by his side,
    he ran up to the well, protected by him.

They looked into the well, upon the water;
    the light of both of them shone on the water.

The lion saw his image in the water,   1315
    the image of a plump hare and a lion.

He saw his enemy down in the water,
   forgot the hare and jumped into the well.

He fell into a well that had been dug –
   his evil was rebounding on his head.

The evil of the wicked is a well
   of darkness – all who know have said this much.

The worse he is, the more his well is ghastly,
   for justice has awarded worse for worse.

1320   And you who use your rank to practise evil,
   be well assured you dig yourself a well.

Don't spin cocoons around yourself like
   silkworms –
   you dig yourself a well, so dig with caution.

Don't reckon that the weak have no revenge.
   Recite the verse 'When comes the help of God'.

If you're an elephant and foes escaped you,
   requital of 'the birds in flocks' arrived!

If on the earth a weak man begs for mercy,
   his cry goes up to meet the hosts of heaven.

1325   So if you bite someone and make them bleed,
   toothache will strike you just as you are biting.

The lion saw himself inside the well,
   he could not tell him and his foe apart.

He saw his own reflection as his foe,
   and so he drew his sword against himself.

How many an evil that you see in others
   is your own nature which you see in them!

Your very being's being beamed at them,
   your cant, your evil and your dissoluteness.

That's you, and you are punching at yourself;   1330
   you spin the thread of curses round yourself.

You cannot see that evil clearly in you,
   or else you'd be *your very soul's* worst foe.

You ignoramus! You attack yourself
   just like the lion who set upon himself.

When you get to the bottom of your nature,
   why, then you'll know that worthlessness was
      yours.

Down at the bottom of the well the lion saw
   his image, which he'd thought was someone else.

Whoever knocks a weaker person's teeth out   1335
   does what that crooked-sighted lion did.

You've seen a blemish on your uncle's face –
   your uncle is not bad. It's you! Don't vanish!

The faithful are a mirror to each other –
   this saying is reported from the Prophet.

If you hold up blue glass before your eye,
   because of that the world is blue to you.

Unless you're blind, this blueness is from you –
   insult yourself, not others anymore!

1340   And if the faithful did not see by God's light,
            how could they see the unseen world unveiled?

        Because you're seeing by the fire of God,
            you can't discriminate the good and bad.

        So softly sprinkle water on the fire,
            so that your fire is turned to light, poor man.

        O Lord, you sprinkle on the cleansing water
            so that this world alight becomes all light.

        The waters of the sea are at Your call;
            O Lord, the water and the fire are yours.

1345   If You should wish, the fire becomes sweet water,
            or, if not, water turns to fire instead.

        The quest in us is also Your conception.
            Lord, freedom from injustice is Your gift.

        You've given us this quest without our asking
            and opened up the treasure-house of kindness.

        *The Hare Relates to the Animals the News That
        the Lion Has Fallen Down the Well*

        The hare was overjoyed at his escape.
            He ran across the plain towards the beasts.

        He'd seen the lion dead inside the well
            and tripped along so happy to the grassland.

1350   Like leaves and branches dancing in the air,
            he clapped his hands, for he'd escaped death's grip.

The branch and leaf got free of earthy gaol,
   held high their heads, were playmates of the wind.

And when the leaves erupted from the branch,
   they hastened to the summit of the tree.

And in the language of the verse '*its shoots*',
   each fruit and leaf will sing in thanks to God.

The Lord of Giving nourished all our roots
   until the tree grew '*stout and firm*' of stature.

The souls that are bound up in clay and water   1355
   are overjoyed when they escape that mud.

They're dancing in the air of love of God,
   as unmarked as the round face of the moon.

Their bodies dancing and their souls – don't ask!
   And that which is around the soul – don't ask!

The hare consigned the lion to the gaol,
   a shameful lion thwarted by a hare!

In such a shameful state and yet, surprise!
   He'd like to keep the title 'King of Beasts'.

O lion, down the well of separation,   1360
   your hare-brained self has drained and drunk
      your blood.

Your hare-brained self is grazing on the plain,
   and you're down in the well of 'why?' and 'how?'.

That lion-tamer ran towards the beasts:
   '*Rejoice, the bringer of good news is come!*

What joyful news, my band of revellers!
    That dog from hell has gone back to his hell.

And joyful news, our life's sworn enemy
    has had his teeth pulled by his maker's wrath.

1365   And he who beat so many heads with punches
    has had a brush with death and been swept off.'

The Gathering of the Animals around the Hare and Their Praising of Him

The beasts then gathered round all full of joy,
    in ecstasy and effervescence, laughing.

They made a circle round him like a candle
    and bowed to him and said to him, 'Indeed,

Are you a heavenly angel or a witch?
    No, you're the Ezrā'il of rampant lions!

Whatever you may be, our souls are yours.
    You triumphed here, more power to your arm!

1370   And God diverted water to your stream –
    a blessing on your hand and on your arm.

Now tell us how you plotted your deceit
    and how by tricks you rubbed the tyrant out.

Retell it so the story will be healing,
    retell it as a dressing for our souls.

But tell! From that oppressor's violence
    our souls have got a hundred thousand wounds.'

He said, 'O gentlemen, it was God's help –
    if not, well what in all the world's a hare?

He gave me power and gave my heart the light;   1375
    my heart's light gave my hands and feet their
      strength.

Advancements come forth from the bosom of God
    – again, reversals come from God as well.

In time and in the course of things, God gives
    this help to doubtful ones and visionaries.'

The Hare Advises the Animals Not to Be Too Happy with This

'Beware! Don't celebrate this fickle world.
    O slave to change, don't act as if you're free.

He whom they raise above the fickle world,
    they ring the changes higher than the planets.

The eternal kings are higher than fickle worlds,   1380
    their spirits ever circling with the Sāqi.

If you declare you'll quit *this* drink a while,
    you'll dip your lips in everlasting wine.'

Commentary on 'We Return from the Lesser Jehād to the Greater Jehād'

Your Majesties, we've slain the outer foe:
    within us there remains a foe who's worse.

To slay this one's not work for mind and wits,
    the inner lion's not the hare's affair.

This *nafs* is hell, and hell is like a dragon
  that seas cannot extinguish or decrease.

1385   It drinks the seven oceans dry, and still
  that creature-burning fire will not die down.

Both stones and stony-hearted unbelievers
  fall into it all wretched and ashamed.

It is not satisfied with nourishment
  like this until God's invitation comes:

'Are you full up, are you replete?' 'Not yet!
  Behold the fire, the heat, the conflagration.'

It gobbled up a world and swallowed it,
  its belly calling, '*Are there any more?*'

1390   God steps upon it from No Place, and then
  it is made peaceful by '*Be and it was.*'

For since this self of ours is part of hell,
  and all parts have the nature of the whole,

It is for God to step on it and kill it.
  Except for God himself, who'd draw the bow?

For arrows which are straight go on the bow.
  This bow has crooked and distorted arrows.

Be true like arrows flying from the bow –
  true arrows leave the bow, without a doubt.

1395   I turned my back upon the outer combat;
  I turned my face towards the inner combat.

'*Indeed we've come back from the lesser struggle*'
  and now we're with the Prophet in the greater.

I seek from God the power and grace and prowess
to dig up this Mount Qāf with just a needle.

For lions to break the battle lines is easy.
True lion is he who breaks the lines of selfhood.

THE COMING OF THE BYZANTINE AMBASSADOR TO THE COMMANDER OF THE FAITHFUL, OMAR, MAY GOD BE PLEASED WITH HIM, AND HIS SEEING THE BLESSED POWERS OF OMAR, MAY GOD BE PLEASED WITH HIM

To explain this will you listen to a story,
to get some sense of mysteries I've mentioned?

1400 An envoy came to Omar from the Caesar,
into Medina from the desert wastes.

'Where is the caliph's palace, O attendants,
where I may take my horse and my equipment?'

The people said to him, 'He has no palace,
for Omar's palace is his radiant soul.

And though he has a princely reputation,
he has a hut to live in like the poor.

O brother, how will you perceive his palace,
when hair has overgrown your inner eye?

1405 Your heart's eye must be cleansed of hair and error,
then go and have a look and see his palace.

Whoever has his soul free from desires
soon sees the presence and the sacred precincts.'

Mohammed, once made pure from fire and smoke,
'God's face' was everywhere he turned his face.

While you are privy to malicious whisperings,
    how will you ever know 'There is God's face'?

And he who has the opening of his breast,
    he will behold the sun from every quarter.

The truth of God appears among the others,   1410
    just like the moon among the other stars.

You put two finger-tips upon your eyes,
    and you see nothing, as you will admit.

If you do not observe this world – no matter;
    at fault's the fingers of your wicked self.

So take away your fingers from your eyes,
    and see whatever you may wish to see.

The people said to Noah, 'Where's the gain?'
    He said, 'Beyond "*They hide behind their
        garments*".'

You have wrapped clothing round your head   1415
        and face;
    no wonder you are blind though you have sight.

For man is sight and all the rest is skin;
    his sight is that he has the Friend in sight.

Without the Friend in sight, sight's better blind.
    The friend who will not stay is better gone.

The envoy of Byzantium, having heard
    these limpid syllables, grew yet more ardent.

He set his sights on seeking Omar out;
    he let his horse and baggage go astray.

1420   He ran in all directions like a madman,
      inquiring after that accomplished man.

'Is there a man like this in all the world,
      and hidden from the world just like the soul?'

He sought him with a view to be his slave,
      and so the seeker turns into the finder.

A Bedouin woman spotted the intruder
      and said, 'There's Omar underneath the palm-tree.

Beneath the date palm, separate from the people,
      see God's own shadow sleeping in the shade!'

The Byzantine Ambassador Finds the Commander of the Faithful Omar (May God Be Pleased With Him) Asleep under the Tree

1425   He came and stood there at some distance from him;
      he looked at Omar and began to tremble.

A fear came on the envoy for that sleeper,
      an ecstasy of sweetness on his soul.

Though love and fear are mutual contradictions,
      he saw the two united in his heart.

He said, 'I have been seen with many a king,
      been honoured and exalted before sultans.

I never had a fear or dread of kings,
      but fear of this man robbed me of my wits.

1430   I've gone through forests full of lions and panthers;
      my face's colour was not turned by them.

I've often been on battlefields in action –
　when things were at their worst, I was a lion.

I've often dealt and suffered heavy blows;
　I was a braver heart than all the rest.

This sleeping man's defenceless on the ground.
　I shake in all my seven limbs – why so?

It's fear of God, it is no fear of creatures,
　nor of this man in patchwork dervish cloak.

He who fears God and chooses piety,　　　　　　　1435
　the *jinn* and humankind who see him fear him.'

He pondered this and put his hands together.
　An hour later Omar rose from sleep.

He bowed to Omar saying, '*Peace be with you.*'
　The Prophet said, 'The greeting then the meeting!'

He said, '*Also with you,*' and called him forward;
　he welcomed him and sat him down beside him.

'*Be not afraid*' is kindness to the fearful;
　it is consideration for the fearful.

Whoever is afraid, they reassure him;　　　　　　　1440
　they pacify the heart of him who fears.

Why say 'Fear not' to him who has no fear?
　Or why give lessons if he needs no teaching?

He cheered the heart that had been sorely troubled,
　and he repaired his shattered state of mind.

And then he uttered subtle words to him,
　the holy names of God, most Gracious Friend,

And God's caresses for the holy servants,
   so he would know the Stations and the States.

1445 *Hāl* is the unveiling of the lovely bride;
   maqām is when he's with the bride in private.

The king will see the bride unveiled with others;
   in private there is no one but the king.

The bride's unveiled to noblemen and commons;
   the king is with his bride in privacy.

Among the Sufis many have had *hāl*,
   but rare are those who have *maqām* among them.

He taught him of the stages of his soul,
   and also of the journeys of his spirit,

1450 And of the time that is devoid of time,
   and of *maqām* that is magnificent,

And of the air in which the spirit's Simorgh
   saw flight and victories before all this.

Its every flight exceeded the horizons
   more than the yearning lover's hopes and longings.

When Omar saw the strange face was a friend,
   he saw his soul was looking into mysteries.

The sheikh was perfect and the pupil keen –
   the man was swift, his mount a thoroughbred.

1455 That guide saw he was open to his guidance.
   He sowed the purest seed in purest ground.

The Byzantine Ambassador Interrogates the Commander of the Faithful Omar (May God Be Pleased With Him)

'Commander of the Faithful,' said the man,
    'how did the soul come from on high to earth?

How did the matchless bird go in the cage?'
    'God chanted spells and stories to the soul.'

And when He chants the spells to those non-beings
    who have no eyes nor ears, they start to boil.

His spells will quickly make the non-existents
    impel themselves headlong into existence.

Again, when He regaled his spell to beings,   1460
    they fled to non-existence at the double.

He whispered to the rose and made her laugh,
    and to the stone and made her a cornelian.

He gave the flesh a sign to make it soul,
    and to the sun He spoke to make it shine.

He breathes into its ear a dreadful word
    and makes its face eclipse a hundred times.

What did that speaker whisper to the cloud
    that tears streamed from its eye like wine from
        wineskins?

What did God whisper to the ear of earth   1465
    that it became contemplative and quiet?

Whoever is confused in vacillation,
    God uttered in her ear perplexity.

To imprison her between these two ideas:
  'Shall I do what He said or the reverse?'

And one side gets from God an inclination
  from which it chooses one of those two sides.

If you don't want your soul's mind in dilemma,
  don't stuff this cotton-wool into your soul's ear,

1470 So that you'll understand those complications,
  so that you'll see the manifest and hidden.

The soul's ear is the place of revelation.
  What's revelation? Speech remote from senses.

Soul's ear and eye are not like other senses;
  the ear of mind and thought are bankrupt of this.

My saying 'jabr' made me mad for love;
  it trapped in jabr one who's not in love.

It is communion with the Truth, not jabr;
  it is the brilliance of the moon, not clouds.

1475 And were it jabr, it is not common jabr;
  it's not the headstrong, self-determined jabr.

God opens insight in the hearts of those
  who recognize what jabr is, my son,

Unseen and future things are shown to them;
  remembrance of things past is meaningless.

Their free-will and their jabr are quite different;
  in oyster shells the drops of rain are pearls.

Outside, the raindrop may be large or small;
　　inside the shell a large or tiny pearl.

Those people have the nature of the musk-gland:　　1480
　　blood in appearance, inside there is musk.

Don't say this stuff is outwardly just blood.
　　How could it turn to musk inside the gland?

Don't say this copper's outwardly just dross.
　　How could it turn to gold in alchemy?

Free-will and *jabr* are fancies in *your* mind:
　　it went to *theirs* and was the light of God.

Bread which is but a lump inside a cloth
　　becomes the joyful spirit in our bodies.

Within the cloth it has no transformation;　　1485
　　by means of Salsabil the soul transforms it.

The power of the soul is this, true reader,
　　so what's the power of that Soul of soul?

A man, a piece of flesh, with mind and soul
　　splits mountains for a channel or a mine.

The power of mountain-splitting souls splits rocks;
　　the power of Soul of souls 'can split the moon'.

But if the heart untied this bag of mystery,
　　the soul would rush towards the throne to raid it.

How Adam Took the Blame upon Himself,
Saying, 'O Lord, We Have Wronged
Ourselves,' and How Eblis Blamed
God Most High for His Own Sin, Saying
'You Have Led Me into Sin'

1490   Consider both God's action and our own.
          Know that our acts exist, and that is clear.

          If creatures' actions have no real existence,
             then don't ask someone, 'Why did you do that?'

          As God's creating gives rise to our actions,
             our actions are the effects of God's creation.

          A speaker sees the meaning or the word –
             how can he comprehend the two at once?

          He goes with meaning and ignores the word;
             no eye can see both back and forth at once.

1495   Just then, when you look forward, at that moment,
          how can you look behind you – don't you see?

          As soul cannot embrace both word and meaning,
             how can soul be creator of this pair?

          God comprehends them both at once, my son;
             one task does not prevent Him from the other.

          When Satan said, '*You led me into sin,*'
             the vicious demon hid his shameful deed.

          But Adam said, '*O Lord we've wronged ourselves.*'
             He was not blind, as we are, to God's action.

Respectfully he hid it in the sin; 1500
  with sin upon his head he ate the fruit.

When he repented, God addressed him: 'Adam!
  Have I created sin and toil in you?

Was that not My decree and My command?
  Why did you hide it at the time of pardon?'

'I was reluctant to forgo respect.'
  He said, 'I've shown the same regard for you.'

For he who shows respect shall have it shown him,
  and he who brings the sugar eats sweet cake.

For whom are *the good women* meant? For
    good men. 1505
  Be good to friends; annoy them at your peril!

Dear heart, imagine this for your instruction:
  know how compulsion differs from free-will.

A hand may tremble from a nervous twitch,
  or else because you shake the hand about.

Be sure that though both movements are from God,
  comparison cannot be made between them.

You may be sorry that you've shaken him,
  but who should be held sorry for the twitch?

It's searching of the mind – what's mind? It's
    cunning, 1510
  so that weak men may feel they've got somewhere.

The mental quest may be like pearls and coral,
  but it is different from the spirit's quest.

The spirit's quest is on another level;
　　the spirit's wine has quite a different substance.

That time when searching of the mind was right,
　　Omar was confidant of Bu'l Hakam.

When Omar went from mind towards the soul,
　　Bu'l Hakam turned into Bu Jahl for this.

1515　He's perfect in regard to mind and senses,
　　but as regards his soul he's ignorant.

The mental, sensual search is secondary;
　　the spiritual quest is quite miraculous.

Receiver of the light, the soul's light comes;
　　correlatives and refutations go.

Because the seer whose inner light is shining
　　does not require the blind man's stick of proof.

Commentary on 'And He Is with You Wherever You Are'

So one more time we've come back to the tale
　　– when did we ever take our leave of it?

1520　His gaol is if we come to ignorance,
　　and if we come to knowledge it's His palace.

We're drunk on Him if we succumb to sleep;
　　we're in His hands if we remain awake.

If we should weep, we're clouds of hypocrites,
　　and if we laugh, then we're His lightning flash.

And we reflect His wrath in war and anger,
His love in peace and reconciliation.

Who are we in this convoluted world?
Like *alef*, what's the point? No point at all.

The Ambassador Asks Omar (May God Be Pleased With Him) the Cause of the Misfortune of the Spirits in This Water and Clay of the Body

'Omar, what secret and what sense is there   1525
to gaol that pure one in this muddy place?

Pure water's been secreted into clay;
pure soul has been encased within our carcase.'

He said, 'You make a most astute inquiry –
you have the meaning captured in a word.

You have restrained the meaning that is free;
you've made a word the fetter of the mind.

You've done this for a beneficial purpose,
you who are shrouded from such benefit.

The One from whom such benefit is sprung,   1530
could He not see such things as we have seen?

A hundred thousand benefits there are;
a hundred thousand's nothing to the One.

Your speech's breath, which is a part of parts,
became a gain – why is the whole a void?

Your action as a part is beneficial.
Why raise your hand to castigate the whole?

Don't speak if there's no benefit in speech,
    and, if there is, stop carping and give thanks!

1535   For thanks to God's a necklace for us all.
    Don't fight with it and pull a sour face.

If giving thanks will only make you sour-faced,
    then vinegar's the best of all thanks-givers.

If vinegar must come into your heart,
    then make it turn to oxymel with sweetness.'

The meaning in a poem's only fumbling:
    it's like a sling, it is not in control.

On the Meaning of 'Whoever Wants to Sit with God Let Him Sit with the Sufis'

That envoy lost himself in cups like this;
    his mission and his message were forgotten.

1540   He was astonished at the power of God –
    that envoy came and turned into a king.

Down by the sea the stream turns into ocean;
    the seed upon the field turns into crops.

When bread connects itself with humankind,
    dead bread is come to life and consciousness.

When wax and wood get closer to the fire,
    their own essential darkness turns to light.

Antimony is smeared upon the eyes
    and turns to sight and keeps a lookout there.

Happy the man who has escaped himself,   1545
    united with a living world of being!

Alas for him who lives but sits with dead men!
    He's moribund and life's abandoned him.

When you have fled to God in the Quran,
    you've mixed among the spirits of the prophets.

The Holy Book's the lives and times of prophets,
    the fishes of the holy sea of greatness.

And if you read yet don't accept that Book,
    so what, if you have seen the saints and prophets!

But if you're open when you read the stories,   1550
    the caged bird of your soul will be afflicted.

The bird who is a captive in a cage
    and does not seek to flee – that's ignorance.

The spirits who have gone and fled their cages,
    they are the prophets, guides, dependable.

The voice comes to them from outside, from spirit,
    which says, 'This is the way of your escape.'

And thus we have escaped this narrow cage –
    there is no other way out of this cage.

So make yourself distressed; lament, lament,   1555
    so you will be released from reputation.

For worldly reputation is a shackle
    no less than iron chains upon the way!

THE STORY OF THE MERCHANT
WHOSE CAGED PARROT GAVE HIM
A MESSAGE FOR THE PARROTS OF
HINDUSTAN AT THE TIME OF HIS
GOING THERE FOR TRADE

There was a merchant once – he had a parrot
  imprisoned in a cage, a gorgeous parrot.

And when the merchant packed his bags to travel
  and was about to go to Hindustan,

He kindly said to all his maids and servants,
  'Now, tell me quickly, please, what shall I bring you?'

1560 Each servant asked him for something she wanted.
  The good man gave his word to all of them.

He asked the parrot, 'What gift would you like
  that I could bring you back from Hindustan?'

The parrot said, 'When you see parrots there,
  explain to them my plight and say to them,

"A certain parrot's desperate to see you,
  who by the fate of heaven is in my prison.

She sends you greetings and demands some justice
  and asks for help and means of guidance from you.

1565 She said, 'Is it correct that I should languish,
  give up the ghost and die here all alone?

And is this right, that I'm in painful chains
    while you can flit about from bush to tree?

Is loyalty of friends to be like this:
    I in this gaol, and you in beds of roses?

O sirs, will you remember this poor bird,
    and in the meadow drink a draught to me!

Friends' memory of their friend is most auspicious,
    more so when one is Layli, one Majnun.

O partners of your own beloved fair ones!   1570
    I drink from cups filled with my own dear blood.

Drink just one cup of wine in memory of me
    if you do not see fit to give me justice.

Or when you've drunk, pour on the dust a drink
    in memory of me grovelling in the dust.

Where then, I wonder, is that bond and oath?
    Where are the vows of those with lips like sugar?

A servant is dismissed for bad behaviour:
    if *You* behave oppressively, what's different?

The harm You do in anger and in strife   1575
    is sweeter than an ecstasy of harp strings.

Your cruelty is better than a victory,
    Your scolding's more desired than life itself.

This is Your fire – what does Your light look like?
    This is the funeral – what's Your wedding like?

As for the sweetness which Your violence holds,
    and for Your subtlety, none plumb your depths.

I weep and then I fear He will believe me,
    and then from kindness moderate His violence.

1580   I love so much His violence and His grace –
    how wonderful, I love these two extremes!

If I forsake this thorn-bush for the garden,
    I'll sing for sadness like the nightingale.

How wonderful, this nightingale, who lifts
    his beak to eat the thorns among the rosebeds.

What kind of nightingale is this? A dragon!
    In love all bitter things are sweet to him.

He's lover of the whole; He is the whole.
    He's Lover of Himself; He seeks His Love.'"'

Description of the Wings of the Birds of the Divine Intelligences

1585   Such is the story of the soul – the parrot –
    where is the one who knows the birds so well?

And where is such a bird, so frail and sinless,
    in whom is Solomon with all his host?

She weeps in anguish, thankless, uncomplaining,
    and in the seven heavens above there's uproar.

Each moment God sends her a hundred missives,
    God's sixty *'Here I am!'* to her *'O Lord!'*

Her lapse is better than obeying God;
    before her lack of faith all faiths are thin.

She makes her own ascension every moment 1590
    and puts a hundred crowns upon her own.

Her form's on earth, her soul is in the No Place –
    a No Place is beyond the mind of travellers.

But not a 'no place' of the imagination,
    whose images are born at any moment,

But Place and No Place under His control,
    just like the four streams in divine control.

Leave off explaining this, avert your face,
    don't breathe another word, '*And God knows
      best*'.

Let us retrace our steps from here, my friends, 1595
    back to the bird, the merchant and to Hind.

The merchant undertook to take this message
    and give his greetings to the parrot's kin.

The Master Sees the Parrots of Hindustan on the Plain and Brings the Message from His Parrot

When he was in the heart of Hindustan,
    he saw a host of parrots on the plain.

He brought his camel to a halt and called
    to give the greeting and the entrusted message.

One of the parrots started trembling so
    that she gave up the ghost, collapsed and died.

The master was most sorry that he'd spoken. 1600
    He said, 'I've gone and killed the living creature.

Perhaps she was related to my parrot;
    perhaps they were two bodies and one spirit?

What have I done, why did I break this news?
    I've scorched the poor thing with these bitter
        words!'

This tongue is like a stone and iron together;
    what's leaping from the tongue is like a fire.

Do not strike iron and stone together idly;
    do not be gossiping or showing off!

1605   Because it's dark, with cotton fields around you,
    how could you risk a spark amid the cotton?

How cruel are those who sew their eyes together
    and with their words incinerate a world.

A single word may devastate a world
    and make a lion from a fox's corpse.

Our souls have Jesus' breath at their foundation –
    one breath's a wound, the other is a salve.

If you should raise the veil from the souls,
    all souls would be Messiah-like in speech.

1610   So if you wish to speak with words of sugar,
    hold back. Do not eat sugar out of greed.

Restraint is what's desired in the wise –
    a craving after sugar is for children.

Whoever shows restraint attains to heaven;
    whoever eats the sugar's left behind!

*Commentary on the Lines of Faridoddin Attār
(May God Sanctify His Spirit): 'You Are a Man
of Self, O Ignoramus, Drink Blood Down in
the Dust / For Even if the Man of Perfect
Heart Should Drink a Poison, for
Him It Is an Antidote'*

It does not harm the man of perfect heart
    if he should drink a lethal dose in public.

Because he's found good health, he's free of care,
    while wretched students languish there in fever.

The Holy Prophet said, 'Desirous man,   1615
    beware! Don't strive with one who is desired.'

Don't enter fire, there is a Nimrod in you,
    and if you would, first be an Abraham.

Since you are not a swimmer or a sailor,
    do not go overboard in your vainglory.

He brings the scarlet rose out of the fire;
    He brings advantage out of what is lost.

A Perfect Man will dig – earth turns to gold.
    A fool will dig for gold – it turns to dust.

And since that man of truth is one with God,   1620
    in all his works his hand's the hand of God.

The fool's hand is the devil's and the demon's
    because he's in the snare of strife and trouble.

The sage turns ignorance to wisdom,
    but wisdom turns to ignorance in fools,

9

And all the sick man gets is turned to sickness.
  A Perfect Man turns unbelief to faith.

O you who've fought a mounted man from standing,
  you shall not make it through, so now desist!

*The Magicians Honour Moses (Peace Be
Upon Him), Saying, 'What Do You Command?
Will You First Throw Down the Staff?'*

1625 Back in the time of Pharaoh the accursed,
  magicians were in bitter strife with Moses.

But they regarded Moses very highly –
  he was a holy man to these magicians.

For they told him, 'It is for you to say
  if you should wish to cast your staff down first.'

He answered, 'No, magicians, you go first;
  you throw your bag of tricks into our midst.'

So great was their respect, it bought their faith
  and put an end to all their disputation.

1630 And when his truth was known by the magicians,
  they sacrificed their hands and feet in penance.

The perfect are allowed to taste and speak,
  but you're not perfect; do not eat, keep silence!

Since you're an ear, He is the tongue, not like you.
  God told the ears to '*Listen silently!*'

When first the child is born and sucks on milk,
  a while it must be silent and all ear.

It must be that its lips are sealed a while
  from speaking, till it learns the act of speech.

And if it does not listen and it babbles,   1635
  it makes itself the dumbest in the world.

The deaf who have no hearing from the start
  are silent – how could *they* burst into speech?

Because for speech the act of listening's needed,
  by listening come towards the act of speech!

'*And enter through the doors into the houses*
  and seek the motivations in the causes.'

There is no act of speaking free of hearing,
  except the speech of the sublime Creator.

He is the author, pupil of no master;   1640
  He is the throne of all, defers to no one.

The rest are busy in negotiations;
  they have a master and they need a model.

If you are not a stranger to this talk,
  take up the robe and weep in desert places.

Because of Adam's tears he escaped chastisement –
  fresh tears are like the breath of the repentant.

For lamentation Adam came to earth,
  that he'd be grieving, mourning, melancholic.

He went from Paradise and highest heaven;   1645
  he went to stand in shame and ask for pardon.

If you're of Adam's stock and from his loins,
  then seek to be among his company.

Prepare a dish of fiery hearts and tears –
　　the garden's made to bloom by sun and clouds.

How should you know the taste of tear-filled eyes?
　　Like eyeless men you crave for bread alone.

If you would rid this basket of its bread,
　　you'd fill it to the brim with jewels of beauty.

1650　So wean your infant soul off Satan's milk,
　　then put it in the tender care of angels.

So long as you are dark, depressed and sombre,
　　you suck upon the teat the devil sucks.

The morsel that enlightens and perfects
　　is that which honest livelihood supplies.

The oil that comes and then puts out our lamp
　　you may call water when it puts it out.

And lawful food bears wisdom and bears knowledge,
　　and love and tenderness are born from it.

1655　But when it bears illusion and ill-will,
　　neglect and ignorance, know it's forbidden.

You'll not sow wheat for barley to come up!
　　And does a mare produce an ass's colt?

Food is the seed, and thoughts are all its fruits;
　　food is the sea, and thoughts are all its pearls.

From lawful food within the mouth is born
　　the will to serve and go towards the next world.

The Merchant Reports Back to His Parrot What He Saw of the Parrots of Hindustan

The merchant finished all his merchandising
    and travelled homeward full of fellow-feeling.

To every serving-boy he brought his present;   1660
    to every maid he gave a little something.

The parrot said, 'Where is the gift for me?
    Describe all that you saw and what you said.'

He said, 'No, I'm so sorry for what happened.
    I'm gnawing at my hands and at my fingers.

Why, out of ignorance and thoughtlessness,
    did I so glibly bear so raw a message?'

She said, 'O master, what's this sorriness?
    What brings about this anger and this sadness?'

He said, 'I spoke of those complaints of yours   1665
    with parrots in a group who looked like you.

There was a parrot who could sense your pain;
    her heart burst and she trembled and she died.

Full of regret, I asked why did I do this,
    but, having spoken, what good does regret do?'

A word that in an instant slips the tongue
    is like an arrow flying from the bow.

That arrow does not swerve off course, my son;
    the flood must be obstructed at the source.

1670 For once it's left the source it floods a world,
   and it's no wonder if the world's destroyed.

  Results of what we do spring up unseen;
   the effects are not in creaturely control.

  Though these effects are thought to be from us,
   they all belong to God, our peerless Maker.

  An arrow wings its way from Zayd to Amr;
   his arrow seizes Amr like a leopard.

  Then pain will be produced the whole year long.
   Such pains derive from God and not from man.

1675 Had Zayd the archer died of fright just there,
   the pains would last until the victim's death.

  And since he perished from the wound's effect,
   you may call Zayd the slayer for this reason.

  Attribute all the blame for wounds to him,
   though all of it is action of the Almighty.

  Like crops and inhalation, sex and traps,
   the outcomes of these things depend on God.

  The holy ones have power from the Lord;
   they can divert the arrow in full flight.

1680 The holy ones repent – the Lord's hand shuts
   the doors of the results of this causation.

  By opening the door, he makes things said
   unsaid – and does not burn the spit and meat.

He wipes away those words and makes them vanish
    from all the hearts of those who heard the
        utterance.

If you should need an argument and proof, sir,
    recite, '*If we should abrogate a verse . . .*'

Recite, '*they wiped My memory from you,*'
    and know their power of making men forget

Since they have power of memory and oblivion,   1685
    and have control of every creature's heart.

And when He's closed the way of sight like this,
    you cannot act, though virtue may be yours.

'*You have made fools of those exalted ones*';
    recite Quran down to '*made you forget*'.

The landlord is the king of all the bodies;
    the lord of hearts is king of all your hearts.

Since, doubtless, action is a type of seeing,
    man's no more than the pupil of the eye.

I shall not risk declaring all of this,   1690
    prevented by the masters of the centre.

Forgetting and remembering by us creatures
    depend on Him, and when they call He comes.

Each night that Splendid One takes from their
        hearts
    a hundred thousand things of good and bad.

And in the day their hearts are filled by Him;
    He makes those oyster shells full up with pearls.

All of those thoughts which had been there before
   are guided so they recognize their souls.

1695   Your calling and experience return;
   the door of capability is open.

The goldsmith's skill does not go to the blacksmith;
   the lovely nature's not for the ill-tempered.

All skills and dispositions, like the world
   on Resurrection Day, come to their partner.

So skills and dispositions after sleep
   come swiftly back to their own counterpart.

And in the morning skills and thoughts return
   to that same place where good and evil were.

1700   Like carrier-pigeons back from other cities,
   they carry to their city wondrous things.

The Parrot Hears about the Actions of Those Parrots, and the Death of the Parrot in Its Cage, and the Master's Mourning for Her

That bird heard what had happened to that parrot;
   she trembled and she fell – her blood ran cold.

And when the master saw her like this, fallen,
   he leapt and flung his turban to the ground.

To see her in this pallor and this state,
   the master leapt about and tore his collar.

He said, 'My lovely sweetly crying parrot!
   What happened to you? Why are you like this?

Alas for you, my sweetly singing bird!   1705
   Alas, my darling friend and confidante!

Alas, my bird of sweetest melodies!
   My spirit's mead and meadow, my sweet basil!

If Solomon had owned a bird like this,
   could he have ever looked at other birds?

And O alas! the bird I bought so cheap,
   I turned my face from hers with such rude haste!

O tongue, you are so hurtful to all mortals.
   When you are speaking, how am I to answer?

O tongue, you are at once the fire and haystack.   1710
   How can you throw this fire into this haystack?

My soul's lamenting secretly for you
   though it is doing everything you say.

O tongue, to me you are an endless treasure!
   O tongue, you are a pain with no relief!

For birds you are the birdsong and the decoy,
   companion in the solitude of exile.

How can you reassure me, insecure one,
   O you who've strung the bow with vengeance
     for me?

Look, see how you have put my bird to flight!   1715
   Stop grazing in the pastures of oppression!

Give me an answer! If not, give me justice,
   or else remind me of the means of joy.

Alas for you, my darkness-burning light!
  Alas for this my day-igniting dawn!

Alas for you, my sweetly soaring bird,
  who's flown to my beginning from my end!

The stupid man's in love with pain forever.
  Go, read from "*I do swear*" to "*in affliction*".

1720   With your face I was free from all the suffering,
  untainted in your stream by any froth.

These groans are mirages of seeing, and
  the act of severance from my own true being.

It was God's jealousy; there is no way round God.
  Where is the heart not shattered by His love?

It's jealousy, for He's unlike all others,
  much more than explanation or report.

Alas! I wish my tears became an ocean
  to shower down upon my lovely sweetheart.

1725   My parrot, O my most sagacious bird,
  interpreter of all my thoughts and secrets!

Whatever comes to me that's just and unjust,
  she told me from the first so I'd remember.'

A parrot with a voice from revelation
  began her life before the first existence.

This parrot is concealed inside yourself;
  you've seen her image in phenomena.

She takes your happiness, yet you are glad;
  you take her blows as if she gave you justice.

O you who burned your soul all for the body,   1730
   you burned the soul and you inflamed the body.

I'm burnt, and anyone in need of tinder
   can set alight their rubbish using me.

Since tinder is amenable to fire,
   take tinder which most quickly sets ablaze.

Alas! and O alas! and O alas!
   that such a moon as this went into cloud!

How can I breathe with such a flaming heart,
   the lion of absence wild and shedding blood?

The one whose sober state is wild and drunk,   1735
   what happens when he takes the cup in hand?

The drunken lion who goes beyond all telling
   is too much for the confines of the plain.

I'm contemplating rhymes – my lover tells me,
   'You only contemplate your vision of me!'

Relax, dear rhyming-couplet-contemplator,
   for in my couplet you are rhymed with triumph.

What's in a word that you should contemplate?
   What's in a word? The thorns around the
      vineyard.

I throw the words and strains and speech together   1740
   so that without them I can sigh with you.

That sigh which I did keep concealed from Adam,
   I'll say to you, O mystery of the world!

That sigh I never breathed with Abraham,
   that sadness Gabriel has never known,

That sigh which the Messiah never breathed,
   God never mentioned, in His zeal, without us.

What's 'we' in words? The 'yes' and 'no'. I'm not
   affirming. I am essenceless negation.

1745   I found identity in the impersonal state;
   I wove it into the impersonal state.

All kings become the servants of their servants,
   and all become deceased in their own dead.

All kings are humbled by their humble servants,
   and all are drunk on those who swoon for them.

The catcher of the birds becomes their prey,
   and suddenly he'll make them prey to him.

With all their souls the amorous seek the lovelorn,
   and all beloveds are their lovers' prey.

1750   The one you saw as lover is beloved;
   he's both of these in terms of the relation.

The thirsty may seek water in the world,
   and in the world the water seeks the thirsty.

So since He is the Lover, you be silent!
   Be ear, since He is tugging at your ear!

Restrain the torrent when it starts to flood,
   or it will cause disgrace and desolation.

Why should I care if there be desolation?
   For underneath there lies a princely treasure.

The one who drowns in God desires more
      drowning,   1755
  his soul tossed up and down like ocean waves.

It's better under or above the sea?
  His shaft's more captivating or His shield?

You will be split apart by whisperings,
  dear heart, if you distinguish joys and trials.

Though your desire is for the taste of sugar,
  is not desirelessness the lover's true desire?

His stars atone a hundred crescent moons;
  He is allowed to shed the world's life-blood.

And we obtained our price and the atonement,   1760
  and quick we were to play our souls away.

How much of lovers' lives is spent in dying!
  You only win the heart by losing it.

With a hundred loving looks I sought His heart.
  He wearily excused Himself from me.

I said, 'My mind and soul are drowned in You.'
  He said, 'Be off, don't chant such spells at me.

Do I not know what you have contemplated?
  Ah, how could your two eyes behold the Friend?

O leaden soul, how you looked down on Him   1765
  because you bought Him at so cheap a price.

Whoever buys for nothing sells for nothing;
  a child will sell a jewel to buy a loaf.

For I am drowned in love which does contain
    the loves of former times and future times.'

I spoke in brief, I gave no full account,
    lest it consume your tongue and understanding.

When I say 'lip', I mean the ocean's shore;
    when I say 'no', the intention is 'except'.

1770   I'm sitting down and grimacing from sweetness;
    I'm silent from a surfeit of my speech

So that our sweetness may be kept disguised
    from both worlds in the veil of grimacing.

This discourse does not fall on every ear;
    I tell one in a hundred heavenly secrets.

*The Commentary on the Saying of Hakim Sanā'i,
'Whatever Word Detains You from the Way, Be It
Belief or Unbelief, Whatever Image Separates you
From the Friend, Be It Beautiful or Ugly'. On the
Meaning of the Saying of the Prophet (Peace Be Upon
Him), 'Indeed Sa'd Is Jealous and I Am More Jealous
than Sa'd, and God Is More Jealous than Me and
Because of His Jealousy He Has Forbidden Vile Deeds
Whether They Are Outward or Inward'*

And all the world was jealous in this way,
    and God surpassed this world in jealousy.

He's like the soul, the world is like the body;
    the world gets good and evil from the soul.

1775   He who is certain in his prayerful focus
    is surely shamed in going back to faith.

He who is Master of the Royal Robes
   would be demoted trading for the king.

Whoever was the sultan's boon companion
   would be quite wronged and duped to wait on him.

When granted leave to kiss the kingly hand,
   were he to kiss his foot, it were a sin!

It is respect to bow down to the king's feet,
   but it's a fault compared to other gestures.

The king would become jealous if the one   1780
   who's seen the royal face preferred his fragrance.

The jealousy of God would be like wheat,
   and human jealousy like straw in haystacks.

The root of all our jealousies is come
   from God Who is beyond comparison.

I leave this explanation to bewail
   the cruelty of that ten-hearted sweetheart.

And I lament – laments are sweet to Him –
   He needs laments and sadness from both worlds.

I must lament His fraud with bitterness   1785
   since I'm not in the circle of His revellers.

Why should I not be night without His day,
   without the union of His day-igniting face?

His nastiness is sweet within my soul –
   soul, victim of the Friend who tortures me.

I am in love with both my grief and pain,
   all for the pleasing of my Matchless King.

I make an eye-balm from the earth of sorrow;
   both oceans of my eyes are filled with pearls.

1790   The tears that people shed on His behalf
   are pearls, and yet the people think them tears.

I am lamenting for the Soul of souls;
   I don't complain, I tell it as it is.

My heart says how I am tormented by Him,
   and I have ridiculed its low hypocrisy.

Be just, O Glory of the righteous ones,
   O You who are the throne and I your shoe-rack.

Shoe-rack and throne? – what do they mean in spirit?
   Both 'we' and 'I' are where our Lover is.

1795   O you whose soul is freed from 'we' and 'I',
   O spiritual grace in men and women.

When lovers become one, You are that one;
   when difference is effaced then there You are.

You made this 'I' and 'we' with this intent,
   that You should play the game of Nard with You,

That all the I's and You's become one soul
   and finally absorbed in the Beloved.

All this exists, and 'Come!', O word of Being,
   You who transcend this 'Come!' and all such
      words.

1800   Flesh sees you only in the fleshly form,
   imagining Your sorrow and Your laughing.

With heart tied down to sorrow and to laughing,
   do not protest that it deserves to see Him.

He who is tied to sorrow and to laughing,
   he lives on these two things which have been
      borrowed.

In love's fresh garden – which is infinite –
   are many fruits apart from joy and grief.

To love is higher than these two conditions,
   and green and tender without spring or autumn.

So pay your lovely face's tax, my beauty,   1805
   and tell the tale of how my soul is torn.

The charms of glances of seductive eyes
   have lately stamped a brand upon my heart.

And I did sanction Him to shed my blood.
   I kept on saying 'sanctioned' and He'd flee.

You flee the cries of scrabblers in the dust.
   Why heap more sorrow on the hearts of grievers?

Each dawn which shone its rays up from the East
   found You erupting like the solar fountain.

Why did You spurn this madly love-sick one,   1810
   O You whose lips of sugar have no price?

O You, the new soul for the ancient world,
   now hear the soulless, heartless body's cry.

Leave off your talk of roses, for God's sake;
   tell how the nightingale was parted from it.

Our fervour does not come from grief and joy,
   nor is our mind on fancies and conjectures.

There is another state which is most rare.
   Do not deny this; God is full of power.

1815 Do not compare this with the human state;
   don't set up house in wickedness and virtue.

For wickedness and virtue, pain and joy,
   are things which pass away and God inherits.

It's dawn, O dawn and refuge of the dawn;
   ask pardon of Hosāmoddin my lord.

Excuser of the universal mind
   and soul, You're Soul of souls and coral's brilliance.

The light of morning shone, and in Your light
   our morning draught of Your Hallāj's wine.

1820 And as Your gift takes hold of me like this,
   what other wine could bring me such delight?

And wine fermenting craves our fermentation,
   and heaven turning craves our understanding.

The wine got drunk on us, not we on it;
   the body came from us, not we from it.

We're like the bee, the body's like the hive,
   and like the hive each body cell's constructed.

Returning to the Story of the
Gentleman Merchant

It's very long, so tell the master's story –
   what happened to that kindly gentleman.

The master was on fire in pain and passion;   1825
   he said a hundred things distraught like this,

Sometimes undone, sometimes puffed up or
      pleading,
   now passionate for truth, now for appearance.

The drowning man is fighting for his life;
   he stretches out his hand to grasp at straws.

That anyone will grab his hand in danger,
   he lunges out with hand and foot in fear.

The Friend is fond of seeing such commotion,
   preferring useless struggle to inaction.

The One who's King is not without his work;   1830
   a groan would be surprising – He's not ill.

On this my son, the Merciful said,
   'Each day He is engaged upon some labour.'

Be always scraping on this path and scratching,
   not idle once until your final breath.

Your final breath may be the final breath
   in which God's favour will be your true friend.

Whatever human beings struggle for,
   the King of Soul's all eyes and ears attending.

The Merchant Throws the Parrot out of
Her Cage and the Parrot Flies

1835   And after that he tossed her from the cage –
     the parrot flew up to a lofty branch.

     The dying parrot rose in soaring flight
     like sunshine dawning on the Turkish landscape.

     The bird's behaviour stupefied the master, who,
     uncomprehending, saw the parrot's secret.

     He lifted up his face, 'O nightingale,
     give me some explanation of our state!

     What was it that she did that you have learnt?
     You played a trick on us and burnt us up!'

1840   The parrot said, 'Her actions told me this:
     "Escape your voice's beauty and devotion,

     Because your voice has put you into chains."
     She put herself to "death" for this advice:

     "O you, who have become the world's musician,
     become 'deceased' like me, to gain release.

     If you're a seed, the chicks will peck at you;
     if you're a rosebud, you'll be picked by children.

     So hide the seed; become completely snare.
     And hide the rose; be moss upon the roof!

1845   Whoever puts her beauty up for auction,
     a hundred ugly fates go after her.

And evil tempers, eyes and jealousies
  pour on her head like water out of skins.

In jealousy her enemies devour her,
  and even friends will rob her of her living.

And she who turned her back on spring and sowing,
  how could she know the value of this life?

You must escape to shelter in God's grace
  Who poured a thousand graces on our spirits,

To shelter you – what shelter will you need then?   1850
  The fire and water will become your allies.

Was not the sea a friend to Noah and Moses,
  and to their foes it was a vengeful tyrant.

For Abraham, was not the fire a fortress
  that caused the smoke to pour from Nimrod's
        heart?

Did not the mountain summon up the Baptist?
  And, raining stones, it drove off his assailants

And said, 'John Baptist, come and flee to me,
  I'll be your refuge from the sharpest sword.'"'

The Parrot Bids Farewell to the
Master and Flies Away

The parrot gave him bits of sound advice   1855
  and then she sang him the *salām* of leaving.

The master said, 'Depart in God's protection.
  You've shown a whole new way of life to me.'

The master told himself, 'That's good advice!
I'll take her path, this path is radiant.

How could my soul be less than such a parrot's?
My soul must have a noble path like hers.'

THE DANGER OF BEING
HONOURED BY PEOPLE AND
BEING IN THE LIMELIGHT

The body's like a cage, a thorn inside
  the soul, with all the things that come and go.

One says to her, 'I shall become your soul-mate';   1860
  another says to her, 'No, I'm your partner.'

One says, 'There's no one like you in existence,
  in beauty, grace or virtue or good nature.'

One says, 'Both this world and the next are yours,
  and all our souls are hangers-on of yours.'

And when she sees the people swooning for her,
  she loses self-control in her conceit.

And she has no idea the devil's thrown
  a thousand like her to the flowing torrent.

Delicious are the world's delights and frauds.   1865
  Eat less of them, for they're a fiery mouthful!

Its fieriness is hid, its taste is strong,
  and in the end it starts to give off smoke.

Don't say, 'How could I fall for such applause?
  He speaks from envy and I know his game!'

Your praiser may lampoon you to the crowd
  and burn your heart for days by such a scorching.

Though you may know he spoke resentfully
   and all his envy of you cost him dear,

1870   The whole effect of this will stay within you,
   the influence of praise on your condition.

And that effect will stay with you for days;
   it causes pride and falsehood in the soul.

Though it does not appear when praise is sweet,
   yet ill appears because reproach is bitter.

It's like the pills and medicines you take –
   the nasty taste and pain of them will linger.

If you eat halva then its taste is instant,
   yet its effect does not remain like that one.

1875   It does not stay and yet it stays in secret –
   know opposites through their own opposite!

As when the effects of sugar stay in secret,
   a while and it brings boils that must be lanced.

From too much praise the self became the Pharaoh.
   Be meek in modesty; don't overbear.

As far as possible, be slave, not sultan:
   receive the hit; be polo ball, not stick!

Or when this grace and beauty are no more,
   those friends of yours will grow annoyed with you.

1880   That group of people who were fooling you,
   when they set eyes on you will call you 'demon'.

They'll tell you, when they see you at the door,
   'A corpse has raised his head out of his tomb.'

Just like the beardless youth they dub 'My Lord'
 so that they trap him by their trickery,

When, in disgrace, his beard comes to his face,
 the devil himself's reluctant to pursue him.

The devil came to Man to work his evil;
 he does not come because you're worse than him.

As long as you're a man, he's after you;   1885
 he chases you and gives you wine to taste.

When you're won over to his devilish ways,
 he flees from you, you wicked little devil!

And he who held on to your hem before
 will run away from you when you're like this.

EXPLANATION OF THE
TRADITION 'AS GOD WILLS
SO IT COMES TO PASS'

All this we've said, yet it is preparation.
　　Without God's care we are as nothing – nought.

Without the care of God and His elect,
　　his page is blank though he may be an angel.

1890　O God whose Grace supplies our every need,
　　the thought of all apart from You is wrong.

So much direction have You given us,
　　till now our many faults are hidden by You.

And make the drop of wisdom You once gave us
　　connected to the oceans of Your Being.

There is a drop of knowledge in my soul.
　　Free it from lust and from the body's earth!

Before this earth attempts to swallow it,
　　before these winds attempt to draw it up,

1895　Though when they draw it up, You can
　　reclaim it and redeem it all from them.

How could a drop that vanished in the air,
　　or spilled, escape the stronghold of Your power?

It may come to the hundredth non-existence,
　　but when You call it back, it comes full pelt.

A hundred thousand opposites are slaying
    their opposites and Your command reclaims them.

There's caravan on caravan, O Lord,
    continually from nothingness to being.

Especially each night when thoughts and minds   1900
    are vanishing, and drowned in oceans deep.

Again, when morning breaks, those god-like ones
    lift up their heads like fishes from the sea.

In autumn, boughs and leaves, a hundred thousand,
    have all been routed to the sea of death.

The crow all cloaked in black like hired mourners
    has grieved for all the greenness of the garden.

The order comes back from the local ruler
    to nothingness, 'Give back what you've
        consumed!'

Give up all that you have consumed, black death,   1905
    of plants, medicinal herbs and leaves and grasses.

Come to your senses for a while, O brother;
    each moment you are full of spring and autumn.

The garden of the heart is green and moist
    with buds and blooms of jasmine, rose and cypress.

The boughs are hidden by a mass of leaves,
    a mass of flowers conceals the plain and palace.

These words that come from universal mind
    are roses', hyacinths' and cypress' scents.

1910   Have you smelt roses where there were no roses?
      Have you seen foaming wine where there was none?

     The fragrance is your guide and your companion;
      it bears you up to Paradise and Kawsar.

     The fragrance is a light-bestowing eye-balm,
      as Jacob's eyes were opened by a fragrance.

     An evil stench brings darkness to the eyes,
      but Joseph's fragrance benefits the eyes.

     So you who are not Joseph, be a Jacob!
      Lament and be distraught just as he was!

1915   Give heed to this advice from Sanā'i,
      so that your ageing body may have vigour.

     As haughtiness demands a rose-like face,
      since yours is not, don't go about bad-tempered!

     It's ugly to be plain of face and haughty;
      it's cruel to be blind and suffer eye-pain.

     In Joseph's presence don't have airs and graces;
      confine yourself to Jacob's prayers and sighs.

     The meaning of the parrot's death was longing.
      Make yourself dead in poverty and longing,

1920   So that the breath of Jesus shall revive you
      and make you good and blessed as she is.

     How could the stone be overgrown by Spring?
      Be earth and grow the many-coloured blooms.

     For years you've been the stone that scratches hearts.
      For once be earth, as an experiment.

THE TALE OF THE OLD HARPIST
WHO IN THE TIME OF OMAR (MAY GOD BE PLEASED WITH HIM) ONE DAY WHEN HE WAS PENNILESS PLAYED THE HARP FOR GOD IN THE GRAVEYARD

In Omar's time, perhaps as you have heard,
　　there was a harpist with a splendid voice.

The nightingale would swoon to hear his voice;
　　one joy became a hundred with his song.

His breath would beautify the hall and concourse –　1925
　　the dead would rise again to hear his songs –

Like Esrāfil whose voice so skilfully
　　brings souls into the bodies of the dead,

Or like the accompanists of Esrāfil
　　whose playing made the elephant grow wings,

As one day Esrāfil will sound the blast
　　that brings to life the hundred-year-old corpses.

The prophets also have such sounds in them
　　for those who seek to gain the priceless life.

The sensual ear does not perceive those tones;　1930
　　the sensual ear's polluted by oppression.

And man does not perceive the peri's tone,
　　for he is foreign to the peri's mysteries.

Whereas the peri's tone is of this world,
  the heart's tone is above both of these sounds.

The peri and the man are prisoners,
  for both are inmates of this ignorance.

Recite: 'O *tribe of jinn*' from *Ar-Rahmān,*
  and know '*If you are able to pass through*'.

1935 The tones that are within the Friends will say,
  'O particles of non-reality,

Quick, lift your heads above the "not" of nothing;
  extract your heads from this deluded thinking.

All you who fester in decay and being,
  the eternal soul has neither birth nor growth.'

Were I to whisper something of their tones,
  the souls would thrust their heads out of their graves.

So put your ear up close; this is not far,
  and yet I'm not allowed to say this to you.

1940 Behold the Friends are Esrāfils for now;
  from them the dead have strength to live and grow.

The deadened souls inside the body's tomb
  spring up within their shrouds to hear their voice.

He says, 'This voice is set apart from others.
  It is the voice of God, which will revive us.'

We died and we were absolutely finished.
  God's summons came, and we were resurrected.

God's summons to us, either veiled or unveiled,
  gives what He gave to Mary from His heart.

And you, who rot in death beneath your skin,
   come back from non-existence at His Voice.

In truth that Voice is from the King Himself,
   although it's voiced by him who is God's servant.

He said to him, 'I am your tongue, your eye;
   I am your feelings, pleasure and your anger.

Go on, you are *"By me you hear and see"*;
   you are the secret, not the secret's keeper.

In fondness you became *"Who is for God"*;
   for you I am become *"God is for him"*.

Sometimes I say "It's You," sometimes "It's I" –   1950
   for all I say, I am the shining sun.

Where I shine from the lamp-niche of a moment,
   a whole world's problems disappear from there.

My Breath transformed that darkness into noonday,
   the darkness which the sun could not disperse.'

To Adam He Himself divulged the names;
   the others had the names revealed through Adam.

So either take His light from Him or Adam –
   take wine straight from the jar or from the cup.

This cup and jar are intimately linked,   1955
   and, not like you, that lucky cup is happy.

The Prophet said, 'What joy for him who saw me,
   and him who looked on him who saw my face.'

As when a lantern takes the candle's light,
   whoever sees it truly sees the candle.

So, till a hundred candles are transmitted,
　　to see the last is to confront the source.

With all your heart you either take the last light
　　or take it from the candle – there's no difference –

1960　You either see the light of this last lamp,
　　or see His light from the ancestors' candle.

In Explanation of This Hadith: 'Indeed Your Lord Has Breaths in the Days of Your Time: Attend to Them'

The Prophet said that in these days of ours
　　God's inspirations come before all else.

Give rapt attention in these precious moments
　　and seize upon such kinds of inspiration.

The inspiration came, saw you and went,
　　revived whoever longed for it and went.

Another inspiration came, for sure –
　　don't miss this one as well, my fellow servant!

1965　The soul that is on fire is quenched by this;
　　the soul that passed away is moved by this.

From this the fiery soul obtained extinction;
　　the dead man wore the garment of forever.

Fresh stirring of the Prophet's heavenly tree
　　which is not like the stirrings of the creatures.

If they should fall to earth or fall in heaven,
　　their courage turns to water straightaway.

Indeed from fear of this eternal breath
    recite: *'but they refused to carry it'*

Or how is it *'they were afraid of it'*   1970
    unless the mountain's heart had bled from fear?

Last night this came to pass quite differently –
    some piece of food arrived and blocked the path.

For food's sake Loqmān turned into a pledge
    – it is the time of Loqmān: food be gone!

All this affliction for the sake of food –
    will you pull out the thorn from Loqmān's foot!

There is no thorn, nor hint of one in it,
    but you, with your desire, cannot see that.

What you saw as a date was just a thorn,   1975
    because you are ungrateful and unseeing.

The soul of Loqmān, garden of the Lord:
    why is his soul's foot troubled by a thorn?

This thorny state of being's like a camel –
    a son of Mostafā rides on this camel.

You're loaded with a bale of roses, camel;
    its scent would grow a hundred blooms in you.

But you prefer the desert thorns and sand.
    What roses will you pick from barren thorns?

O you who've gone from here to there in   1980
        searching,
    how long will you repeat, 'Where are the roses?'

Until you get this thorn out of your foot,
  your eye is blinded – how can you proceed?

A man is more than all the world can hold,
  yet in a thorny point he disappears.

For harmony the Holy Prophet came:
  '*Homayrā, speak to me, O speak to me.*'

Homayrā, put your horseshoe in the fire
  so that it turns the mountain into rubies.

1985   The word *Homayrā*'s feminine in gender –
         The Arabs use the feminine for 'soul'.

The soul is not at risk from femaleness;
  the soul does not partake of male and female.

Above the feminine and masculine,
  it's not a soul of moist and dry conditions.

It's not the soul that grows by eating bread,
  that's now like this and then again like that.

The sweetener, it is sweet, the soul of sweetness.
  Without it there's no sweetness, O bribe-taker.

1990   Though sugar sweetens you, there comes a time
         when all that sugar disappears from you.

But when, from so much faith, you turn to sugar,
  then how can you be parted from the sugar?

The lover drinks on vintage wine within,
  and intellect is at a loss and friendless.

The partial intellect opposes love,
  though it pretends to be its confidant.

Intelligent and clever, but not nothing,
   demonic till the angel disappears.

In speech and action it is our companion,   1995
   but when you come to inward states, it's nothing.

It's nothing, since it's not escaped from being,
   not willingly – unwillingly will do.

The soul is perfect and its calling's perfect.
   Mohammed said, '*Belāl bring comfort to us!*'

Belāl, lift up your voice of liquid tones
   gained from that breath I breathed into your heart.

That breath which rendered Adam thunderstruck
   struck dumb the minds of heaven's occupants.

Mohammed was so taken by that voice   2000
   that prayer eluded him that night of halting.

He could not wake from that enchanted sleep
   until the morning prayer became the noon.

The night of halting, and before that bride,
   their pure souls did attain to kissing hands.

Both love and soul are hidden and concealed.
   If I have called Him 'bride', do not blame me.

I'd spared the Friend vexation and kept silent,
   had he just let me have a moment's respite.

But yet He says, 'Speak out, there's nothing   2005
      wrong –
   it's what the hidden destiny decrees.'

He would be wrong to see the fault alone.
　　Could spirit pure and unseen see such fault?

Fault is related to the witless creature,
　　not in relation to the Lord of Favour.

For the Creator unbelief is wisdom;
　　accusing us of unbelief is sinful.

If there's one fault among these hundred boons,
　　it's like the stalk inside the sugar-cane.

2010　　Together both are put into the scales
　　because, like soul and body, both are sweet.

And so the great have not said this in vain:
　　'The pure are pure in body as in soul.'

Their words and selves and personalities
　　are all, without a trace, soul absolute.

The soul opposed to them is merely body;
　　just like the 'plus' in Nard it's just a name.

As this one went to earth and turned to earth,
　　so this one went to salt and turned out pure,

2015　　The salt that made Mohammed more refined –
　　he is more eloquent than fine hadith.

This salt endures in his inheritance;
　　those heirs of his are with you – seek them out!

He sits in front of you – where is the 'front'?
　　In front – where is the forward-thinking soul?

If you imagine you have 'back' and 'front',
　　you're bound to body and deprived of soul.

'Down', 'up', 'behind', 'in front' describe the flesh;
at heart the radiant soul has no directions.

Release your vision to the King's pure light;   2020
don't fantasize like one who cannot see,

That you're no more than all these griefs and joys
beyond! Where is before and after there?

It is a day of rain – go on till nightfall,
not in this earthly rain but in the Lord's.

The Story of Ā'isha (May God Be Pleased With Her), Asking Mohammed (Peace Be Upon Him): 'Today It Rained. Since You Went to the Graveyard, Why Are Your Clothes Not Wet?'

One day Mohammed visited a graveyard
accompanying the coffin of a friend.

He piled the earth inside the grave to fill it;
he made his seed alive beneath the earth.

Those buried in the earth are like these trees,   2025
for they have raised their hands above the earth.

They send a hundred signs to humankind
and they make clear to him who has an ear.

With tongues of green and with extended hands
they speak the secrets from the earth's interior.

Like ducks who have their heads plunged into
        water,
    they were like ravens; they've become like
        peacocks.

For though in winter he imprisoned them,
   the Lord would make those ravens into peacocks.

2030   Although they were consigned to death in winter,
   in spring he made them live and gave them leaves.

The atheists say, 'This process is eternal.
   Why should we link this to a generous God?'

In spite of them, within the friendly ones
   the Lord makes vineyards and rose-gardens grow.

In them each rose, which is so sweetly smelling,
   each rose describes the universal secret.

Their fragrance, noxious to the atheist's nose,
   will pass around the world and rend the veils.

2035   The atheists flee that rose-scent like a beetle
   or like a fragile brain before a drum.

They make themselves seem busy and absorbed,
   and from this flashing lightning steal their eyes.

They steal their eyes, but no eye's really there;
   the eye is what can see a place of refuge.

Now when the Prophet came back from the
     graveyard,
   He went to his Seddiqe and confided.

As soon as his Seddiqe saw his face,
   she came to him and put her hand upon him,

2040   Upon his turban and his face, his hair,
   his collar, chest and then upon his arm.

The Prophet said, 'Why search me in such haste?'
    She said, 'Today a rain came from the clouds.

I'm making an inspection of your clothes;
    I see no moisture from the rain – a marvel!'

He said, 'What covering did you throw upon your
        head?'
    She said, 'I took your mantle as my head-dress.'

He said, 'Pure heart! It was because of this
    God showed to your pure eye the unseen rain.'

It's not the rain that's from these clouds of yours –   2045
    there is another cloud, another sky.

*Commentary on the Verse of Hakim Sanā'i
    (May God Be Pleased with Him):*
'Within the Kingdom of the Soul Are Skies
Which Are Commanders of These Worldly Skies
And Heights and Valleys on the Spirit's Way
The Highest Mountains and the Deepest Oceans'

The unseen world has other clouds and waters,
    another heaven and another sun.

But they appear to the elect alone,
    the rest *'in doubt as to the new creation'*.

There is the rain which is in aid of nurture;
    there is the rain in aid of decomposing.

The boon of rain in spring is wonderful,
    but autumn rain's like fever to the garden.

The spring rain nurtures it so tenderly;   2050
    the autumn rain will rot and yellow it.

And so like this the cold and wind and sunshine
   do different things – now do you get the point?

It's also different in the unseen world,
   in loss and benefit and gains and tricks.

This breath of saints arises from that spring;
   a garden springs up in the heart and soul.

The action of the spring rain on the plants
   will come upon the lucky from their breaths.

2055   If in this place there is a dried-up plant,
   it's not the soul-reviving wind's mistake.

The wind blew over, having done its work.
   The human soul preferred it to her self.

On the Meaning of the Hadith 'Take Advantage of the Coolness of Springtime . . . etc.'

The Holy Prophet said, 'O friends beware,
   don't shield your bodies from the cool of spring!

Because it has the effect upon your soul
   that springtime has upon the trees and plants.

But flee from autumn's chill lest it should do
   what that chill did to gardens and to vines.'

2060   Narrators took the outward sense of this
   and were contented with the surface meaning.

That lot were ill informed about the soul:
   they saw the mountain, not the mine within.

With God, that autumn is the self and lust;
   the mind and soul are spring and life eternal.

There is a partial mind concealed in you –
   go seek the perfect mind within the world!

Your part shall be made whole by His perfection.
   The perfect mind's a yoke upon the self.

To understand this, then, the holy breaths   2065
   are like the spring and life in leaves and tendrils.

Don't shield your body from the words of saints,
   for, rough or smooth, they are your faith's support.

Both hot and cold He speaks, but take it gladly.
   Escape the hot and cold, escape hellfire!

His hot and cold are new springtimes of life,
   the source of truth and certainty and service.

He makes the garden of our souls alive;
   He fills the ocean of the heart with pearls.

The knowing heart would grieve a thousand griefs   2070
   if just one leaf were lacking in its garden.

Seddiqe (May God Be Pleased With Her) Asks Mohammed (Peace Be Upon Him), 'What Was the Mystery of Today's Rain?'

Seddiqe said, 'O you, the cream of being,
   what was the wisdom of today's downpour?

Was this a rain of mercy, or was it
   to threaten and affirm majestic justice?

Would it be from the favour of the springtime,
    or from an autumn full of misery?'

He said, 'This is to soothe away the sorrow
    of the afflictions on the race of Adam.'

2075   If humankind remained on fire like that,
    much desolation and much loss would come.

Immediately this world would be laid waste,
    and out would come our greedy human vices.

Forgetting is the pillar of this world,
    intelligence the ruin of this world.

Intelligence is from that world and when
    it dominates, this world is brought down low.

Intelligence is sunshine, greed is ice,
    the world is filth, intelligence is water.

2080   It comes in trickles from that unseen world
    to stop the roar of greed and envy here.

And if the trickle from that world increases,
    no virtue and no vice stay in this world.

This has no end – go back to the beginning,
    return to tell the tale of the musician.

The Rest of the Story of the Harpist and
Explanation of Its Import

The world was filled with joy by the musician,
  whose voice created fantasies of wonder.

To hear his voice the bird of soul would soar,
  its reason devastated by his sound.

When years went by and he grew elderly,   2085
  his falcon soul made do with catching gnats.

His back became as rounded as a barrel,
  his brows like leather straps upon his eyes.

His lovely soul-uplifting voice became
  a hideous thing, no use to anyone.

That voice which even Venus envied once
  was like the braying of an aged mule.

Indeed what lovely thing does not decay?
  What roof does not one day become a floor?

Except the voice of holy men within them,   2090
  from which the trumpet blast reflects their
     breath.

The heart that makes all hearts intoxicated,
  the nothingness that makes our beings real.

Magnet of thought and voice, He is the joy
  of inspiration, revelation, secret.

Now when old age and weakness plucked the harpist,
  so destitute he could not buy his bread,

He said, 'You've given me much life and leisure,
   O God; You've shown much favour to a knave.

2095   I have been sinning threescore years and ten,
   and not one day have You withheld Your gift.

I have no means, today I am Your guest.
   I'll play the harp for You, for I am Yours.'

He took his harp and went to look for God
   around the graveyard of Medina, sighing,

'I ask from God the price of playing silk,
   for in his mercy He accepts base coin.'

He played his harp and, weeping, bowed his head
   and fell on to a tomb, his harp a pillow.

2100   Sleep took him, and his soul's bird fled the cage;
   it left the harpist and the harp and flew,

Released from body and from worldly pain
   into the pure world and the soul's expanses.

His soul was singing there of what had passed:
   'If only they'd allow me to remain here,

How glad my soul would be in this spring garden,
   so drunk on this expanse of heavenly flowers,

I'd make the journey without head or feet,
   I'd eat the sugar without lips or teeth.

2105   My thought and conscience free of mental fever,
   I'd revel with the residents of heaven.

I'd see a universe with eyes tight shut,
   without a hand I'd pick the rose and basil.'

This seabird plunged into a honeyed sea
  to drink the fount of Job and purify him.

Job was made pure by this from head to foot,
  washed clean of pains as in the dawning light.

And were the *Masnavi* as great as heaven,
  it would not yet contain one half of this.

That land and sky of such expansiveness,   2110
  their narrowness has torn my heart to shreds.

This world, revealed to me in what I've dreamt,
  has opened up my wings with its unveiling.

If this world and the way to it were known,
  no one would stay down there another moment.

The order came: 'No, do not be so greedy.
  The thorn's extracted from your foot, so go!'

His soul was hesitating in that place,
  residing near His goodness and His mercy.

*The Voice from Heaven Spoke to Omar (May
God Be Pleased With Him) in Sleep, Saying,
'Give Some Gold from the Treasury to That
Man Who Is Asleep in the Graveyard'*

Just then God cast a drowsiness on Omar   2115
  so that he could not keep himself from sleep.

He was astonished: 'This is unaccustomed;
  it must come from above, it's not for nothing.'

He bowed his head, sleep took him, and he dreamt
  there came a voice from God – his soul was listening.

That voice which is the root of every calling,
    that is the true voice – all the rest are echoes.

The Persian speaker, Turk and Kurd and Arab
    can know that voice with neither ear nor lip.

2120   Why stop at Turks, Tajiks and Ethiopians?
    The wood and stone can understand that voice.

Each moment '*Am I not your Lord?*' comes from Him,
    the substance and effect come into being.

And if the 'Yes' does not come back from them,
    their coming out of nothing is their 'Yes'.

Now pay attention to this tale explaining
    what I have said of mind in wood and stone.

*The Complaint of the Yearning Pillar When They
Made a Pulpit for the Prophet (Peace Be Upon Him),
for the Crowd Had Become Great and They Said,
'We Cannot See Your Blessed Face at the Time of
your Sermon,' and the Prophet and Companions
Heard That Complaint and the Clear Questions
and Answers of Mohammed (Peace Be Upon
Him) to the Pillar*

As it cried out about the Prophet's absence,
    the yearning pillar seemed intelligent.

2125   The Prophet said, 'What do you want, O pillar?'
    It said, 'My soul is bleeding from your leaving.

When I was your support, you ran away;
    you made the pulpit top your leaning place.'

'Then would you like to be a date-palm tree,'
    he said, 'and East and West shall pick your fruit?

Or in that world would you be made a cypress
    and stay in leaf and green forever more?'

It said, 'I want the life that is eternal.'
    O careless, listen, don't be less than wood.

He had the pillar buried in the ground   2130
    that it shall rise like man on Judgement Day,

So you may know that all whom God has called
    will be untroubled by this worldly toil.

Whoever has his duty from the Lord
    gains access there and leaves his worldly work.

But one who is not privy to the mysteries,
    how could he countenance the cry of matter?

He says, 'Yes,' not sincerely but conforming,
    so that they shall not call him 'hypocrite'.

If there were none who know the order 'Be!'   2135
    these words would be rejected in the world.

A hundred thousand hypocrites and sophists
    are thrown off into doubt by half a thought.

For their hypocrisy and arguments,
    their wings and arms are fixed in their
        conjectures.

That good-for-nothing devil stirs up doubt,
    and all the blind men tumble in head first.

The leg of those who argue is of wood –
    a wooden leg is very insubstantial,

2140   Not like the Pole of insight of the age,
    whose firmness makes the mountain feel light-
        headed.

The stick is acting as the blind man's leg
    so he does not fall head first on the gravel.

Who was the knight who made the army triumph
    and men of faith as well? The man of insight.

Though blind men 'see' the way with blind men's
        sticks,
    they are protected by the men of insight.

If visionaries and kings did not exist,
    then all the blind men in the world would perish.

2145   No sowing and no harvest are produced,
    no building and no trade come from the 'blind'.

Had He not shown you mercy and indulgence,
    your wooden arguments would break in two.

What is this staff? It's argument and inference.
    Who gave it? The All-seeing, Glorious One.

The staff became the means of war and strife.
    O you who have been blinded, break the staff!

He gave the staff to you to come to Him,
    but in your wrath you struck Him with that staff.

2150   What are you up to, circle of the sightless?
    Invite the One who's keeping watch to join you.

And grasp His hem – He gave the staff to you.
  See what resulted from the Fall of Adam!

Reflect on Moses and Mohammed's wonders:
  the staff became a snake, the pillar spoke.

Out of the staff a snake, the pillar yearning!
  Five times a day they drum it for religion.

If this perception were not so absurd,
  what need were there for miracles at all?

The mind will swallow all that's logical   2155
  without support of marvels or convulsions.

This virgin path's beyond the reason, see –
  see how the chosen hearts have all received it.

As beasts and demons, out of fear of Adam,
  stampeded to the islands in their envy,

So have the sceptics hidden in the grass,
  intimidated by prophetic wonders,

So they can live pretending to be Muslims
  deceptively, so you don't find them out,

Like forgers who rub silver on base coin   2160
  and stamp the name of kings upon the fakes.

Outside their speech is Oneness and The Law,
  its inside's like the darnel seed in bread.

Philosophers don't have the gall to say so,
  or, if so, true faith knocks them all together.

Their hands and feet are fossils, and whatever
  their souls may say, they're both in its control.

Though with their tongues they're spreading evil
    thought,
    their hands and feet give evidence against them.

*The Performing of a Miracle by the Prophet
(Peace Be Upon Him) When the Gravel in
the Hand of Abu Jahl (May He Be Cursed)
Spoke up and Testified to the Truth of
the Message of Mohammed
(Peace Be Upon Him)*

2165   There was some gravel in Bu Jahl's fist.
    He said, 'Mohammed, quickly, say what is this –

If you're God's envoy, what hides in my fist? –
    since you're informed of heaven's mysteries.'

'Would you prefer I tell you what it is
    or that it tells you I am true and just?'

Bu Jahl said, 'This second thing is rarer.'
    He said, 'Yes, God is mightier than that.'

And from within his fist each piece of grit
    at once began to say the *Shahādat*,

2170   '*Except for God there is no god*,' it said,
    and threaded pearls, '*Mohammed is his Prophet.*'

And when Bu Jahl heard this from the stones,
    he threw the stones in fury to the ground.

*The Remainder of the Story of the Musician
and the Sending of a Message by the
Commander of the Faithful Omar
(May God Be Pleased with Him), Which the
Heavenly Voice Had Spoken to Him*

Go back and hear the plight of the musician.
    In waiting, the musician had despaired.

To Omar came the voice that said, 'O Omar,
    redeem Our servant from his state of need.

We have a special servant, much respected.
    Please take the trouble, go down to the
      graveyard.

Get up, Omar, and from the public coffers   2175
    take out the sum of seven hundred dinars.

Take it to him, say, "We have chosen you;
    accept this sum now, with apologies.

Lay out this sum to pay the price of silk,
    and when it has been spent, come back to me."'

Omar leapt up in panic at the voice
    to gird himself to carry out this service.

He turned to make his way towards the graveyard,
    the purse under his arm and running, seeking.

He ran around the graveyard several times;   2180
    he saw no one except that old man there.

'Not him,' he said, and ran around again.
    Worn out, he saw no one except the harpist.

He said, 'God has decreed, "We have a servant,
and he is pure and fine and fortunate."

How could an aged harper be God's chosen?
How good, O hidden mystery, how good!'

And one more time he went around the graveyard,
just like the lion prowling on the plain.

2185   Convinced there was no one except the harpist,
he said, 'In darkness there are many shining hearts.'

He came and sat down with a hundred bows,
then Omar sneezed, and made the old man jump.

He saw Omar, and in astonishment
he made as if to leave and started quaking.

His heart declared, 'O God, from You comes justice.
A judge has come to get this aged harpist!'

And when he looked upon that old man's cheek,
he saw him pale of face and full of shame.

2190   Then Omar said, 'Don't fear, don't flee from me,
for I have brought good news to you from God.

Your nature has been praised so much by God,
He's made Omar the lover of your face.

Sit next to me and do not keep your distance;
I'll whisper in your ear His Grace's secret.

God sends you His *salām* and asks of you
how are you in this toil and endless sorrow?

Some golden pieces for the price of silk, see!
Go buy it, then be sure to come back here.'

The old man heard this and he quaked all over.   2195
   He bit his hands and tore apart his clothes.

'O God without an equal!' – so the old man
   cried out as he dissolved in shamefulness.

When weeping and distress became too much,
   he smashed the harp upon the ground and broke it,

And said, 'O you who've been my veil from God,
   who highway-robbed me on the king's highway,

O you who drank my blood these seventy years,
   who shamed my face in perfect company!

O God of generosity and faith,   2200
   have mercy on a life run on injustice.

God gave a life, and every day of it
   has value no one knows except for Him.

I poured my life away in breath on breath;
   I blew it all on bass and treble clef.

My head full of Iraqi modes and scales,
   our parting's bitter moment slipped my mind.

Ah, from the limpid minor *zirafgand*
   my heart's seed withered and my heart has died.

Alas, caught up in these two dozen modes,   2205
   the caravan has left; the day is gone.

God save me from this yearning to be saved.
   I seek for vengeance only from the vengeful.

I get my justice from no one except
   from Him who's closer to myself than me.

This "I" arrives in me from Him each moment.
  I see Him then, when this abates in me.

As when someone is counting gold for you,
  you fix your gaze on him, not on yourself.'

Omar (May God Be Pleased With Him)
Made Him Turn His Gaze from the Station
of Weeping, Which is Existence, to the
Station of Immersion

2210   Omar then said to him, 'Your lamentation
          is all a mark of your sobriety.

The self-negating path's another path;
  sobriety's another kind of sin.

Sobriety is mindful of the past;
  the past and future states are veils from God.

Set fire to both of them! How long will you
  be knotted up like reeds by these two states?

A knotted reed is not your instrument.
  It's not the partner of the lip and voice.

2215   When you go round, you are wrapped up in it;
          when you come home, you're still inside yourself.

Your news is ignorant of the informer;
  your penitence is worse than your offence.

O you who have remorse for past conditions,
  say when will you repent of this repentance?

There was a time you made sweet tones your focus –
  and now you kiss the lips of lamentation.'

As Omar was the mirror of the mysteries,
the soul of the old man awoke within.

Now free of tears and laughter like the soul,   2220
this soul was gone. Another came to life.

Just then amazement seized his inner state
so much, he took his leave of earth and heaven.

The search and quest beyond the search and quest,
I do not understand – do you? Tell me!

Such words and states beyond all states and words,
he drowned within the beauty of His splendour.

One drowned beyond all hope of being found,
and none would know him now except the ocean.

The partial mind could not tell of the whole   2225
if waves of impetus did not appear.

Since impetus on impetus is coming,
that ocean's waves are coming to this place.

With this much telling of the old man's state,
he and his state withdrew behind a veil.

The old man freed himself from words and speech –
and half the tale has stayed within my mouth.

In order to obtain such joy and pleasure
you'd need to lose a hundred thousand souls.

In hunting for the spirit be a falcon!   2230
And like the world's sun gamble with your soul!

The sun on high is radiating life,
each moment emptying and filling up.

O sun of spirit, radiating soul,
   direct your newness to the worn-out world.

The soul and spirit come to man's existence
   like flowing water from the world unseen.

Commentary on the Prayer of the Two Angels
Who Every Day in Every Bazaar Make a
Proclamation – 'O God Give Every Generous
Giver a Reward' *and* 'O God Give Every
Greedy One Some Harm' – *and to Explain*
That the Generous One Is He Who Strives
on the Way of God, Not the One Who Is
Greedy on the Way of Desire

The Prophet said, 'All for the sake of counsel,
   two angels are proclaiming evermore:

2235   "O God, pay back in full the generous;
             reward each dirham with a hundred thousand.

O God, as for the misers of this world,
   afford them only ruin upon ruin!" '

O many a saving's better than expense –
   give what is God's at His command alone,

And claim as yours the treasure without end.
   Do not be numbered with the infidels.

Seek God's command from him who is in union.
   Not every heart attains to God's command.

2240   In the Quran the negligent are warned
             that their expenditure will be their grief.

The Meccan chiefs, at war against the Prophet,
    made sacrifice in hope of winning favour.

They made a camel sacrifice so that
    their swords might overcome the Holy Prophet,

Just like the rebel slave who acted justly
    and gave the king's possessions to his foes.

The 'justice' of this rebel with his king
    achieved just what? A stern and angry face!

In fear of this, the faithful always say   2245
    in prayer, '*Direct us on the righteous path!*'

To give their wealth is fitting for the rich;
    the lover's gift's to give the soul itself.

You'll earn your bread if you give bread for God;
    you'll earn your soul if you give soul for God.

And if the plane tree scatters all its leaves,
    God gives to it the gift of leaflessness.

So if your hand has nothing left from giving,
    how could the grace of God leave you
        downcast?

The barn of him who sows is emptied out,   2250
    but there is goodness growing in his field.

But leave it in the barn and save it up:
    misfortune, mouse and weevil clean it up.

This world is void – look into permanence.
    Its form is empty – look into your spirit!

Put to the sword your briny, bitter soul!
   Acquire the soul sweet as freshwater seas!

And if you cannot yet frequent these halls,
   I only wish you listen to my story.

THE STORY OF THE CALIPH WHO
SURPASSED HĀTEM OF TAYYI
IN GENEROSITY AND HAD
NO EQUAL IN HIS TIME

In days of old there was a certain caliph   2255
  whose generosity enslaved the noblest.

He'd raised the flag of kindness and of justice
  and banished need and poverty from Earth.

His bounty swept the oceans of its pearls;
  his justice reached the world's extremities.

To a world of dust he was the cloud and rain,
  outpouring of the Benefactor's bounty.

The seas and mines were shaken by his giving,
  and countless travellers came for his abundance.

As need had targeted his door and gate,   2260
  his fame for giving spread across the world.

Greeks, Persians, Arabs, Turks and all were left
  astonished at his generosity.

He was Life's water, sea of human kindness;
  he brought to life both Arab and barbarian.

The Story of the Poor Bedouin and His Wife's Quarrel with Him Because of Their Indigence and Poverty

One night a Bedouin wife addressed her husband
    and in her speech exceeded all the bounds:

'We suffer all this poverty and hardship,
    and all the world is well and we're the worse.

2265   We have no bread, our salt is pain and envy;
    we have no jug, our water is our tears.

Our clothing is the sun's ray in the daytime;
    by night our bed and blankets are the moonbeams.

We thought the round moon was a disc of bread,
    and so we held our hands up to the sky.

Our misery puts mendicants to shame;
    day turns to night in thoughts of our survival.

Both family and strangers fled from us,
    just as Sāmeri fled from humankind.

2270   If I beg someone for a cup of lentils,
    he tells me to shut up and die in pain.

For Arabs war and charity are glorious.
    As Arabs go, you're like a scribal error!

What warfare? We are killed without a war!
    We've lost our heads to deprivation's sword.

What charity? We are enmeshed in begging!
    We slit the veins of flies caught in mid-air.

If someone comes to visit, it is certain that
    at night when he's asleep I'll have his cloak.

How Novices Are Deceived in Their Needs by Impostors, and How They Imagine Them to Be Sheikhs and Worthy, Holy Men, and How They Do Not Know the Difference between Fact and Fiction and What Has Been Stuck On and What Has Developed Naturally

'And so it is, the wise have said acutely: 2275
    "You must become the guest of virtuous men."

You are the follower and guest of him
    who out of meanness makes off with your goods.

He's not robust; how could he make you so?
    He gives no light; he covers you in darkness.

And since there is no light in his direction,
    how can another take the light from him?

Like some dim-sighted doctor of the eyes,
    what does he stuff in eyes except for wool?

This is our state in poverty and tiredness;   2280
    I pray no guest is taken in by us.

If you've not seen what ten-year famines do,
    then feast your eyes and take a look at us!

Our outside's like the impostor's inner state,
    all darkness in his heart and silver-tongued.

With not a whiff or trace of God about him,
    he claims more for himself than Seth or Adam.

The devil himself's not shown his face to him,
   yet he announces, "We are saints" and more.

2285   He has purloined the speech of dervishes
   to give the impression he is one himself.

In talking he belittles Bāyazid,
   who would be mortified at his existence.

He is deprived of heavenly bread and fare –
   God has not thrown a single bone to him.

He's claimed, "I have laid out the heavenly feast;
   I am God's vicar and the caliph's son.

The feast awaits, you writhing simpletons.
   Fill up on . . . nothing, at my ample banquet!"

2290   Tomorrow's pledge keeps people waiting years
   around the door – tomorrow never comes.

And long it is before the human secret
   is ever known in outline and in detail.

Behind the body's wall is there a treasure,
   or just a nest of ants and snakes and dragons?

When he discovered there was nothing there,
   the seeker's life had gone – what good was
      wisdom?'

In Explanation of How It Very Occasionally
Happens That a Novice Sincerely Puts His Trust in an
Impostor, Believing Him to Be Someone Special, and
by This Act of Trust Comes to a Level of Attainment
of Which His Sheikh Has Never Dreamed, and Water
and Fire Do Not Harm Him but Harm the Sheikh –
but This Happens Very Rarely

A novice sometimes comes who has such radiance
    that falsehood counts as something in his favour.

With his good will he gets what he deserves,   2295
    though what he thought was soul was merely
        matter.

Like looking at the qibla in the darkness:
    there is no qibla, but the prayer is heard.

The impostor's running short of soul inside,
    while we are running short of bread outside.

Why should we cover up like the impostor,
    lay down our lives for notoriety?

The Bedouin Orders His Wife to Be
Patient and Explains the Virtue of Patience
and Poverty to Her

Her husband asked, 'How long will you seek gain?
    What life remains to us? – It's mostly gone.'

The wise man does not stare at gain and loss,   2300
    because, like flooding waters, both subside.

No matter if the flood be clear or murky,
    it does not last – don't dwell on it a moment!

The creatures in their thousands in this world
 live happily without such ups and downs.

The ring-dove in the tree will thank the Lord,
 yet it has no provision for the night.

The nightingale will sing to God its praise,
 'For food I trust in You who are attentive.'

2305 The falcon's made the king's hand his reward;
 he's given up the hope of any kill.

They're all like this, from flies to elephants,
 God's family – how well does God provide!

These griefs which are within our breasts are all
 the mist and dust and wind of our existence.

These griefs are tearing like a scythe through us –
 we're duped that things should be a certain way.

You know that every pain's a little death.
 Drive out this partial death, if well you can.

2310 If you cannot escape the partial death,
 they'll pour the whole of death upon your head.

But if you treat the partial death as sweet,
 be sure that God will make the whole one sweet.

For pains are come as envoys sent from death.
 Do not ignore His envoy, boastful one!

Whoever lives in ease will die in pain;
 whoever serves the flesh will lose his soul.

They drive the flocks of sheep from off the plain;
 the fattest ones are those they slaughter first.

The night has passed, and morning's come,
   Tamar.   2315
How long until the tale of gold again?

'Once you were young and you were more contented.
   At first you were the gold – then turned prospector.

Full-fruited vine – how did you turn out worthless?
   Just as your fruit matured, you were corrupted.

But your fruit should have had a greater sweetness,
   not turning round like those who make up rope.

You are my spouse, and spouses must conform
   so that events turn out successfully.

The couple must resemble one another –   2320
   just think about a pair of boots or shoes.

If one shoe is too tight upon the foot,
   the pair of them are of no use to you.

You've seen a pair of doors, one big, one small?
   A wolf united with a savage lion?

A pair of bags, one small and one full-size,
   cannot be balanced on a camel's back.

I'm marching to contentment, proud of heart;
   why are you heading for humiliation?'

The happy man, inflamed by his own candour,   2325
   addressed his wife like this till break of day.

The Wife Advises Her Husband, 'Do Not Say Any
More about Your Progress and Your Station: "Why
Do You Say What You Do Not?" for Although These
Words Are True, You Have Not Attained to the
Station of Trust in God, and to Say Such Things
above Your Station and Your Business Is Harmful
and Is "Very Hateful to God"'

The wife cried out, 'O devotee of fame,
    I shall no longer swallow your deceits!

Don't speak of foolish things in your pretence.
    Enough! Don't speak such proud and boastful words!

How long the pompous, self-important speech?
    Look at your deeds and state, and have some shame!

For pride's repulsive, more so in a beggar,
    like wet clothes on a cold and snowy day!

2330 How much more boasting, steaming bluster is there,
    O you whose house is like the spider's web?

When has contentment filled your soul with light?
    Contentment is a name that you have learnt.

The Prophet said, "What is contentment? Treasure."
    But you can't tell this treasure from distress.

Contentment is the treasure of the soul.
    Don't boast, O pain and torture of my soul!

Don't call me wife and take me in your arms.
    I am the wife of fairness, not corruption.

2335 How can you walk with princes and with chiefs
    and slit the veins of locusts in mid-air?

You're in dispute with dogs about a bone;
    you're groaning like the hollow-hearted reed-flute.

Don't look at me so meanly and so feebly,
    or else I'll broadcast what goes through your veins.

Have you assumed your mind is quite beyond me?
    Why have you reckoned I am feeble-minded?

Don't pounce upon me like a crazy wolf!
    With shame for brains you would be better
        brainless!

It is not "mind" to be a snake and dragon,   2340
    for your "mind" is a fetter on mankind.

May God oppose your darkness and deceit!
    May we be spared the favour of your "mind"!

Amazing how you are both snake and charmer!
    Disgrace to Arabs! Snake and serpent-catcher!

The crow would melt away in grief and sorrow
    like snow, were he to see his ugliness.

The charmer calls his spell down on the snake,
    and in return the snake charms him, like rivals.

Had not the snake spell been a trap for him,   2345
    how would he have been prey to snaky charms?

The charmer in his lust to get his way
    does not perceive the snake's spell in the moment.

The snake says, "O seducer, save yourself.
    You've seen your spell, so see my spells as well."

You do deceive me in the name of God
　　to bring me into bitter, wicked shame.

God's name took me, not any ploy of yours.
　　You made God's name a trap – alas for you!

2350　　For me God's name exacts revenge from you.
　　I trust my soul and body to God's name.

It cuts your vein of life as by my blow,
　　or puts you into prison just like me.'

And in this way the wife recited volumes
　　of such acerbic speech to her young husband.

The Husband Advises His Wife, 'Do Not Look upon the Poor with Contempt, but Regard God's Work as Perfect, and Do Not Scoff at Poverty and the Poor with Your Impoverished Imagination and Opinions'

'Wife, are you woman or a man of woe?
　　I'm poor and proud, don't beat my head!' he said.

'For wealth is just a hat upon the head.
　　The bald man takes his refuge in a hat.

2355　　But she whose hair is curly and attractive
　　looks prettier when her hat is off her head.

The man of God is likened to the eye;
　　the naked eye is better than the blinkered.

The trader, when he's showing off his slaves,
　　will strip the slaves of garments masking faults.

But if there were a fault, why would he strip them?
   He'd rather trick the buyer with the garments.

He'd say, "This one is shy of good and bad,
   and stripping him would scare him off from
      you."

The rich man's sunk up to his ears in faults,   2360
   but he has wealth, which covers up his faults.

The greedy, in their greed, don't see his faults;
   they are united in their hearts by greed.

Yet though the beggar utters golden words,
   his goods will not admit him to the shop.

Such poverty's beyond your understanding.
   Don't look on poverty with such contempt.

For dervishes transcend material wealth;
   they have an ample living from the Lord.

For God Most High is just. How can the just   2365
   then be unjust to those who've lost their hearts,

And give to one the favour and the means
   and then consign the others to the fire?

The fire is burning him who has this thought
   about the Lord and Maker of both worlds.

Is "*Poverty's my pride*" so incorrect?
   No! Glorious hidden glances in their thousands!

In anger you have hurled your slanders at me;
   you've called me charmer of both friends and
      snakes.

2370   If I should catch the snake, I'll draw its fangs,
            lest it be hurt by having its head crushed.

        Because its fangs are hostile to its life,
            and, knowing this, I make the foe a friend.

        I do not chant this spell out of desire,
            for I have turned desire upon its head.

        And God forbid I want something from others.
            There is a world of peace within my heart.

        Up in the pear tree things may seem like this.
            Come down from there to banish such a thought!

2375   When you whirl round, you make your head confused;
            you see the house as spinning, yet it's you!

*Explaining How Everyone's Movement Is from
the Place Where He Is; He Sees Everyone from
the Circle of His Own Self-existence. A Blue Glass
Shows the Sun as Blue, a Red Shows Red, but
When the Glasses Are Other than Coloured,
It Becomes White, and It Is Truer than All
Other Glasses, and It Is the Principal*

        'Abu Jahl saw Mohammed and he said,
            "From Hāshem's line an ugly form has sprouted."

        Mohammed answered him, "You are correct.
            You've spoken truly, though you've gone too far."

        Seddiqe, seeing him, said, "Shine in beauty,
            O sun not of the East nor of the West."

        Mohammed said, "You've spoken truly, dear one,
            O you who've left the world of nothingness."

Those who were present said, "O chief of men,   2380
    why did you say both opposites were true?"

"I am the mirror polished by His hand –
    in me all nations see reality."

O wife, if you think me so avaricious,
    then overcome this womanly concern!

What looks like avarice is really mercy;
    where is the avarice when there is grace?

Experiment a day or two with poverty;
    in poverty you'll see your riches double.

Be patient with it, give up your vexation;   2385
    in poverty there's majesty and greatness.

Do not be bitter, see a thousand souls
    sunk in tranquillity in honeyed seas!

A hundred thousand souls, like roses steeped
    in rose syrup, have staunched their bitterness.

And oh, I wish you had the depth of mind
    that I could tell you all about my heart!

These words are milk within the breast of soul
    that will not flow without the one who drinks.

As when a listener finds his thirst and craving,   2390
    then even half-dead preachers find their tongues.

And when the listener's fresh and vigorous,
    the silent, tongue-tied, find a hundred voices.

When strangers make to enter by my door,
    the women hide themselves behind the veil.

If relatives come in who pose no threat,
    the ones who are concealed lift up their veils.

And all that they make fair and fine and lovely
    is made so for the sight of him who sees.

2395   How could the sound of treble, bass and harp
    be for the ears of those who have no hearing?

God did not make musk's heavy scent in vain;
    He made it for the sense, not for the scentless.

For God has formed the heavens and the earth
    and in between set up great fire and light.

He made this earth for creatures made of earth,
    and heaven He made the home for heavenly beings.

The inferior man is enemy of the heights –
    a man is known by where he's to be found.

2400   You've never been inclined, O modest one,
    to decorate yourself for someone blind!

If I should fill the world with hidden pearls,
    since they're not to your taste, what should I do?

Be done with strife and anguish, O my wife,
    and if you'll not say so, then say good-bye!

What place is there for strife on rights and wrongs,
    when this my heart is even scared by soothing.

You will be quiet or, if not, I'll go
    this very minute from my house and home!'

The Wife Acknowledges Her Husband and Begs Forgiveness for What She Had Said

Now when the wife saw him so bold and tough,   2405
   she wept – indeed tears are a woman's snare.

She said, 'How could I have imagined this?
   I must have had the wrong idea of you!'

The wife came to the path of self-negation
   and said, 'I am your dust and not your lady.

My soul and body, all of me, are yours;
   commands and orders all belong to you.

And if my heart was tired of being poor,
   it was on your behalf, and not on mine.

In suffering you have been my remedy.   2410
   I would not wish you to be destitute.

Upon my soul this was not done for me;
   these cries and wails of mine were all for you.

By God, my every breath desires that I
   should die right here before you for your sake.

I wish your soul, on which my spirit dotes,
   were conscious of my soul's profoundest thoughts.

And since you've held me in such low esteem,
   I am disgusted by my soul and body.

I have contempt for gold and silver, now   2415
   you treat me so, O solace of my soul.

O you who live within my heart and soul,
   will you abandon me for such a thing?

Abandon me – you have the power to do so.
   O how my soul protests against your leaving!

Remember that there was a time when I
   was your fair idol, you my worshipper.

This slave inflamed her heart devoted to you:
   though you would say it's cooked, she'd say it's
      burnt.

2420   In everything you cook I am your spinach:
   you may cook me in sweet or sour dishes.

I did blaspheme; I've come back to the faith.
   With all my soul I've come to your dominion.

I did not know your kingly disposition;
   Presumptuously I drove the ass before you.

Now I have made a lamp of your forgiveness.
   I do repent and cast away reproach.

Before you I lay down my sword and shroud;
   I hold my neck before you – strike me down!

2425   You talk about a bitter separation –
   do what you will, but this you must not do.

Your inner conscience pleads forgiveness for me,
   constant defence against you in my absence.

My intercessor's in your inner nature,
   committed, though my heart committed sin.

Show unselfconscious mercy, angry one,
　　whose nature's sweeter than a ton of honey.'

She spoke with grace agreeably like this,
　　and as she did a weeping overwhelmed her.

As tears and sobs became unbearable,   2430
　　from her who'd ravished hearts without a tear,

A lightning flash appeared from that deluge,
　　a spark struck at her lonely husband's heart.

The woman whose fair face enslaved the man,
　　what happens when she starts to act the slave?

And whose magnificence will quake your heart –
　　how will you be when she breaks down before
　　　you?

When hearts and souls are bleeding for her glances,
　　how will it be when she's the one in need?

Her cruel tyranny has us entrapped –   2435
　　how will we plead when she gets up to plead?

'To men alluring' as God fashioned things,
　　how can they flee what God has made for them?

He made her that 'he might take comfort in her',
　　so how can Adam now be cleaved from Eve?

A Rostam son of Zāl, greater than Hamze,
　　he's still a captive in his wife's command.

And he whose words enraptured all the world
　　would yet cry out, 'Please speak to me, Homayrā!'

2440   The water vanquishes the fire by shock,
           but fire will make it boil up in the pot.

       And when a cauldron comes between the two,
           it makes the water vanish in thin air.

       Outside, like water, you may quench your wife;
           inside, controlled, you long for her – like fire.

       Such are the qualities of humankind;
           the beasts lack love, they are the lower species.

Explanation of the Tradition, 'Indeed Women Dominate the Wise Man, but the Ignorant Man Dominates Them'

       The Prophet said that women dominate
           completely wise and well-intentioned men,

2445   While fools are overweening with their wives,
           as they will treat them fiercely and perversely.

       There's little gentle, kind or warm in them,
           because the beastly in them rules their nature.

       For love and gentleness are human traits,
           and lust and anger marks of beastliness.

       She is a ray of God, not just the loved one.
           You might say she's creative, not created.

How the Man Surrendered Himself to What
His Wife Requested – that He Seek a Livelihood –
and How He Understood Her Criticism of
Him as a Sign from God:
It is within the Mind of All Who Know
That in amidst the Turning There's the Turner

The husband felt remorse for what he'd said,
    just like the oppressor at the hour of death.

'How could I end up hostile to my darling?   2450
    How could I land a kick upon her head?'

When fate ordains, the vision is obscured
    so that the mind cannot tell head from foot.

When fate has passed, you eat yourself alive;
    the veil is torn, your garment ripped apart.

The man declared, 'O wife, I am remorseful.
    If I was faithless, now I turn to faith.

Show mercy to the one who sins against you;
    once and for all don't tear me from my root!

If the old infidel becomes remorseful,   2455
    he will become a Muslim when he's sorry.

For God is full of mercy, full of bounty,
    and being and non-being are His lovers.

Belief and unbelief adore His greatness –
    the copper and the silver serve the elixir.'

Explaining That Both Moses and Pharaoh Are
Subject to the Will of God like Poison and
Antidote, and Darkness and Light, and
Pharaoh's Silent Prayer in Solitude That He
Should Not Ruin His Reputation

Both Moses and the Pharaoh serve the spirit:
    it seems that one is guided, one is wayward.

By daylight Moses cried aloud to God;
    at midnight Pharaoh also took to weeping.

2460   'O God, what chain is this around my neck?
    Were there no chain, who would say, "I am I"?

Just as You have illuminated Moses,
    You have made me the one who brings disturbance.

As You endowed the moon's face unto Moses,
    so did You then eclipse my own soul's moon.

My star was nothing better than a moon;
    eclipse occurred, so what resort had I?

And though they beat the drums for me as king,
    they beat the pans beneath the moon's eclipse.

2465   They strike those pots and make a pandemonium,
    and with those blows of theirs they shame the
        moon.

Woe comes to me, the Pharaoh, from my people:
    they beat *"Exalted Lord!"* out on a pan.

We are the household servants of the master;
    your axe is cleaving through your forest boughs,

It plants the one bough firmer in the ground;
　　it leaves another bough annihilated.

The bough has no resistance to the axe;
　　no bough could leap back from the axe's force.

Then by the power invested in Your axe,   2470
　　please make this twistedness be straight again.'

Again the Pharaoh said, 'How wonderful!
　　Do I not spend all night in "*O my Lord*"!

In private I am meek and moderate.
　　When I encounter Moses, then what happens?

The coats of gilt are overlaid ten times;
　　why does its face turn black before the fire?

Are not my heart and body in his power
　　to make me now a kernel, now a husk?

When he says, "Be a field," I'm turning green,   2475
　　and when He says, "Be hideous," I turn yellow.

He makes me moon one moment, next I'm black:
　　what else indeed could be the work of God?'

As from the bats of the creative word,
　　we're driven into matter and to spirit.

For colour-free is prisoner of colour:
　　a Moses is in conflict with a Moses.

When you become quite free of your own colour,
　　then Moses and the Pharaoh are at peace.

If you should have a question on this point,   2480
　　could colour be devoid of disputation?

The wonder is that hues come from the hue-less.
How did the hue arise against the hue-less?

The source of oil is much increased by water,
so how has it become its opposite?

Since oil has been concocted out of water,
how is it water is oil's opposite?

The rose is of the thorn, the thorn of roses:
why are they at each other's throats in mischief?

2485   Or may this not be war but higher wisdom,
and be pretence like donkey traders' quarrels?

Or it is neither this nor that – confusion!
The treasure must be sought – this is the ruin.

That which you speculate to be the treasure
is treasure that you lose in speculation.

Be sure, your dreams and fancies are like buildings,
and treasure's never found in built-up places.

In buildings there are strife and goings-on;
non-being is disdainful of such life.

2490   It's not that being took against non-being,
but that non-being did despise that being.

Don't say I am escaping from non-being,
but it escapes from you – and now desist!

In outward form it calls you to itself
when really it expels you with a cudgel.

The shoes are on the wrong feet, my good man.
Take note that Pharaoh's horrors were from Moses.

The Reason the Wicked Are Disappointed in Both Worlds, according to the Text 'He Loses this World and the World to Come'

The charlatan philosopher's convinced
  the sky's an egg and earth is like a yolk.

The doubter asked him, 'How does this world stay   2495
  within the ocean of the firmament?

Suspended in mid-air just like a lamp,
  it does not rise and neither does it drop.'

That sage declared, 'The attraction of the sky
  supports it in the air from six directions,

As when an iron idol is suspended
  beneath an archway of magnetic stone.'

The other said, 'How could serenest heaven
  draw down upon itself the darkest earth?

No, it repels it from the six directions,   2500
  and so it stays between the stormy blasts.'

So, through rejection by perfected hearts,
  the souls of Pharaohs languished in perdition;

Rejected by both this world and the next,
  these wayward ones have neither this nor that.

Though you might spurn the servants of the Lord,
  be sure that they despise your very being.

They have the amber, and when it's revealed,
  they drive the stuff of your existence wild.

2505   And when they hide the amber in themselves,
          they make your self-surrender mutinous.

        This is the stage of animality,
          imprisoned and in awe of humankind.

        The human stage is in the saints' control:
          we are in awe of them like animals, you know.

        Quite rightly did Mohammed call the world
          'my servant'. Read the passage 'Say, my
            servants . . .'

        Your mind's a camel driver – you're the camel;
          in its tight grip it drives you everywhere.

2510   The saints are those who are the Mind of mind,
          and minds are just like camels in the end.

        So look upon them with all due respect:
          one guide there is, a hundred thousand souls.

        What is the guide? What is the camel driver?
          Now get yourself an eye to see the sun!

        A world has been abandoned, nailed to night;
          it waits, devoted to the sun and day.

        Here is a sun concealed within a speck,
          a rampant lion hidden in a sheepskin.

2515   Here is a sea concealed beneath some straw –
          don't step upon this straw in hesitation.

        The inner kind of doubt and hesitation
          is God's compassion for the sake of guidance.

Each prophet came alone into the world;
    alone he was, his guidance hid within him.

He brought the universe under his spell;
    he squeezed himself into a tiny figure.

The foolish thought him all alone and weak.
    How could the king's companion be alone?

The foolish said, 'He's no more than a man.'   2520
    O woe to those who care not for the future!

*How the Eyes of the Senses Saw Sāleh and His
She-camel as Contemptible and Defenceless.
When God Wishes to Destroy an Army, He
Makes the Enemy Appear as Contemptible and
Paltry, even though that Enemy Might Be Superior:
'And He Made You Appear as of Little Account
in Their Eyes so That God Might Accomplish a
Thing to Be Done'*

As Sāleh's camel looked just like a camel,
    that bitter people hamstrung her, not knowing.

For water's sake they had become her foes;
    ungrateful, they were blind to bread and water.

God's female camel drank from streams and clouds;
    they staunchly held God's water back from God.

And Sāleh's camel, just like righteous bodies,
    became an ambush to destroy the unrighteous.

See what that people suffered from that order   2525
    of death and pain, '*Let God's she-camel drink!*'

The worker of God's vengeance sought from them
   the blood-price for the camel, a whole town.

The spirit's like Sāleh, flesh is the camel –
   the spirit is in union, flesh in trouble.

The righteous Sāleh's spirit has no hardship;
   the blow falls on the camel, not the essence.

The righteous Sāleh's spirit feels no hurt;
   the light of God is not in awe of heathens.

2530   In secret God is joined to him in body,
   so when he's harmed by them and suffers trials,

They're unaware that harming him harms God –
   the water of this jar flows in the river.

Divinity engaged itself with flesh
   that He would then become the whole world's
     refuge.

Be servant to the saintly form, the camel,
   that you may be the righteous spirit's servant.

'Since you have shown such envy,' Sāleh said,
   'in three days' time revenge will come from God.

2535   In three more days there will appear three signs
   that bring misfortune from the Alluring One.

The face of every one of you will change
   to various different colours to behold.

The first day you will have a face like saffron,
   red like the Judas tree upon the second.

The third day all your faces will turn black,
  and after that will come the wrath of God.

If you require a sign of what I threaten,
  the camel's foal has run towards the mountains.

If you can catch him, there's a fighting chance;   2540
  if not, the bird of hope has flown the snare.'

No one could catch up with that camel foal –
  it went into the hills and disappeared

Just as the pure in spirit flee, ashamed
  of flesh, towards the Lord of Bounty.

He said, 'You've seen that fate has been declared
  and it has cut the throat of hope's illusion.

What is the camel's foal – it is the heart
  that you bring back with virtue and affection.

If his heart should return, you're saved from
      that,
                                                        2545
  or else no hope, and you may gnash your teeth!'

When they heard tell of that impending threat,
  they lowered their eyes and stood in wait for it.

The first day they beheld their faces yellow;
  they breathed a chilling sigh of hopelessness.

The second day their faces all turned red;
  the chance for hope and penitence was lost.

And on the third their faces all turned black,
  and Sāleh's words came true without contention.

2550   As all hung down their heads in hopelessness,
            they sat with legs drawn up like sitting birds!

        In holy scripture Gabriel has brought
            the story of this kneeling, '*fallen prostrate*'.

        Kneel down that instant when they're teaching you
            and putting you in fear of such a kneeling.

        They'd been awaiting vengeance's attack –
            when vengeance came it vaporized the town.

        From his retreat Sāleh came to the town;
            he saw the town engulfed in smoke and fire.

2555   He heard the grieving coming from their limbs;
            laments were heard, the source of them was
                hidden.

        He heard the grieving coming from their bones;
            the tears cascaded from their souls like hail.

        Sāleh heard this and was about to weep,
            his grieving welling up for those who grieved.

        He said, 'You people who have lived in vain
            and you for whom I've wept before the Lord!

        God said, "Be patient with their tyranny
            and counsel them – they have not much time left."

2560   I told them, "Counsel's stopped by cruelty.
            The milk of counsel flows from love and peace.

        How many a cruelty did you do to me!
            The milk of counsel's curdled in my veins."

God told me, "I bestow on you a favour,
    I lay a dressing on those injuries."

And God has made my heart as pure as heaven,
    and He has swept your violence from my heart.

I went back one more time to give advice;
    I spoke in words and parables like sugar.

I caused fresh milk to be produced from sugar;   2565
    I mingled milk and honey with my words.

In you those words became a kind of poison,
    for you were poison in your very heart.

How should I suffer now that suffering's over?
    You were my suffering, O stubborn people!

Does anyone lament the end of suffering?
    A head wound heals, then do you tear your hair?'

He pondered to himself and said, 'O sad one!
    That people are not worthy of your sadness.'

True reader of the clear text, don't misread,   2570
    'How should I mourn an unbelieving people?'

He found tears welling in his eyes and heart –
    once more, spontaneous mercy shone in him.

It rained in droplets and he was amazed –
    spontaneous droplets from the sea of grace.

His mind would ask, 'Where do these tears come
    from?
    Should tears be shed for scornful men like these?

Why do you weep, tell me? For what they've done?
   For all the hostile mass of wicked men?

2575   Or for their rust-encrusted, blackened hearts?
         Or for the poisoned tongues they have, like snakes?

Or for their dog-breath and their dog-like teeth?
   Or scorpion nests which are their eyes and mouths?

For all their strife and violence and scorn,
   be grateful that the Lord has shut them up.

They have distorted hands and feet and eyes;
   their love and peace and anger are distorted.

To copy intellectual posturing,
   they set their foot against the ancient wisdom.

2580   They sought no guide and all became old asses
         from fawning on each other's eyes and ears.

God brought His servants out of Paradise
   to show them those who are brought up in hell.'

On the Meaning of the Verse: 'He Let Forth the Two Seas That Meet Together, between Them Is a Bar They Do Not Breach'

Although the damned and blessed are neighbours here,
   between them is 'a bar they do not breach'.

He mixed the people of the fire and light,
   and raised the mount of Qāf between them both.

As earth and gold are mixed up in a mine,
   a hundred plains and camel-trains divide them.

Like pearls and beads of jet upon a necklace,   2585
   they're mixed together – guests who stay one
      night.

And half the sea is sweet as sugar is,
   sweet-tasting with a colour bright as moonlight.

The other half is bitter as a snakebite,
   with acid taste and colour black as pitch.

They clash from underneath and from above
   like waves upon the surface of the sea.

This clash takes form within the narrow body,
   the mingling of the souls in war and peace.

The waves of peace are being dashed together,   2590
   and hate is being unleashed from human breasts.

And in a different form the waves of war
   are overturning many ways of love.

Love draws the bitter ones towards the sweet,
   for rightful guidance is the root of loving.

Their fury takes the sweet to bitterness:
   how can the bitter ones deserve the sweet?

With these eyes, sweet and bitter can't be seen,
   but through the next world's window they appear.

The eye that is far-sighted sees the truth;   2595
   the worldly eye is flattering and mistaken.

Oh, many the one who seems as sweet as sugar,
   but poison is concealed within the sugar.

The more discerning know it by its smell,
    the others when it reaches lips and teeth.

The lips reject it then before the throat,
    though Satan roars at you to '*eat it up*'.

To others it's revealed inside the throat;
    for others it comes out inside the body.

2600   It causes others burning in excreting;
    its taste gives them a searing liver pain.

It comes to others after days and months,
    to others after death out of the grave.

And if they give him respite in the grave,
    it comes for sure on Resurrection Day.

For every sweet and sugary thing on earth
    has its appointed day in time's great cycle.

Long years are needed in the sun until
    the ruby gains its lustre, hue and shine.

2605   While vegetables are full-grown in two months,
    a red rose takes a year to come to bloom.

For this Almighty God the Glorious stated
    the term of all things in the sura 'Cattle'.

You've heard this – may you hear with every hair –
    the living water you have drunk: good health!

And call it living water, not mere words!
    In ancient scripture's body see new spirit.

Now listen to another point, my friend,
    which like the soul is simple and yet subtle.

There is a place where even this snake poison   2610
    becomes digestible by God's decree.

It is a poison here, but there a cure;
    in one place unbelief, elsewhere it's lawful.

Although down there it's harmful to the soul,
    when it comes here it is a remedy.

The juice is bitter in young grapes, and yet
    when they become mature it's good and sweet.

In wine-jars it is bitter and forbidden –
    as vinegar how fine a condiment!

On the Meaning of the Unsuitability of the Disciple Presuming to Do and Actually Doing the Same Things That the Saint Does, for Sweets Do Not Harm the Physician but Harm the Sick, and Frost and Snow Do Not Harm the Ripe Grape but Harm Immature Grapes, for He Is on the Way 'That God May Forgive You Your Past and Future Sins'

If saints drink poison, it's an antidote;   2615
    if pupils drink, the mind is darkened by it.

From Solomon came the saying 'Lord, give me . . .
    do not bestow such power except on me.'

'On no one else confer this grace and favour' –
    this does resemble envy – but was not.

Read with your soul the phrase 'may not belong to';
    don't think that 'after me' conceals his greed.

But no, in power he saw a hundred dangers.
    Each hair of worldly power is mortal fear.

2620   With mortal, inward and religious fear,
       for us there are no trials such as these.

       So you will need resolve like Solomon's
       to escape the hundred thousand scents and colours.

       And even with the strength of will he had,
       the waves of that dominion smothered him.

       And when the dust of his remorse was settled,
       he pitied every monarch of this world.

       He pleaded, saying, 'Bestow this sovereignty
       with that perfection which You gave to me.

2625   Whoever is bestowed and graced with this
       is Solomon, and I myself am he!

       He is not after me, but he is with me.
       What is this "*with* me"? I have no opponent!'

       I should explain this, but I now return
       to tell the story of the man and wife.

The Outcome of the Quarrel of the Arab and His Wife

       A man of candid heart would hope to find
       some ending to the quarrel of the couple.

       The quarrel of the man and wife is told
       as an example of your self and mind.

2630   This man and wife, who are the self and reason,
       are much required for good and evil's sake,

And these two, needed in this earthly palace,
  are day and night engaged in war and strife.

The woman always wants domestic things:
  her honour, bread and meat, and social standing.

The self, just like the wife in seeking gain,
  seeks now to be like dust, and now the boss.

Your reason's unaware of all these thoughts,
  with only godly passion on its mind.

Although this story's mystery is a snare,   2635
  hear now the outward story to its end.

If spiritual explanation were enough,
  creation of the world were all in vain.

If love were merely thought and merely meaning,
  your prayer and fasting would not have a form.

The gifts of sweethearts to each other sent
  are nothing else but tokens of their love,

So that a proof is given by the gifts
  of passions hid away in secret places,

Because the outward acts of goodness tell   2640
  of secret passions, O most worthy friend.

Your evidence is true and false at times;
  sometimes you're drunk on wine, sometimes on
      whey.

The one who's drunk on whey displays his stupor;
  he makes a show of revelry and rapture.

The hypocrite is at his prayer and fasting
    to make it seem that he is drunk on God.

The outcome is that outer deeds may differ
    in that they are a sign of what is hidden.

2645   O Lord, give us discernment through Your Will,
    that we may know the true sign from the crooked!

And do you know how sense becomes discerning?
    Because that sense *is seeing by God's light*.

If there is no effect, the cause appears
    like kinship, which announces love.

And he whose leader is the light of God
    will not be slave to causes or effects.

Or else love casts a flame into your depths;
    it waxes great and frees you from effects.

2650   He has no need for tokens of affection,
    since love has set His light upon the sky.

There are fine points to end this conversation,
    but you must seek, and I bid you farewell.

Although the meaning's clear within this form,
    the form is far from meaning yet nearby.

In what they *stand for* they're like tree and sap,
    but as for *what* they are, they're far apart.

Quit talking quiddity and quality,
    and tell of how the moon-faced ones turned out.

The Arab Sets His Heart upon His Own Darling's Entreaties and Swears, 'In My Submission I've No Trick or Test (up My Sleeve)'

The husband said, 'I'm done with opposition!   2655
  You are in charge; unsheathe your sword on me!

Whatever you command I shall obey;
  I care not for its good or bad result.

I will become non-being in your being,
  for I'm your lover, "*love makes blind and deaf.*"'

The woman said, 'You're either being good to me
  or out to get my secret by a trick.'

He said, 'By God who knows the hidden secret,
  He Who made noble Adam out of clay,

In this three-cubit body which He gave him   2660
  all destinies and spirits were displayed.

All that would ever come to pass He taught him
  before all else, by His "*taught him the names*".

The angels were most shocked by his instruction;
  they saw a different holiness in him.

The revelation Adam showed to them
  had never been revealed within their heavens.

Compared to the expanse of that pure soul,
  the seven heavens' space becomes contracted.

The Prophet said that God has so proclaimed,   2665
  "I am contained in neither high nor low,

Nor yet am I contained in earth, nor throne,
   nor firmament, know this for sure, dear one!

I am contained in the believer's heart!
   What wonder! If you seek me, search those hearts."

"Come in among My servants, you shall meet
   My vision's paradise, O pious one."

The throne of God, with its far-ranging light,
   when it set eyes on him, became upset.

2670   The greatness of the throne is truly vast,
   but what is form when spirit has arrived?

Each angel said to him, "Until this moment,
   we had a friendship here upon the earth.

Upon the earth we sowed the seed of service;
   we were amazed at that relationship.

Just what was our relationship to clay,
   when our true nature was celestial?

What was the affinity we had, as lights,
   with darkness? How can light abide with
      darkness?

2675   The affinity was in your fragrance, Adam,
   because the earth was all your body's fabric.

From here they fabricate your form of clay;
   from there they take your light of purity.

The light our souls have garnered from your spirit
   was shining from the earth in former times.

We were on earth, oblivious of the earth,
  oblivious of the treasure buried there.

When He told us to go from that abode,
  the change left us with acid in our throats.

So that we were caught up in disputation,   2680
  'O God, who will be coming to replace us?

Will you sell off this glorifying light
  of praise all for the sake of disputation?'

God's law has rolled the carpet out for us:
  'Speak out and in an open-hearted way,

And fearless say what rises to your tongue,
  like darling only-children with their father.

No matter if these words are not quite proper,
  My mercy overcomes my wrathfulness.

To show you how it overcomes, My angel,   2685
  I put in you an awkward, doubting streak.

So will you speak, and I shall not take umbrage –
  whoso denies My patience will not speak.

A hundred patient fathers, patient mothers,
  are born and die each moment in My patience,

Their patience froth upon My Sea of Patience.
  Froth comes and goes, but yet the sea remains."

What shall I say? Before that pearl this shell
  is no more than the froth of froth of froth.

And by the froth and by the sea that's pure,   2690
  I swear this speech is not a test or trick.

It is from love, respect and purity,
   I swear by Him to Whom I am returning.

If this desire appears to you a test,
   then will you test the test for just an instant?

That mine shall be revealed, don't hide your secret;
   whatever I can do, command me do it.

Don't hide your heart, so mine shall be revealed,
   and I may then receive all that I can.

2695   What shall I do, what recourse do I have?
   Just see what trouble has beset my soul.'

The Wife Sets out for Her Husband the Way to Make a Living, and He Accepts It

'A sun has shone upon us,' said the wife –
   'A world has been illuminated by it!

The regent of the Merciful, God's caliph,
   can turn the city of Baghdad to springtime.

If you sit with that King, you'll be a king!
   How long will you chase after hopeless cases?

To sit with kings is like some alchemy –
   what's alchemy compared to seeing them?

2700   The Prophet's eye was cast on Abu Bakr –
   by this true act he came to be the true one.'

The husband said, 'How might I meet the king?
   How can I go to him without good reason?

I need some introduction, or a trick.
    No piece of work is done without some tool.

Just as Majnun, whose fame you well must know,
    when some slight illness came upon his Layli,

Said, "Oh! How can I go with no excuse?
    And if I stay while she is ill, what then?

I wish I were proficient as a doctor;   2705
    I'd be the first to sit at Layli's bedside!"

God said to us, "*Say, Come!*" That is a sign
    for us that we might overcome our shame.

If bats had vision and they had the means,
    they'd fly around by day quite happily.'

The wife said, 'When the noble king steps out,
    the stuff of useless things will have its use.

Because the means is being and pretension,
    reality is humble, without means.'

He said, 'How can I prosper without means   2710
    unless I demonstrate I have no means?

Then I shall need a proof of my poor state
    so that the king takes pity on a fellow.

Come up with something modest and discreet
    so that the handsome king will show compassion.

Behaviour based on tricks and flashy talk
    will count for nothing with the Almighty Judge.

The truth's required as witness to your state
    so that your light may shine without your words.'

The Bedouin Takes as a Present to the Commander
of the Faithful in Baghdad a Jug of Rainwater
from the Middle of the Desert, Thinking
That There Is a Shortage of Water There

2715   The wife said, 'Truth is when with all your being
            you sacrifice what you have struggled for.

        We have rainwater in a water-pitcher;
            it's your possession, capital and wealth.

        Take up this water-pitcher now and go;
            make it a present for the King of kings.

        Tell him we have no other worldly goods.
            There is no better water in the desert.

        His treasury may be full of precious gems,
            but he'll have nothing like this precious water.

2720   What is that pitcher? Our beleaguered body!
            In it the brackish water of our senses.

        O Lord, accept this jar and jug from us,
            accept it by the grace of "God has purchased . . ."

        It is a jug with five outlets of senses,
            so keep this water free from all pollution.

        Let my jug have an outlet to the sea
            and then acquire the nature of the sea.

        So when you take the present to the king,
            he'll see that it is pure and will accept it.

2725   And after that its water will be endless.
            My jug will satisfy a hundred worlds.

Stop up its outlets, fill it from the source –
God said, "*Cast down your eyes from worldliness.*"'

His beard puffed up: 'Who has a gift like this?
It truly does befit a king like him!'

The woman did not know that on the way
there is the river Tigris sweet as sugar,

And flowing through the city like a sea
all chock-a-block with boats and fishing nets.

Go to the Sovereign, see his situation,   2730
and see the sense '*beneath which rivers flow*'.

Such senses and such vision as our own
are but a single drop in that pure ocean.

The Bedouin's Wife Sews a Pitcher of Rainwater into Felt and Seals It Because of the Strong Convictions of the Bedouin

The husband said, 'Oh yes, seal up the pitcher!
Be careful! It's a gift to bring us riches!

Sew up this pitcher in a felted cover
so that the king will breakfast on the gift.

In all the lands there is no liquid like this;
it is the finest wine and purest nectar.'

Such men who say such things are always sick.   2735
Half-blind, they drink on bitter, brackish waters.

The bird whose home is on the salty sea,
how can she know the place of limpid water?

O you whose home is in the brackish spring,
    what do you know of Oxus and Euphrates?

And you who have not fled this half-way hostel,
    what do you know of ecstasy and passion?

And should you know, it's all inherited –
    to you these names are like the alphabet.

2740   The alphabet and lettering are so clear
    to children, yet their meaning is remote.

The Bedouin then took up his water-pitcher;
    he held it day and night upon his journey.

He trembled for his jug and fate's ill treatment,
    yet took it from the desert to the city.

The wife unrolled the prayer-mat for petition;
    she made 'God save!' her litany for prayer.

She said, 'Protect our water from the villains.
    O Lord, propel that pearl towards the sea.

2745   Although my husband is astute and skilful,
    the pearl has many thousand enemies.

What pearl? It is the stream of Paradise.
    One drop of this is what has formed the pearl.'

Both through the wife's complaints and lamentations,
    and through the husband's toil and steadfastness,

He took it to the caliph's court at once,
    untouched by robbers and unharmed by stones.

He saw a court abundant with largesse
    and needy folk with all their nets spread out.

Each moment, everywhere, the folk in need   2750
   got charity and raiment from that place.

For Magian or for Muslim, fair or ugly,
   it was like rain and sun – no – Paradise!

Some people were dressed up for him to view;
   the rest of them were standing to attention.

The high and low, from Solomon to ant,
   revived just like the world at the last trump.

The worshippers of form were wound in pearls;
   truth-seekers found the ocean of the Real.

Those lacking aspiration were inspired,   2755
   and those aspiring found their heart's desire.

*Explaining How, Just as the Beggar Is in Love with
Generosity and with the Generous Person, so the
Generosity of the Generous Person Is in Love with
the Beggar. If the Beggar Has Great Self-restraint, the
Generous Person Will Come to Him, but while
Self-restraint in the Beggar Is a Virtue, Self-restraint
in the Generous Is a Fault*

A voice was calling him: 'O seeker, come!'
   For giving needs the poor as they need giving.

The giver seeks the beggar and the weak
   just as the beautiful seek shining mirrors.

The mirror beautifies the handsome face;
   the beggar brings to light the face of virtue.

As God said in the sura of 'The Forenoon',
   'Mohammed, do not drive away the beggar.'

2760   And if the beggar is your charity's mirror,
            beware, as breath destroys the mirror's face.

        One kind of charity brings beggars forth;
            the other kind bestows excess on them.

        So mendicants reflect God's bounteousness,
            and those with God are consummate in bounty.

        Apart from these two, all are dead indeed –
            a picture on a veil, not of His court.

The Difference between One Who Is Destitute in God and Is Thirsty for God and One Who Is Destitute of God and Is Thirsty for Something Else

        A dervish picture, not a real live man!
            You won't be throwing bread at some dog's
                picture.

2765   He has a piece of bread, not peace of God.
            Don't offer dishes to a dead man's picture.

        That mendicant of bread is but a land-fish,
            a fish in form but timid of the sea.

        He is a poultry fowl, no heavenly Simorgh;
            he feeds on crumbs, he is not fed by God.

        He is God's lover for the sake of favours;
            his soul is not in love with good and virtue.

        If he should fantasize he loves the Essence –
            to think of names and aspects is not Essence!

Imagining is created and is born.   2770
   God never came to birth – *'was not begotten'*.

How can he be a lover of the Gracious
   and be in love with his imagined fancies?

If he who loves imagined things is truthful,
   his metaphor will lead him to the truth.

A discourse is required to explain these words,
   but I am shy of worn-out understandings,

As worn-out and short-sighted understandings
   bring to their thoughts a hundred evil phantoms.

Not everyone can hear with perfect hearing;   2775
   the fig is not the food for every fledgling,

Especially not a dead and rotting bird
   whose eyes have disappeared, deluded, blind.

What's land or sea to a painting of a fish?
   To a Hindu's colour, what is soap or vitriol?

If you should draw a sad design on paper,
   it feels no sense of sadness or delight.

Its form is sad, yet it is free of this;
   its form may laugh and yet it leaves no trace.

These joys and sorrows written in the heart   2780
   are images before those joys and sorrows.

The picture's smiling form is for your sake;
   that form articulates the meaning truly.

The images that are inside the steam-baths,
   outside the changing rooms resemble clothes.

So long as you are outside, you see clothes;
   take off your clothes, come in, my dear companion.

For there is no way in with clothes. The body
   obscures the soul as clothes obscure the body.

The Guardsmen and Gatekeepers of the Caliph Come Forward to Attend to the Bedouin and Receive His Gift

2785   Just as the Bedouin of the distant desert
     came to the entrance of the caliph's palace,

The palace guardsmen came to him and showered
   his bosom with the rose-water of favour.

They understood his needs without his saying;
   their role was to anticipate requests.

They asked him, 'Arab prince, where are you from?
   How are you after travelling and toiling?'

He said, 'I'm noble if you treat me so,
   and ruined when you turn your back on me.

2790   O you whose faces have the signs of greatness,
     whose glory is more fair than Ja'far's gold,

O you whose glance is worth so many glances,
   for whom gold coins are scattered on your way,

Who all acquired your vision by God's light
   and came forth from the king for charity,

That you may work your glance's alchemy
   upon the copper coin of human selves.

I am a stranger, I am from the desert.
    I've come in hope of favour from the Sultan.

The fragrance of his grace possessed the deserts;   2795
    the grains of sand themselves acquired souls.

I made my way here for the sake of money.
    When I arrived, I swooned at what I saw.

A person ran for bread towards the baker;
    he lost his soul on seeing the baker's beauty.

He went for recreation to a rose-garden;
    his recreation was the gardener's beauty.

Just like the Bedouin drawing well-water,
    in Joseph's face he tasted living water.

When Moses went in order to get fire,   2800
    he saw a fire that rescued him from fire.

And Jesus leapt to escape his enemies,
    which took him to the fourth estate of heaven.

Forbidden fruit became a trap for Adam,
    and then his being made mankind his fruit.

The falcon lands upon the trap for food;
    it finds the king's forearm, fortune and glory.

The child goes to the school to further knowledge
    in hope of father's present of a bird.

At school that pupil rises to the top   2805
    and, having paid her fees, becomes a star.

Abbās went off to war for vengeance's sake
    to quell Mohammed and oppose the Faith.

His and his children's caliphate became
the Faith's defence until the Resurrection.

I came to court in search of gaining something.
I gained the place of honour when I entered.

I brought a gift of water to gain bread;
the smell of bread took me to Paradise.

2810   By bread was Adam driven out of Eden;
bread has reconstituted me in Eden.

Like angels I am freed from bread and water;
like heaven I circle round this court desireless.'

In this world, nothing turns without desire
except the souls and bodies of His lovers.

*Explaining That Lovers of This World Are like
Lovers of a Wall on Which the Rays of the Sun
Fall, and Who Make No Effort or Attempt to
Understand That That Ray and Brightness
Are Not from the Wall but from the Disc
of the Sun in the Fourth Heaven. As a
Result He Sets His Whole Heart on
the Wall, and When the Rays of the Sun
Return to the Sun He Is Desolate Forever:
'They Shall Be Barred from Their Desires'*

The lovers of the whole and part are different:
he who desires the part neglects the whole.

When parts love other parts, then very soon
one part's beloved goes to its own whole.

2815   He was the laughing stock of others' slaves;
he drowned while clinging to a feeble man.

He has no right to be considering him.
Shall he work for his Master or for him?

The Arabic Proverb: 'If You Commit Fornication,
Commit It with a Free Woman, and If
You Steal, Steal a Pearl'

The saying '*fornicate with a free woman*'
was shifted to the saying '*steal a pearl*.'

The slave went to his master, he to grief:
the rose's scent for roses, thorns for him.

And he remained cut off from what he craved,
attempts aborted, useless toil, lame-footed.

He's like a hunter who is catching shadows.   2820
How can a shadow turn into his fortune?

A man holds tight the shadow of a bird;
bewildered is the bird upon the branch,

'I wonder who this bird-brain's laughing at!
How stupid! What a rotten pile of causes!'

If you insist the part and whole are one,
then eat the thorn – the thorn and rose are joined.

In one sense are the part and whole apart,
or else the prophets' missions were for nothing.

The prophets came to bring unification;   2825
how could they join something already joined?

These words go on forever, my dear fellow.
The day is late, so finish off the story.

The Bedouin Presents His Gift, Namely the
Water-pitcher, to the Servants of the Caliph

He now produced the pitcher full of water –
    he sowed the seed of service at that court.

He said, 'Convey this present to the sultan;
    redeem the king's petitioner from need.

Sweet water and a pitcher green and new
    from rainwater collected in the ditch.'

2830   The officers began to smile at that,
    but they received it like a gift of life.

Since all his courtiers had instilled in them
    the manners of that fine, sagacious king.

The ways of kings are placed within their subjects,
    as verdant heaven makes earth like verdant heaven.

The king's a reservoir, his servants pipes
    from which the water's running into pitchers.

When all the water's from a source that's pure,
    each pipe delivers sweet, delicious water.

2835   If water in the source is salt and foul,
    then every pipe will spout the same foul stuff.

Because each pipe's connected to the source,
    immerse yourself in what these words might mean.

The royal grace that is the stateless soul,
    see how it has affected all the body!

And reason's grace, good-natured and well-born,
    see how it civilizes all the body.

How passionate love, without repose and restless,
    brings all the body to a state of madness.

When ocean water is as soft as Kawsar's,   2840
    then all its pebbles are of pearls and jewels.

Each skill for which the teacher is renowned
    is then endowed within the pupils' souls.

Theology is read with theologians
    by students who are keen and talented.

Law students studying with their law professors
    read jurisprudence, not theology.

As for a master who professes grammar,
    his pupils' souls become grammarians.

The teacher who's absorbed upon the Path   2845
    absorbs his pupils' souls into the King.

Of all the kinds of knowledge, when death comes
    the one to have with you is poverty.

The Story of What Happened between the Grammatist and the Boatman

A grammatist once got into a boat.
    That self-regarding man looked at the boatman

And said, 'Do you know grammar?' 'No,' he said.
    'And half your life has gone!' he chided him.

The boatman's heart was broken by the pain,
   but for the moment made his answer silence.

2850   The wind then blew the boat into a whirlpool.
   The boatman hollered to the grammatist,

'Do you know how to swim at all, please tell me?'
   He said, 'I don't, you shrewd and handsome man!'

'Then *all* your life has gone, dear grammatist,'
   he said. 'Our boat is sinking in these whirlpools.'

Absorption's needed here, not grammar, see!
   If you're absorbed, jump in. There is no danger.

The ocean wave will raise the dead aloft.
   How can the living man escape the sea?

2855   And if you've died to human qualities,
   the sea of secrets sets you at its summit.

And you who've called the people asinine,
   now you're the one who's like an ass on ice.

World's greatest scholar of your time you may be,
   but note this world is passing – watch the time!

Now we stitched up the grammatist in order
   to tell you of the grammar of absorption.

The heart of all the learned sciences,
   my learned friend, you'll learn in self-effacement.

2860   That pitcher is our learned sciences,
   that caliph is the Tigris of God's knowledge.

Full jars we're carrying to the river Tigris
   and we're an ass, though we don't know it yet.

At least the Bedouin man could be excused –
    from distant parts, he didn't know the Tigris.

If he, like us, had known about the Tigris,
    would he have lugged his jar from place to place?

No, surely, if he'd known about the Tigris,
    he would have smashed his jar upon a rock.

The Caliph Accepts the Gift and Generously Rewards Him in Spite of the Fact That He Had Absolutely No Need of the Gift and the Pitcher

The caliph saw and heard about his plight,   2865
    and filled the jar with gold to overflowing.

He freed the Bedouin from poverty;
    he gave him gifts and special robes of honour.

That sovereign, world of generosity
    and sea of justice, ordered his official,

'Fill up this jar with gold and give it him.
    When he goes home, convey him on the Tigris.

He came across the desert and on foot;
    it will be quicker sailing up the river.'

When he sat in the boat and saw the Tigris,   2870
    he made himself prostrate with blushing shame:

'That gracious king's benevolence is a marvel!
    And more's the marvel that he took my water!

How could that sea of grace receive from me
    so readily such worthless coin as that?'

The whole world is a pitcher such as this,
   my son, brimful with knowledge and with beauty.

It is a droplet of His beauty's Tigris,
   so full it can't be kept under the surface.

2875   What was 'a hidden treasure' burst in fullness
   and made the earth more brilliant than the heavens.

What was 'a hidden treasure' effervesced
   and dressed the earth a sultan swathed in satin.

If he had seen a trickle of God's Tigris,
   he would have totally destroyed that jar.

Those who have seen it always lose themselves;
   the selfless smash a stone against the jar.

And you whose stone has smashed your jar in envy,
   your own disintegration's made you whole.

2880   The jar is smashed, the water does not spill;
   it's made a hundred times more whole by
      smashing.

Each piece is dancing and in ecstasy,
   though this appears absurd to finite minds.

There is no jug nor water in this state –
   see clearly '*And God knows what's for the best.*'

Knock at the spirit's door and it will open.
   Beat contemplation's wings; fly like the falcon.

For you the wings of thought are clogged and heavy
   because you're eating of the earth like bread.

Since bread and meat are earth, eat less of them   2885
    that you do not remain earthbound like them.

When hunger gets you, you become a dog;
    you're vicious, uncontrollable, ill bred.

And when you're full it's almost like you're dead,
    oblivious as a wall, and useless too.

One moment you're a dog, the next a corpse.
    How will you keep up on the lions' way?

Be sure, the dog's your only means of hunting;
    don't throw the dog a bone if you can help it.

For when it's full and is cantankerous,   2890
    how will it hunt and chase successfully?

The lack of livelihood propelled that Bedouin
    towards that court, and riches came his way.

Our tale has spoken of the king's good deeds
    towards that destitute and helpless man.

The scent of love leaps from the lover's mouth,
    whatever he might say, into love's quarter.

If he talks jurisprudence, it becomes
    the scent of poverty in his sweet phrasing.

If he speaks unbelief, it has faith's scent;   2895
    his talk of doubt gives off the scent of
        knowledge.

The leaping foam has risen from truth's sea;
    the part's made tranquil at the purest source.

That foam is pure and proper, you must know,
   like accusations from your lover's lips.

Uncalled-for accusations became sweet
   all on account of her beloved cheek.

If he should lie he makes the truth appear,
   O falsehood which can beautify the truth.

2900   If you make sugar in the shape of bread,
   it smacks of candy to the taste, not bread.

And if a Muslim finds a golden idol,
   will he just leave it for idolators?

No, he would seize it and set fire to it,
   and he would smash its counterfeit appearance.

So that the idol's form would not remain in gold,
   for form's a hindrance and a highwayman.

Its golden essence is the gift of lordship;
   the graven image on the gold is fake.

2905   Don't burn a whole kelim to kill a flea,
   and do not spend your day on fly-sized headaches.

Idolatry is when you're stuck in forms.
   Pass through appearance; see reality.

If you're a pilgrim, seek out one who's been there,
   be he a Turk or Indian or Arab.

Do not be put off by his form or colour;
   consider his resolve and his intention.

If he is black and shares your inclination,
   then call him white for he is the same colour.

This story has been told all upside-down, 2910
 like lovers' thoughts – it has no head nor foot.

It has no head; it pre-existed all.
 It has no foot; its home is in the eternal.

No, rather it's like water, every droplet
 is both the head and foot, and yet is neither.

But, God forbid, this is no simple story.
 It is the cash between my state and yours.

The Sufi is advancing and retreating;
 he's not concerned with what has come to pass.

We are the jar, the king and Bedouin, 2915
 we are '*at variance and perverted from it*'.

To reason, 'man' and 'wife' are self and greed,
 twin dark deniers of the light of reason.

Hear how the root of their denial grew;
 it was because the whole has many parts.

The whole's parts are not parts within the whole,
 not like the scent that features in the rose.

The flower's beauty shares the rose's beauty;
 the turtle-dove's song shares the nightingale's.

If I am busy with such points and answers, 2920
 how can I give out water to the thirsty?

If you're confused and dazzled by all this,
 be patient, '*Patience is the key to joy.*'

Protect yourself, protect yourself from thoughts.
 Thought is the lion and deer, and hearts are bushes.

Protection is far better than the cure,
for scratching only makes the itching worse.

Protection is the principle of health,
so practise it and see your soul grow strong.

2925   And you receive these words with open ears,
and I shall make a golden earring for you.

You'll be the ring in the great goldsmith's ear;
you'll rise up to the moon and Pleiades.

First hear that all the various creations
are different in their souls as 'A' from 'Z'.

Confusion reigns among the different letters,
though also they're a set from start to finish.

Diverse yet one, depending on your viewpoint,
in both a serious and light-hearted sense.

2930   The Last Day is the day of the great Reckoning.
He who is fair and glorious seeks the Reckoning.

For one like the dishonest Hindu trader,
the Reckoning is the time of his disgrace.

With nothing of the sun about his face
he wants the night alone to be his veil.

His thorns have not a single rose's petal;
his springtime foe exposes all his secrets.

For one who's head to foot in rose and lily,
the spring is like the gaze of two bright eyes.

2935   The soulless thorn is longing for the autumn
to vie with it in striking the rose-garden,

To hide the garden's bloom and thorny shame
   that you'll not see her colour and its rust.

Then autumn is its springtime and its life,
   when rock and purest ruby look the same.

The gardener knows them, even in the autumn,
   – divine eyesight is better than the world's.

That One is all the world, the other's evil.
   Each star in heaven's a portion of the moon.

So all the forms and images are saying,   2940
   'Good news, good news, that spring is coming –
      see!'

So long as blossoms shine like coats of mail,
   how can the fruits reveal their buds and berries?

As blossoms fall and fruits begin to grow,
   so when the body breaks, the soul arises.

Fruits are the meaning, blossoms are their form:
   the blossoms are the news, the fruits their
      substance.

When blossoms fell, the fruits came into sight:
   as one came down, the other was increasing.

How can unbroken bread give nourishment?   2945
   How can untrodden grapes turn into wine?

Till myrobalan's mixed into the drugs,
   how can the drugs have their remedial power?

On the Qualities of the Pir and
Submission to Him

O Light of Truth, Hosāmoddin, take up
an extra page or two about the *pir*.

For though your fragile body has no strength,
without your sun we have no light at all.

And though you have become the *lamp* and *glass*,
you are my heart's commander and my clue.

2950   For since the clue is in your power and will,
the pearls upon the heart's string are your gift.

Write all about the *pir* who knows the way.
You choose the *pir*, you choose the way itself.

The *pir* is summer, fall his followers;
the followers are night, the *pir*'s the moon.

I gave my favoured youth the name of *pir*,
because he's old in truth, not old in seasons.

He is so old that he has no beginning.
There is no rival to a pearl so rare.

2955   Indeed with age, old wine becomes more potent,
especially the wine that is *of God*.

Go choose a *pir*; without a *pir* this journey
is full of dangers, full of fear and dread.

That road which you have travelled many times
confounds you when you are without your guide.

So never go alone upon a road
    you do not know; do not desert your guide.

If you don't stay within his shadow, fool,
    the ghoulish howl will drive you to distraction.

The ghoul casts you to ruin from the road   2960
    – and many a shrewder sort than you was here!

In scripture hear about the travellers' straying,
    what evil-minded Eblis did to them.

He stole them for a hundred thousand years
    from truth, corrupted them and stripped them
        naked.

You see their skeletons, you see their hair.
    Be warned, don't drive your ass in their direction.

Cling to your ass's neck and steer it onward
    to those who know and keep well to the Way.

Don't let the ass escape; hold on to it.   2965
    Beware, it has a passion for green pastures.

But let it go one moment carelessly,
    it will be off for miles in search of grass.

Opponent of the Way, the ass is grass-mad.
    How many riders has it brought to grief!

If you don't know the Way, do the reverse
    of everything the ass wants – that's the right way.

'*Consult them,*' then '*perform the contrary,*'
    for he who does not disobey them fails.

2970   Do not be friends with lust and appetites;
        '*they will divert you from the Way of God.*'

        To break this lust, there's nothing in the world
        to match the help of comrades on the way.

The Prophet (Peace Be Upon Him) Commanded Ali (May God Bestow Grace Upon His Person), Saying, 'When Everyone Seeks to Draw Close to God through Some Kind of Devotion, You Should Seek to Be Near to Him by Means of Associating with His Wise and Special Servant So That You May Be the First to Approach Him'

        The Prophet said to Ali, 'O Ali,
        you are the lion of God, my stalwart champion.

        But do not put your trust in lion-nature.
        Come over to the palm-tree shade of hope,

        And come into the shadow of that Wise One
        Whom no remover pushes from the Way.

2975   His shadow on the earth is like Mount Qāf;
        His spirit is the highest-circling Simorgh.

        Were I to sing His praises till the Last Day,
        do not expect there'd be a pause or ceasing.

        The sun has veiled his face in human nature.
        Please understand "*And God knows what is best.*"

        Among all the devotions of the Way,
        O Ali, choose the man of God's protection.'

        As everyone sought refuge in devotions,
        contrived a place of safety for themselves,

Go on, seek refuge in the Wise One's shadow;   2980
   escape that hidden enemy of strife.

Of all devotions this is best for you.
   You'll be ahead of all who are ahead.

And once the *pir* has claimed you, just
     surrender!
   Behave like Moses under Khezr's rule.

Be patient in all Khezr's guileless deeds,
   that Khezr will not say '*This is the parting.*'

If he should sink the boat, don't breathe a word;
   if he should kill the child, don't tear your hair.

God has declared his hand is His own hand,   2985
   as He has said, '*God's hand is above their hands.*'

God's hand will make him die and make him live,
   and what is life? He makes his soul immortal.

If, rarely, someone goes this Way alone,
   he will arrive thanks to the *pir*'s attention.

The *pir*'s hands do not fail the absent ones;
   his hand's none other than the power of God.

They give such honour to the absent ones –
   those who attend fare better than the absent.

Such food they keep for those who do not come!   2990
   Imagine what delights they give the guest!

And how is he who serves in the king's presence
   compared with him who stands outside the door?

When you have made your choice of *pir*, be bold.
  Do not be liquid-soft like clay and water.

If you're resentful of each blow you get –
  how can your mirror shine without a buffing?

The Tattooing of the Form of a Lion on the Shoulders of a Man of Qazvin, and His Regretting It Because of the Pricking of the Needle

Now listen to this story from its author
  about the ways and manners of Qazvinis.

2995 They prick themselves with tips of bluish needles;
  their bodies, hands and shoulders feel no pain.

A Qazvini went to a tattoo parlour:
  'I'd like a tattoo and I want a beauty!'

'What pattern shall I do, sir, for the tattoo?'
  He said, 'Tattoo me with a rampant lion.

My sun's in Leo – tattoo me a lion –
  and try and tattoo in a lot of blue!'

'Where would you like to have it on your body?'
  He said, 'Prick out the figure on my shoulder!'

3000 When he began to stick the needle in,
  the pain began to set into his shoulder.

Our hero then began to howl, 'For God's sake!
  You're killing me! What shape are you tattooing?'

He said, 'Well, you told me to do the lion.'
  'Which limb have you begun with?' he replied.

He said, 'I've started with the lion's tail.'
    The man replied, 'Leave out the tail, my friend!'

The lion's tail and rump have got my breath;
    I have a nasty rump upon my throat!

O lionizer, leave the lion tail-less;   3005
    my heart is fainting from the needle's pricks.'

The man began to prick the other side;
    he showed no mercy, favour or respect.

He screamed, 'Which of his members is this now?'
    'Well, my good man,' he said, 'this is the ear.'

'Good doctor, then he'll have no ears,' he said.
    'Leave out the ears and do the best you can.'

He started pricking on the other side,
    and once again the Qazvini was whining.

'This is the third place – what limb is it now?'   3010
    He said, 'The lion's belly, Excellency.'

He said, 'The lion shall not have a belly!
    The pain's increased; don't needle me so much!'

The barber was annoyed and quite bewildered.
    He stood there for a while and bit his fingers.

The barber threw his needles down in anger,
    and said, 'In all the world, whoever saw

A lion without a tail or head or belly?
    God never made a lion such as this!'

You must endure the lance's pain, my brother,   3015
    to lance the poison of your pagan self.

The sky and sun and moon all venerate
  that band of men who've gone beyond existence.

The sun and cloud obey the man in whom
  the pagan self has been allowed to perish.

And since his heart knows how to light the candle,
  the sun is now unable to consume him.

God said about the sun that is inclining,
  '*inclining from their cave towards the right*'.

3020 The thorn becomes all beauty like the rose
  before the partial going to perfection.

What is to honour and extol the Lord?
  To know yourself as nothing more than dust.

And what is it to know God's unity?
  It is to burn our self before His Oneness.

If you want incandescence like the day,
  then scorch the sombre darkness of your selfhood.

Like alchemy dissolve your self as copper
  into the Being of Him Who nurtures being.

3025 Both hands are holding tight to 'I' and 'we'.
  This misery is from duality.

THE WOLF AND THE FOX ATTEND
THE LION ON A HUNT

The lion and the wolf and fox had gone
    into the mountains on a hunting trip,

That with each other's help they would be able
    to put the chains of bondage on their victims.

The band of three would roam those boundless
       forests
    and seize great quantities of slaughtered prey.

Although the rampant lion was ashamed
    of them, he was polite and sociable.

For such a king the rank and file are trouble,   3030
    but he joined in, '*community's a mercy*.'

For such a moon the stars are a disgrace;
    he is among the stars just out of kindness.

The order '*Counsel them*' came to the Prophet
    although no counsel can compare with his.

Though gold and barley share the weighing scales,
    it's not because they're of the same material.

The spirit travels with the body now;
    the dog is briefly guardian of the palace.

And so this couple set off for the mountains   3035
    in the most glorious lion's cavalcade.

And things were going well for them, they bagged
  a mountain ox, a goat and a fat hare.

Whoever hangs around a raging lion
  will not go short of meat by day or night.

They brought them from the mountain to the forest,
  the dead and wounded trailing in their blood.

The wolf and fox were harbouring a hope
  that shares would be in line with royal justice.

3040 The hopes of both were picked up by the lion;
  the lion knew their hopes' entitlement.

Whoever is the lion and prince of secrets
  is well aware of all that thought conceives.

Beware, habitual thinkers, that you keep
  your hearts from evil thinking in his presence.

He knows, and drives his donkey quietly onward,
  and in concealment he will smile at you.

The lion, when he knew their expectations,
  said nothing and indulged them for the while.

3045 But to himself he said, 'I'll punish you
  as you deserve, you miserable beggars.

Was my decree not good enough for you?
  Is this your view of my benevolence?

O you whose minds and reasoning are from mine,
  from gifts of mine which beautify the world,

How can the painting estimate the painter
  when it was he who gave it worth and fame?

That you had such ignoble thoughts as these
  for me makes you the outrage of your time.

"And those who harbour evil thoughts of God",   3050
  it is a sin if I do not behead them.

I'll free the sphere of heaven from your shame,
  so that this tale stays current in the world.'

With this in mind the lion beamed his smile –
  do not be trustful of a lion's smiles!

The riches of this world are smiles of God:
  they make us drunk, deceived and down-at-heel.

For you, sir, pain and poverty are best
  for digging out the trap that comes with smiles.

The Lion Tests the Wolf and Says, 'Come Here, Wolf, and Divide Up the Prey between Us'

The lion said, 'Now, wolf, divide this up!   3055
  Devise a new fair deal for us, old wolf.

Be my replacement, doling out the shares,
  so I can see what substance you are made of.'

He said, 'Your Majesty, the ox is yours;
  it's big like you are big and broad and strong.

The goat's for me – the goat is medium-sized –
  and fox, you take the hare – no arguing!'

'Explain what you have said, wolf,' said the lion,
  'How you say "we" and "I" when I am present.

A dog indeed that wolf must be to see
 himself before a matchless lion like me!'

3060 He said, 'Come here, you self-regarding ass!'
 He came, and with his claws the lion tore him.

As he saw no good kernel nor good counsel,
 the lion flayed his head in punishment,

'Since sight of me did not destroy your self,
 a soul like yours must die in agony.

As you've not passed away while in my presence,
 I'm doing you a favour to behead you.'

3065 '*All things are perishing*' except His Face.
 If you're not in it, do not seek existence.

When someone is extinguished in Our Face,
 '*All things are perishing*' does not apply.

Because he's in '*except*' and beyond '*not*'.
 Whoever's in '*except*' is not extinguished.

At heaven's gate to call out 'I' and 'we'
 is to be barred and twisted into '*not*'.

*The Story of Someone Who Knocked at a
Friend's Door. From Inside Someone Said,
'Who Is It?' He Replied, 'It's Me!' The
Other Answered, 'Since You're You I'll
Not Let You in. I Don't Know Any
Friend That Is "Me"'*

A fellow came and knocked at a friend's door.
   His friend said, 'Who are you, trustworthy man?'

He said, 'It's me!' 'Be off!' said he. 'Not now.   3070
   At such a feast there's no room for the raw.'

What cooks the raw and frees him from deception
   except the fire of loss and severance?

The poor man went and travelled for a year,
   burnt by the sparks of absence from his friend.

The burnt one became cooked, and he returned
   and went around to his companion's house,

Knocked at the door, atremble with politeness,
   that no rude word might tumble from his lips.

His friend called out, 'Now who's *that* at the   3075
     door?'
   He answered, '*You* are at the door, heart-stealer!'

He said, 'Now since you're me, come in, O me;
   there's no room in the house for two of me.'

The needle does not take both ends of thread –
   when you are single, come into the needle.

The thread has the connection with the needle;
   '*the needle's eye*' will not accept the camel.

How should the camel's being be slimmed down
    except by means of discipline and practice?

3080   The hand of God is needed for that, reader,
    for all absurdities: '*Be and it was.*'

With *His* hand the impossible is done;
    in fear of Him the obstinate are quiet.

What of the blind, the leper and the dying?
    The Dear Lord's word will bring them back to life.

That nothingness, more lethal than the dead,
    cannot resist the hand of His creation.

Recite: '*Each day He is upon some labour.*'
    Do not think Him inactive and inert.

3085   The smallest act of His is that each day
    He sends three armies marching over here:

One army from the loins of men to mothers,
    so that the plant may grow within the womb;

One army from the wombs into the world,
    so that the world is filled with males and females;

One from earth towards the next existence,
    that all will see the beauty of good works.

These words go on forever. Quickly now,
    return to those pure-hearted bosom friends!

3090   His friend said, 'Enter, you who are all me,
    not enemies like rose and thorn and garden.'

The thread is single – do not be mistaken –
    if you see double in the letters 'BE'

The '*B*' and '*E*' are like a tempting noose
   to draw non-being into life's conditions.

The noose must thus be two-fold in its form,
   although the two are single in effect.

The biped and the quadruped may travel;
   the double-bladed scissors make one cut.

Look at that pair of fellows washing clothes –   3095
   they would appear to work against each other.

The one has thrown the clothes into the water;
   the other fellow's trying to get them dry.

The one will make the dry things wet again,
   as if to thwart his partner out of envy.

But these two opposites who seem in strife
   share one heart and one purpose in agreement.

Each prophet and divine friend has a path,
   but all the paths that lead to God are one.

Since sleep has swept off all my listeners,   3100
   just as the water swept away the millstones,

This flow of water is above the mill;
   its flowing through the mill is for your sake.

Since you had no more need of such a mill,
   He drove the stream back to its origin.

This speech comes to the mouth for education,
   for otherwise it has its separate stream.

It goes without a sound or repetition
   to rose-gardens '*beneath which are the rivers*'.

3105   O God, exhibit to the soul that place
            in which the wordless discourse flourishes,

        So that pure souls may fly headlong towards
            the far-flung space that is beyond existence.

        A very open and extensive space
            provides the source of fantasy and being.

        The fantasies are narrower than non-being,
            and so they are the cause of suffering.

        Much narrower than fantasy is being,
            so here the moon is like the moon that's set.

3110   This world of sense and colour's narrower still;
            it is more narrow than the narrowest gaol.

        The cause of narrowness is form and number;
            the senses are inclined towards formation.

        The world of oneness is beyond the senses.
            If you seek oneness, you must strive to go there.

        One action is the order 'Be'; the sounds
            took place in speech, and meaning was unsullied.

        These words go on forever. Let's go back
            to see what happened to the struggling wolf.

The Lion Teaches the Wolf a Lesson
for Being Disrespectful in
Dividing Up the Kill

The headstrong lion ripped the wolf's head off   3115
  to rid him of two-headedness and preference.

'Old wolf, it is "*So we took vengeance on them*,"
  because you were not dead before your prince!'

The lion turned his gaze upon the fox,
  then said, 'Divide this up to make a meal.'

He made a bow and said, 'This great, fat ox
  could be your breakfast, most exquisite king.

The goat, perhaps, at twelve o'clock, for luncheon,
  could be a dish for our victorious king.

The hare, O kind and gracious Majesty,   3120
  could be your supper later in the evening.'

He answered, 'Fox, you have made justice shine!
  Who taught you how to share things out like this?

Where did you learn this, O most noble sir?'
  He said, 'World-ruler, from the wolf's experience.'

He said, 'Since you are pledged to me in love,
  pick up all three, and take them and be gone.

You've turned completely into me, my fox.
  How could I harm you when you're me myself?

Both I and all the beasts of prey are yours.   3125
  Step up to highest heaven and ascend.

You've learnt a lesson from the wretched wolf –
    you are no longer fox, you are my lion.

How wise is he who learns something from friends'
    deaths in avoidable calamity!'

A hundred times the fox would thank his luck –
    the lion first called the wolf and *then* himself.

'If I had been the first to get the order
    "Divide this up," who could have saved my
       soul?'

3130   So thanks are due to Him that in this world
    He made us after men of former times,

So that we've heard about God's punishments
    in ages past upon our predecessors,

So, mindful of the state of wolves of yore,
    we'll watch ourselves more carefully like the fox.

For this God's Prophet, truthful in explaining,
    called us *'a people who've had mercy shown
       them'*.

See clearly now the bones and fur of wolves,
    and take your counsel from it, gentlemen!

3135   The sage gives up this vanity and being
    on hearing of the fates of Ād and Pharaoh.

If not, then others learn from his experience
    and learn a lesson from his misadventure.

Noah (Peace Be Upon Him) Threatens the
People, Saying, 'Do Not Struggle with Me,
for in Reality You Struggle with God,
Who Is within This, O Forsaken Men'

Said Noah, 'You proud men, I am not I!
   I've died to self and live in the Beloved.

Since I have died to human sense-perception,
   God has become my ears and eyes and senses.

As I am not myself, this breath is His.
   Whoever breathes before this breath blasphemes.'

Inside the fox's image is the lion;   3140
   you should not go too boldly to this fox.

If you do not accept his outward form,
   you will not hear the roaring lions in him.

If Noah did not have the hand of God,
   how did he turn a whole world upside-down?

A hundred thousand lions in one body,
   he was like fire and all the world a haystack.

And when the haystack did not pay its dues,
   he set the stack on fire with such a flame.

Whoever utters something disrespectful   3145
   while in the presence of this hidden lion,

The lion tears him as he tore the wolf
   and reads to him '*So we took vengeance on him.*'

Mauled as the wolf was by the lion's paws,
   a fool to act so bold around a lion!

I wish those wounds would fall upon the body
    so that the faith and heart could stay secure!

My strength is sapped now that we've come this far;
    how can I bring this mystery to light?

3150   Just like the fox, you must ignore your stomach.
    Don't play your foxy tricks when in His presence.

Surrender to Him all your 'I' and 'we'.
    The kingdom is His Kingdom. Give it to Him.

When on the Way of Truth you are the pauper,
    the lion and his prey will both be yours.

For He is holy, glorious is His name.
    He needs no things of beauty, skin or substance.

And every prize and every boon there is
    is for the sake of those who serve the King.

3155   The King has no desires. He made this state
    all for His creatures – happy he that knows this!

What use are states and kingdoms to the One
    Who fashioned both the state and two domains?

Keep watch over your heart before His glory,
    so that you are not shamed by evil thoughts.

For He sees plots and thoughts and scheming ploys
    as clearly as an eyelash in white milk.

The man whose breast is free of images
    is mirror to the unseen images.

He is assured and certain of our secrets,   3160
   for true believers mirror true believers.

If He should strike our coin against the touchstone,
   He can distinguish certainty from doubt.

His Soul's the very touchstone of all coinage,
   and He shall see true hearts and counterfeit.

How Kings Seat Enlightened Sufis before Their Faces So That Their Eyes May Be Illuminated by Them

Such is the age-old custom among kings
   – you will have heard of this if you recall –

That on the left-hand side the heroes stand,
   because the heart is fixed within the left side.

The chancellor and scribes are to the right,   3165
   for this hand does the writing and accounting,

And facing them they place the Sufi masters,
   for they're a mirror to the soul, and more:

Hearts' mirrors polished in divine reflection
   so that the heart reflects the virgin image.

The fair ones who are born of nature's loins
   must have a mirror placed in front of them.

The faces of the fair adore the mirror,
   which lights the soul with 'reverence of their hearts'.

HOW A CERTAIN GUEST CAME TO JOSEPH (PEACE BE UPON HIM) AND CLAIMED FROM HIM A GIFT AND A PRESENT

3170 From distant lands there came a dear friend who
became the guest of Joseph the sincere one.

From childhood they had been the best of friends,
reclining on the couch of intimacy.

He brought to mind the brothers' cruel envy.
He said, 'That was the chain, I was the lion.'

The lion is not made shameful by the chain,
so we do not lament God's destiny.

The lion had a chain upon his neck,
but he is lord of all the chain-makers.

3175 'How were you in the prison of the well?'
He answered, 'Like the moon when it is waning.'

The new moon may be crescent at this time –
won't she be full moon over heaven later?

Although they smash the seed-pearl in the mortar,
it turns into the heart's light and far-sight.

A grain of wheat was buried underground,
then from the ground the ears of wheat were raised,

And then again they ground it with the millstones.
Its value grew as soul-sustaining bread.

Again, the bread they ground between the teeth   3180
   became the wise man's mind and soul and reason.

Again, when that soul disappears in love,
   it's *'pleasing to the sowers'* after sowing.

These words go on forever; let's go back
   to see what that good man declared to Joseph.

When Joseph had regaled him with the story,
   he said, 'Sir, what gift have you brought for me?'

Arriving empty-handed at a friend's
   is just like coming grain-less to the millstone.

Almighty God asks creatures at the Judgement,   3185
   'Where is your present for the Resurrection?'

'Alone and you have come to Us' without
   provision, just as *'We did fashion you.'*

So what have you brought with you as a present?
   An offering for the Day of Resurrection?

Or did you have no hope of going back?
   And did the promise of this day seem empty?

Do you refuse His hospitality?
   Then get the dust and ashes from His kitchen.

And if you don't deny Him, how can you   3190
   set foot in that Friend's court with empty hands?

Show some restraint in sleeping and in eating,
   and for that meeting with Him bring a present.

You must be *'light on sleep'* like *'those who slumbered'*;
   at *'dawn'* be one of *'those who asked forgiveness'*,

And make a little movement like the foetus,
   that they give you the light-perceiving senses.

And then you will depart the womb-like world:
   from earth go to a wide and open space.

3195   The phrase that has declared, '*God's earth is vast*'
   means that expanse in which the prophets dwell.

The heart's not strained by that wide-open space,
   and there the body's palm-tree does not wither.

Just now it is a burden on your senses,
   and you are dull and weary and dejected.

In sleep, when you are borne aloft unburdened,
   exhaustion goes; you have no pain and grief.

Regard the sleeping state as just a taste
   of higher states the Friends of God enjoy.

3200   The Friends are like those of the Cave, O rebel,
   in standing and in turning in their sleep.

He draws them with no effort in their action
   '*towards the right and left*' without their knowing.

What is that *right side*? Action which is noble.
   What is *the left*? The workings of the body.

These two activities come from the prophets,
   but, like the echo, they're aware of neither.

If echoes bring you good and evil sounds,
   '*the mountain's heart is unaware of either.*'

The Guest of Joseph (Peace Be Upon Him)
Says, 'I Brought a Mirror for You So That
Every Time You Look into It to See Your
Own Lovely Face You Will Remember Me'

'Come on,' said Joseph. 'Get your present out!'   3205
   And he cried out in shame at being asked.

'So many gifts,' he said, 'I sought for you,
   but not a single gift could catch my eye.

Could I bring specks of gold-dust to the gold-mine?
   Could I bring droplets to the Arabian Sea?

I would be taking caraway to Kermān
   if I should bring my heart and soul to you.

There is no seed that is not in this grain store
   except your beauty beyond all compare.

I thought it suitable that I should bring you   3210
   a mirror like the light within the heart,

That in it you might see your lovely face,
   O you, the lamp of heaven, like the sun.

O brilliant one, I've brought a mirror for you
   so when you see your face you'll think of me.'

He drew it out from underneath his arm –
   the mirror is the business of the fair ones.

What is the glass of being? Non-existence.
   Bring non-existence if you are not stupid.

Existence can be shown in non-existence   3215
   as rich men shower kindness on the poor.

Bread's true reflection is the hungry man,
    and tinder is the mirror of the flint.

All nothingness and damage that arise
    are mirrors of the goodness of all arts.

If you have clothes which fit and are well sewn,
    when will they demonstrate the mender's skill?

Must not the trunks of trees be hacked to bits
    for carpenters to use their stems and boughs?

3220 The master bonesetter will pay his call
    where there is someone with a broken leg.

When there's no sickly patient, how then can
    the beauty of the healing arts be known?

And how can alchemy be seen if copper's
    low-grade, inferior nature is not known?

Deficiencies are mirrors of perfection;
    the vilest things are mirrors of His glory.

For opposites make known their opposites
    as honey's taste is known in vinegar.

3225 Whoever understands his own defects
    has galloped to perfection with ten horses.

And why he is not flying to his Lord
    is that he thinks himself already perfect.

There is no sickness of the soul that's worse
    than being convinced of your perfection, sir!

Much blood must flow out of your heart and eyes
    until this smugness takes its leave of you.

Eblis' mistake was saying '*I am better*' –
   all creatures have this sickness in their selves.

Though he may see himself as very broken,   3230
   beneath the stream see filth and purest water.

But when he makes you stirred up in temptation,
   just then the water turns a filthy colour.

The bottom of the stream is filthy, man! –
   although to you the stream appears pristine.

The *pir* who knows the path, who is all-wise,
   digs channels for the gardens of all selfhood.

Who can make pure the streams that are our selves?
   Our knowledge is dependent on God's knowledge.

How can the sword design itself a hilt?   3235
   Go now and take your wounds off to a surgeon.

Flies come and swarm all over any wound
   so no one sees the wound's disgusting state.

Those flies are thoughts and they belong to you;
   your wound is the dark state of your condition.

The *pir* applies a plaster to your wound;
   at once your pain and agony subside.

So you imagine you have got your health back,
   but it's the healing ray that shines upon you.

Hey, don't ignore the plaster, suffering sore-back!   3240
   It's from the ray, you know, not of your doing.

The Apostasy of the Scribe of Revelation on
Account of That Ray of Revelation Falling
on Him as He Read That Verse in the Presence
of the Prophet (Peace Be Upon Him), Then
Said, 'I Am the Abode of Revelation'

Before Osmān there was a certain scribe,
　　most diligent in copying revelation.

The Prophet would dictate from revelation,
　　and he would write it down upon the leaf.

The ray of revelation shone upon him,
　　and he discovered wisdom in himself.

The Prophet gave the essence of that wisdom,
　　and this much wisdom led that fool astray.

3245　Saying, 'All that the enlightened Prophet says,
　　its truth already lies within my heart,'

The ray of his conception struck the Prophet
　　and brought the wrath of God upon his soul.

He quit his scribal work and quit the faith,
　　turned hostile to the faith and to Mohammed.

Mohammed said, 'Rebellious man, how could you
　　become so black if light came out of you?

If you had been the spring of the divine,
　　you would not have released such bilge as this.'

3250　In case his reputation in the world
　　should be destroyed, this comment shut him up.

His insides were ablaze with this affair;
    he was unable to repent – surprise!

He sighed, but sighing was no help, until
    the sword came down and made off with his head.

God made esteem a hundredweight of iron;
    how many languish in that hidden chain!

The path is blocked by pride and unbelief
    so much that he cannot express a sigh.

He said, '*The chains . . . by which their heads*   3255
    are raised' –
those chains on us are not outside ourselves.

'*In front of them a barrier . . . we have covered . . .*'
    Behind, in front, the barrier is not seen.

The risen barrier has the hue of space –
    he does not know that it belongs to Fate.

Your lover masks the face of the Beloved;
    your master masks the voice of your true Master.

How many an infidel is mad for Islam!
    Their chains are fame and pride in this and that.

The chain is hidden but it's worse than iron;   3260
    the axe can cut to bits the chain of iron.

It's possible to take off iron chains,
    but no one has the axe for unseen chains.

If any man should suffer from a wasp sting,
    immediately his nature strains to stop it.

But when the sting is from your own existence,
    the stinging's fierce; the pain does not abate.

The telling of this leaps out of my breast.
    I fear that it will bring you to despair.

3265   Do not despair. Be happy in yourself,
    and call for help from Him who will respond.

Saying, 'You who love forgiveness, forgive us,
    O healer of the pain of this old gangrene.'

Reflected wisdom sent that wretch astray.
    Do not admire yourself; don't rake up dust.

My brother, wisdom's flowing over you;
    it's from the saints and it is lent to you.

Although the house has found its light within,
    it shines from its illuminating neighbour.

3270   Give thanks; do not be flattered or turn up
    your nose. And listen, do not be conceited!

It is a hundred pities that this loan
    has distanced faithful people from the Faith.

I am his servant who at every hostel
    does not claim he's enlightened at the table.

And many's the hostel must be left behind
    so that one day the man will reach his home.

Though iron glows red, it is not red itself –
    it is the borrowed ray from something burning.

3275   Although a window or a house is bright,
    you know the sun's its only luminescence.

Each door and wall announces, 'I am bright.
I have nobody else's ray, it's me.'

And then the Sun will say, 'Misguided one,
when I have set, then all will be revealed.'

The plants say, 'We are green all by ourselves.
We're happy, laughing and so fair of face.'

And summertime will say to them, 'My people,
observe yourselves when I have passed away.'

The body relishes its health and beauty;   3280
the spirit hides its glory, wings and plumage,

And asks, 'Who are you, pile of excrement?
You live a day or two thanks to my ray.

Your coquetry and boasts exceed this world.
Just wait until I leave you and take off.

The ones who've made you warm will make your
grave;
they'll make a meal of you for worms and ants.

The one who would have died for you one time
will hold her nose to keep your stench away.'

The spirit's powers are speech and sight and   3285
hearing;
the fire's power is in the boiling water.

Just as the power of soul comes to the body,
so does the power of saints come to my soul.

As my Beloved draws back from my soul,
my soul becomes just like a lifeless corpse.

And so I lay my head upon the earth
    to be my witness on the Day of Judgement.

This earth shall be the witness of our states
    on Judgement Day when 'shaken with a shaking'.

3290   And 'She shall tell her tidings' publicly –
    the earth and rocks will find the words to speak.

In thoughts and views philosophers deny –
    well, let them bang their heads against the wall.

The sounds of earth and clay, the sounds of water:
    the senses of the open-hearted hear them.

Philosophers deny the Moaning Pillar;
    they're strangers to the senses of the Friends.

They say the power of melancholia
    brings much illusion into human minds.

3295   But no, these sceptical illusions strike them,
    reflections of rebellious blasphemy.

Philosophers deny the devil exists
    while all the time they're in the devil's service.

You've never seen the devil? – See yourself!
    No blueness in the temples without madness.

He who is doubting, twisting in his heart,
    is secretly a sophist of this world.

Professing his convictions now and then,
    his thinker's vein will make his face go black.

3300   Beware believers, for you have that too;
    within you there is many an endless world.

In you are all three-score-and-twelve religions:
   make sure they never take control of you.

Whoever has the blessing of belief
   would tremble like a leaf in fear of this.

You scoffed at Eblis and the devils since
   you thought yourself to be a virtuous man.

And when the soul inverts its coat of skin,
   how many woes will come up from the faithful?

The shop has golden-coloured things all smiling   3305
   because the touchstone's not in evidence.

O Veiler, do not lift the curtain from us.
   Be our protector in the final test.

Fake gold rubs shoulders with real gold at night –
   until the daylight, gold will bide its time.

With golden tongue the gold says, 'Wait awhile,
   O flashy one, until the dawn is golden.'

A hundred thousand years the accursed Eblis
   was one of the élite and prince of Muslims.

He, wrestling out of self-conceit with Adam,   3310
   was cast away like night-soil in the morning.

The Prayer of Bal'am Son of Bā'ur – 'Make Moses and His People Return from the City They Have Besieged without Success' – and the Answering of His Prayer

The people of the world became the subject
    of Bal'am Bā'ur like Jesus in his day.

They would bow down to no one except him;
    he had a charm that made the sickly strong.

He wrestled, out of pride and pomp, with Moses;
    his state turned out to be as you have heard.

The world has had, concealed and seen like this,
    a hundred thousand Eblises and Bal'ams.

3315   The Lord has made them both notorious
            so that they are a moral for the rest.

He hanged these robbers high up on a gibbet,
    or many others would have faced His wrath.

He dragged them by the forelock to the city;
    the victims of His wrath are numberless.

You are belov'd, but stay within your limits
    for God; for God's sake do not stray beyond.

If you should strike one more belov'd than you,
    you'll be cast down the pit of deepest earth.

3320   What does the tale of Ād and Thamud mean?
            That you should know that prophets are beloved.

These signs of sinkings, stonings, thunderbolts
    explain the stature of the rational self.

Kill all the animals for mankind's sake,
    but kill all humankind for reason's sake.

What? – universal reasonable mind –
    the partial reason's reason, but it's feeble.

All animals untamed by humankind
    are placed below the rank of human species.

Their blood is fit for humankind to shed   3325
    because they lack the higher intellect.

The honour of wild animals diminished
    because they came to be our enemies.

What's happening to your honour, *homo sapiens*,
    since you've become like '*frightened asses fleeing*'?

The ass should not be killed, because he's useful.
    If he turns wild, his killing is permitted.

The ass has no sagacity to warn him,
    and yet the Loving God lets nothing pass.

Then how, my noble friend, can we be pardoned   3330
    when we are running wild against that breath?

And so it is that heathen blood is lawful,
    like beasts before the arrow and the lance.

Their wives and children all are sitting targets;
    they're stupid, abject and recalcitrant.

And reason which abandons Reason's reason
    is sent from reason into beastliness.

How Hārut and Mārut Trusted in Their
Own Protection and Desired the Leadership
of the People of the World and
Fell into Temptation

As Hārut and Mārut once famously
    fell to the poison arrow of their pride,

3335   They were relying on their holiness –
    what kind of buffalo would trust a lion?

Though it may lunge its horns a hundred times,
    the rampant lion tears it limb from limb.

Its horns may be as spiny as a hedgehog –
    the lion slays the hapless buffalo.

Although the Sarsar wind uproots the trees,
    it brings the benefit of verdant freshness.

Frail grass is pitied by that stormy wind.
    O heart, do not be boastful of your vigour.

3340   Why should the axe fear thickness in the bough?
    It cuts it through a little at a time.

It does not strike itself against a leaf;
    it only strikes its blade against an edge.

Does fire fret before the woodpile's height?
    What butcher runs away from flocks of sheep?

Before the spirit what is form? Not much –
    the spirit of the sky keeps it inverted.

Take, for comparison, the heavenly wheel.
    What makes it move? The guiding intellect.

The movement of this shield-like human body   3345
   is from the spirit that is veiled, my son.

The movement of this wind is from its spirit.
   It's like the wheel, the prisoner of the stream.

The ebb and flow, this in and out of breath,
   comes only from the soul filled with desires.

Sometimes it makes the 'j' or 'h' or 'd';
   sometimes it makes for peace, sometimes for struggle.

Now to the right, now to the left it goes,
   and now it makes the rosebed, now the thorns.

So in this way our God had made this wind   3350
   to be just like a dragon *versus* Ād.

Again that self-same wind for the believers
   He fashioned as respect and peace and refuge.

Religion's leader said, '*God is the Real*'
   the ocean of the real, '*Lord of the Worlds*'.

The strata of the heavens and the earth
   are debris on the surface of that ocean.

The swirling of the debris in the ocean
   comes from the water at the time of turmoil.

When He desires to quell them in their writhing,   3355
   He has the debris cast upon the shore.

He drags them from the shore into the waves;
   He treats them like the fire will treat the grass.

This story has no end – go back again,
   young man, to be with Hārut and Mārut.

The Rest of the Story of Hārut and Mārut
and Their Public Chastisement and Punishment
Down in This World in the Pit of Babylon

As soon as both of them had realized
    the sin and viciousness of worldly creatures,

In fury they began to gnaw their hands.
    They did not see their faults with their own eyes.

3360   The ugly see themselves caught in the mirror
    and turn their face away from it in anger.

The arrogant will see someone's offence
    and there appears in him a hellish fire.

He calls his arrogance religion's safeguard;
    he does not see the pagan self within him.

Religion's safeguard has another stamp,
    and from its fire there is a world of greenness.

God said to them, 'If you are shining beings,
    do not look so askance at heedless sinners.

3365   Be grateful, O my multitude of servants,
    that you've escaped from lust and genitalia.

If I put something on you of that nature,
    then Heaven will let you enter in no more.

The self-defence that you have in your bodies
    reflects My self-defence and preservation.

See how it comes from Me, not you. Beware
    the accursed devil does not win you over.'

Like him who wrote the Prophet's revelation,
  who saw true light and wisdom in himself,

And took himself – a whistle like an echo –   3370
  to be the very birdsong of God's birds.

If you become the mimic of their birdsong,
  how will you understand the birds' desires?

If you learn how the nightingale is singing,
  will you know what he feels towards the rose?

And if you know, it's all from supposition
  like deaf men reading movements of the lips.

A Deaf Man Visits His Poorly Neighbour

A well-to-do man told a certain deaf man,
  'Your next-door neighbour has become unwell.'

The deaf man said, 'But I am hard of hearing.   3375
  What can I grasp of what that young man says,

Especially if he's sick and softly spoken?
  But I must go; there's no escaping it.

When I can see his lips begin to move,
  I'll have a guess myself at what he says.

When I inquire, "Poor soul, how are you feeling?"
  He'll answer, "Very well" or "I am fine."

And I shall say, "Thank God! What are you taking?"
  And he will say, "Some medicine or broth."

And I shall say, "Good health to you – who is   3380
  the doctor treating you?" He'll name someone.

Then I shall say, "He has got magic hands.
    If he's around, you will be better soon.

We have experienced his healing hands –
    wherever he has been it's a success."'

That good man made these theoretical
    replies and visited the sickly man.

'How's things?' He said, 'I'm dying.' 'Oh, thank God,'
    which made the patient outraged and nonplussed.

3385   'What thanks is this? Perhaps he is my foe!'
    The deaf man made a guess and got it wrong.

He said, 'What have you taken?' 'Poison,' he said.
    'Good health!' he said. The sick man's fury grew.

And after that he questioned him: 'Which doctor
    is coming to take care of your condition?'

– 'The angel Ezrā'il is coming. Go!'
    – 'Then may his healing touch be very blessed!'

The deaf man left. Most cheerfully he said,
    'Thank goodness I have made this timely visit.'

3390   The sick man said, 'He is my mortal foe.
    I did not know his malice ran so deep.'

The sick man's mind was seething with abuse
    to get his message out in any way.

When someone's eaten meat that has gone off,
    it churns his stomach till he throws it up.

'To curb your anger' means do not throw up,
    and in return sweet words will fill your mouth.

But since he had no patience, he was rattled:
    'Where is that pup, that prostituting pimp,

That I may pour on him all that he said when   3395
    the lion of my consciousness was sleeping?

If visiting is meant to soothe the heart,
    this was no visit but an act of hatred

To see his enemy reduced to this,
    so that his hateful heart would be consoled.'

How many lose themselves in their devotions
    who set their hearts on paradise and blessings!

In truth their sinfulness is hidden,
    and what you think is very pure is murky,

Like that deaf fellow who imagined that   3400
    he'd done some good when it was the reverse.

He sat down happy: 'I have done my service;
    I have performed my duty to my neighbour.'

He has ignited for himself a fire
    within the sick man's heart and scorched himself.

Beware then of the fire you have ignited;
    in truth you have increased your sinfulness.

The Prophet said this to a boastful man:
    'Perform the prayer, sir, you have not begun.'

In order to protect us from these fears,   3405
    'Guide us' occurs in every act of prayer,

Which is 'Do not, O God, mix up our prayer
    with prayers of those who stray, the boastful ones.'

The deaf man, by the guesses he had made,
    wrote off ten years of friendship by his action.

Sir, sensual guessing is especially low
    for revelation, which exceeds all bounds.

If your perception follows just the letter,
    you'll know your subtle ear is surely deaf.

The First Person to Introduce Analysis of the Quran Was Eblis

3410   The person who was first to bring conjecture
    upon the radiance of God was Eblis.

He said, 'No doubt the fire's superior
    to earth. I am of fire. He is dark earth.

So let's compare the branches with the root:
    his is from darkness, ours from shining radiance.'

God said, 'But no! There shall be "*no relations*".
    Fear and renouncing are the door to virtue.'

It's not what comes down from the mortal world
    to be had by relation; it is spirit.

3415   No, these are things which are bequeathed by
        prophets.
    The heirs of these are spirits of the God-fearing.

And, famously, Bu Jahl's son was pious
    while Noah's son was one of those who strayed.

'The child of earth was lit up like the moon.
    You are the child of fire. Be off, O blackface!'

The wise use such conjectures and surmises
　　on cloudy days and nights to find the qibla.

But when the sun and Ka'bah both appear,
　　do not look for conjectures and surmises!

Don't turn your face; do not ignore the Ka'bah　　3420
　　in your surmise, for God knows what is best.

As when you hear the singing of God's bird,
　　you hold its form in mind just like a lesson.

From it you then make some analogies;
　　you make something essential from pure fancy.

The holy ones can grasp the subtleties
　　that verbal formulations do not reach.

You've only learnt the speech of birds by rote;
　　you've set on fire a hundred lusts and guesses.

Their hearts are pierced by you, just like the sick　　3425
　　　　man's;
　　the deaf man's drunk on thought of his
　　　　achievement.

The scribe of revelation heard that birdsong
　　and thought he was the equal of that bird.

It flapped a wing at him and blinded him,
　　and plunged him to the depths of death and pain.

Mind you don't also fall from heaven's realms,
　　beguiled by echoings and by reflections.

Though you be Hārut and Mārut and more
　　than all those on the terrace of 'we're ranged,'

3430   Have mercy on wrong-doers for their wrongs,
           and curse them for their selfishness and pride.

       Beware lest envy take you by surprise;
           you'd fall headfirst into the earth's abyss.

       Both said, 'You are the one who orders, Lord.
           Where is our safety without your protection?'

       They said this and their hearts were palpitating:
           'How could wrong come from us, the best of
               servants?'

       The irritation did not leave these angels
           until the seed of self-conceit was sown.

3435   And then they said, 'O elemental creatures,
           oblivious of the purity of spirits,

       We draw the veils around this wheeling sky;
           we'll come to earth and set up royal court.

       We'll mete out justice and we'll offer worship,
           and every night we'll fly back up to heaven.

       And we shall be the marvel of the age,
           and bring peace and protection to the world.'

       Their likening of the states of heaven and earth
           does not ring true. There is a hidden difference.

To Explain That You Should Keep Your Inner State and Your Intoxication Hidden from the Ignorant

Now hear the words of Hakim Sanā'i: 3440
   'Lay down your head where you were drinking
     wine.'

The drunkard who has wandered from the tavern
   becomes the butt of jokes and children's plaything.

He lurches in the mud upon the road,
   and every idiot is laughing at him.

The children trailing him like this don't know
   his ecstasy or how his wine might taste.

Except those drunk on God, all men are children:
   no one's adult till he's escaped desire.

It's said, 'This world's a play and a diversion,   3445
   and you are children,' and God speaks the truth.

You are a child if you've not left off playing –
   without soul-slaying, how can you be sharp?

And see, this lust which men indulge in here,
   young man, is like the sexual play of children.

Then what is children's sexual play? – A game,
   compared to Rostam's or a hero's union.

The wars of man resemble children's fights,
   all meaningless and empty and in vain.

And all their wars are fought with wooden swords,   3450
   and all their ventures founder on the futile.

They are the cavalry on hobby-horse:
  'Hey, look at us on Doldol and Borāq!'

They are the mounts, these ignorant upstarts,
  who think they're mounted riders on a road.

Wait till the day when those whom God lifts up
  will gallop to the ninth degree of heaven.

The spirit will ascend to him with angels,
  and heaven shall tremble at the spirit's flight.

3455   You are all riders of the hem like children –
  you've seized the corner of a hem to ride on.

From God came forth *'surmise does not avail . . .'*
  When did surmise's steed attain to heaven?

You may prefer the best of two opinions;
  don't doubt you see the sun when it is shining.

And at that time you'll see that your own mounts
  are mounts that you have made of your own feet.

Your thoughts and fancy, feelings and perception
  are like the hobby-horse of children's play.

3460   The sciences of spiritual men support them;
  the sciences of worldly men oppress them.

When knowledge strikes the heart, it is a friend;
  when knowledge strikes the body, it's a burden.

God said, *'It's like the ass that carries books.'*
  The knowledge that is not of God is leaden.

The knowledge that is not direct from Him
  does not remain; it's like a woman's make-up.

But when you bear this burden with good grace,
   they will unburden you and give you joy.

Don't bear that weight of knowledge from
      ambition;   3465
   make sure you see the fruits of inner knowledge,

And ride upon the vehicle of wisdom,
   and then the burden tumbles from your shoulders.

Without His cup will you be free from cravings,
   O you who are content with just His name?

What comes of qualities and names? Illusion.
   Yet that illusion signifies the union.

Have you seen signs without a signifier?
   When there's no road, there is no ghost to haunt it.

And have you seen a name without its essence?   3470
   From 'r', 'o', 's', 'e' have you picked a rose?

You've named it, now go find the thing you've
      named!
   The moon is in the sky, not in the river.

If you would pass beyond the name and letter,
   then cleanse yourself of self, once and for all.

Be rust-free like the sheen of polished iron;
   be rust-free in your practice, like a mirror,

And cleanse yourself of qualities of self
   so that you see your pure and holy essence.

You'll see within your heart the prophets' science   3475
   without a book or tutor or a master.

The Prophet said, 'There are those of my people
   who share a nature and intent with me:

Their souls can see me by the very light
   by which I also look into their souls,

Without the tomes, traditions and their scholars
   but where the living water is imbibed.'

Recall the mystery of 'a Kurd by night',
   And then recite 'an Arab by the morning'.

3480   If you should like a dose of hidden knowledge
      then tell the tale of Greek and Chinese painters.

THE STORY OF A DISPUTE BETWEEN THE GREEKS AND CHINESE ON THE ART OF PAINTING AND DRAWING

The Chinese said, 'We are the better painters.'
   The Greeks replied, 'Ours is the power and glory.'

The sultan said, 'I wish to test you on this,
   to see who of you lives up to your claim.'

And when the Chinese and the Greeks were ready,
   the Greeks were more experienced in the skill.

The Chinese said, 'Will you consign to us
   a whole apartment, also one for you?'

There were two such adjacent sets of rooms,   3485
   and one the Chinese had, the Greeks the other.

The Chinese begged the king for a hundred colours;
   that dear man opened up his vaults to them.

Each morning from his treasury the colours
   were paid out to the Chinese as a gift.

The Greeks said, 'In our work no paint materials
   are suitable, except to clean the rust.'

They closed the doors and took to burnishing,
   and they became as pure and clear as sky.

There is a path from many hues to none: 3490
   a hue is like a cloud, a moon is hueless.

And all the light and shining in the cloud
    is from the stars and moon and sun, you know.

Now when the Chinese had performed their task,
    they took to beating drums in celebration.

The king came in and there he saw the paintings;
    they robbed him of his mind and understanding.

And after that he went to see the Greeks;
    they drew the curtain back between the rooms.

3495   The image of those pictures and those works
    was mirrored on those walls with clarity.

And all he'd seen in there was finer here –
    his eyes were stolen from their very sockets.

The Greeks are like the Sufis, my dear father,
    free from contention, books and artifice.

Instead they've stripped their hearts and purified
      them
    of lust and greed and hate and avarice.

The mirror's purity is like the heart's,
    receiving images beyond all number.

3500   The endless formless form of the unseen
    shone from the heart's mirror on Moses' breast,

Although that form is not contained in heaven,
    nor on the throne nor earth nor sea nor Pisces.

Because they have a boundary and a number,
    the mirror of the heart is free of limits.

The mind is silenced here, or led astray,
   because the heart's with Him, or is Himself.

No image is eternally reflected
   as one or many except within the heart.

Each image newly formed on it forever   3505
   appears in it with no concealment there.

The burnishers are free from scent and colour;
   each moment they see instantaneous beauty.

They left behind the form and husk of knowledge
   and raised the flag of certainty itself.

Mere thought is gone. They have attained to light;
   they've got the strait and sea of recognition.

And death, of which the masses are in dread –
   these people make a laughing-stock of it.

And no one is the victor of their hearts: 3510
   the harm comes to the shell not to the pearl.

They gave up jurisprudence, flouted grammar,
   but they took up ascetic self-abandon.

Since images of all eight heavens shone forth,
   the tablets of their hearts have been receptive:

They're higher than the Throne and Seat and Void,
   they occupy '*the Sure Abode*' of God.

THE PROPHET (PEACE BE UPON HIM) ASKS ZAYD, 'HOW ARE YOU TODAY, AND HOW DID YOU RISE?' AND HIS REPLY: 'I WOKE UP A BELIEVER, O MESSENGER OF GOD'

The holy Prophet said to Zayd one morning,
　　'How do you feel this morning, my good friend?'

3515　He said, 'A faithful slave.' Again he asked him,
　　'If your faith's garden blossomed, where's the sign?'

And he replied, 'By day I have been parched;
　　by night I have not slept, from love and fever.

And so I passed through day and night just as
　　the spearhead's tip will penetrate the shield.

For on the other side all creeds are one;
　　a hundred thousand years is like an hour.

Eternity before and after time
　　is one – the mind cannot go there inquiring.'

3520　He said, 'Bring out the souvenir from travelling
　　to match your understanding of these realms.'

He said, 'When other people see the sky,
　　I see the throne and those who sit in heaven.

Eight paradises, seven hells appear
　　to me as clear as idols to the shaman.

I recognize the creatures one by one,
   like wheat among the barley in the mill.

The strangers from the guests of Paradise
   I see like serpents swimming among fish.'

This time has been revealed for this assembly,   3525
   'the day their faces turn to black or white'.

However wicked was the soul before this,
   it was within the womb, concealed from people.

*'The damned are damned inside their mother's
     womb,
   their state is known from marks upon the body.'*

The flesh – a mother – bears the infant soul;
   death is the pain and trauma of its birth.

The souls of all who've gone before watch out
   to see how that exultant soul is born.

The Ethiopians say, 'He's one of us.'   3530
   The Anatolians say, 'No, he's too fair.'

When born into the spirit-world of grace,
   there is no difference between white and black.

If he is black the Ethiops take him off;
   if he's a Greek the Greeks take him themselves.

Unborn, it is a puzzle for the world,
   for those who know the unborn are but few.

But surely *'he is seeing by God's light'*;
   he has the way beneath his outer skin.

3535   The human seed is white and fair in substance,
            but it reflects both Greek and savage soul.

        It colours those who have '*the fairest stature*'
            or drags the other half to deepest hell.

        These words go on forever; go on back!
            Let us not miss the caravan of camels.

        '*The day their faces turned to black and white*',
            the Turk and Hindu will be known among them.

        They are not known when they are in the womb;
            at birth the strong and weak come into view.

3540   'I see, as on the Day of Resurrection,
            all of them face to face as men and women.

        So shall I speak or shall I save my breath?'
            Mohammed bit his lip at him: 'Enough.'

        'God's Prophet! Shall I tell the assembly's secret?
            I'll show the world today the Resurrection.

        Will you allow me to draw back the veils
            and, like a sun, my substance will shine out,

        So that the sun will be eclipsed by me,
            that I may show the date-palm and the willow?

3545   I'll demonstrate the Resurrection mystery,
            the precious coin and that with alloy mixed.

        Companions of the left with severed hands,
            I'll show their faithless and deceitful colours,

        Reveal the seven holes of their deception,
            in moonlight neither waning nor declining.

I shall reveal the woollen cloak of thieves;
  I'll sound the drum and tabla of the prophets.

I'll bring before the eyes of infidels
  clear sight of hell and heaven and what's between.

I'll show the seething reservoir of Kawsar,   3550
  whose sound and water hit their ears and faces.

And those who run around it parched with thirst,
  I shall identify them clearly there.

And now their shoulders rub against my shoulders;
  their screams are penetrating both my ears.

Before my eyes the folk of Paradise
  embrace each other of their own free will.

They visit one another's place of honour,
  and then they plunder kisses from their lips.

My ear is deafened by the noise of sighing   3555
  of wretched men and cries of "I am suffering."

These words are hints and I would speak in depth,
  but yet I fear I might annoy the Prophet.'

He spoke like this, half-drunken and half-mad.
  The Prophet turned his collar up at him.

He said, 'Beware, hold back, your horse is hot.
  When "God is not ashamed!" has struck, shame
    goes.

Your mirror has been sprung out of its case –
  how can the mirror contradict the scales?

3560   How could the scales and mirror stop the breath
           to spare someone offence and spare their feelings?

       The scales and mirror are the brilliant touchstones
           were you to use them for two hundred years.

       If one should say, "Conceal the truth for me,
           display the increase, don't display the loss",

       They'll say, "Don't mock your own moustache and
               beard,
           the scales and mirror, counsel and deception!"

       Since God has elevated us so that
           through us reality may be discerned,

3565   Or else, if not, what are we worth, young man;
           how shall we be the showcase of the fair?

       But put the mirror back inside its case.
           Illumination's made your heart a Sinai.'

       'How could the Sun of Truth, the Sun eternal,'
           he said, 'be kept eclipsed beneath an armpit?

       It tears the underhand and underarm;
           no madness and no wisdom can survive it.'

       He said, 'Put up one finger to your eye –
           the world appears to be without the sun.

3570   A single fingertip obscures the moon
           – this is a symbol of how God conceals.'

       Just as the world is hidden by a point,
           the sun becomes eclipsed by one mistake.

You, close your lips and see the ocean's depth –
  God made the ocean subject to mankind.

As Salsabil and Zanjabil's outpourings
  are subject to the Lord of Paradise,

Four streams of Paradise are in our power,
  not from our might but by command of God.

We keep them flowing everywhere we will,   3575
  like magic at the will of the magicians,

As these two fountains flowing from the eyes
  are subject to the heart and soul's command.

If it desires, it goes to poisonous snakes,
  or it may wish to go to take good counsel.

If it desires, it goes to sensual things,
  or it may wish to go to subtle things.

If it desires, it goes to universals
  or stays within the gaol of partial things.

So all five senses are just like a channel: 3580
  they're flowing at the heart's command and will.

Whatever way the heart is telling them,
  the senses move and trail their skirts behind them.

The hands and feet are in the heart's control
  just like the staff held in the hand of Moses.

The heart desires – and feet are made to dance
  or flee to increase from deficiency.

The heart desires – the hand is brought to book
  with fingers so that it shall write a book.

3585   The hand is subject to a hidden hand –
            from inside this controls the outer body.

          If it desires, it is a snake to foes,
            or it may be a comrade to a friend.

          If it desires, it is a spoon in food
            or else a mace that weighs a hundredweight.

          I wonder what the heart will say to them –
            such strange conjunctions, stranger hidden causes.

          The heart must have the seal of Solomon
            that it can hold the reins of all five senses.

3590   Five outward senses are controlled by it,
            five inward senses at its beck and call.

          Ten senses and ten limbs and many others –
            you may count up the ones I've overlooked.

          Since you're a Solomon in sovereignty,
            O heart, then cast your spell on sprite and demon.

          If you are not deceitful in this kingdom,
            three demons will not take the seal from you.

          And after that your name will seize the world;
            you shall possess the two worlds like your body.

3595   But if the demons take the seal from you,
            your sovereignty is gone, your fortune dead.

          And after that 'O sorrow!' and 'O servants!'
            are fixed for you until 'the day of gathering'.

          If you deny your own deceit, how will
            you save your soul before the scales and mirror?

How Servants and Staff Acted Suspiciously towards Loqmān, Saying, 'He Has Eaten the Fresh Fruit Which We Have Brought'

To his own master, Loqmān seemed to be
one of the feeblest of his serving boys.

His lordship sent his servants to his orchards
to bring him fruits so he could savour them.

In servant circles Loqmān was a nuisance,   3600
his face as dark as night, so spiritual.

The serving boys would take enormous pleasure
in eating all the fruits with greedy relish.

They told their master, 'Loqmān's eaten them.'
The master was annoyed and cross with Loqmān.

When Loqmān made enquiries of the reason,
he ventured into speech to chide his master:

'O Lord, the faithless servant,' said Loqmān,
'is not accepted in the sight of God.

Test all of us, O you who are so generous,   3605
by filling up our bellies with hot water.

Then make us run around the desert wastes,
you riding, and us running round on foot.

Then keep an eye out for the evil-doer,
the acts of "the revealer of the mysteries".'

The master served his servants with hot water;
they drank the draught and drank it out of fear.

And then he drove them to the desert wastes.
　　That group ran up and down and round about.

3610　They all began to vomit in distress;
　　the water brought up all the fruit in them.

Loqmān began to vomit from his stomach;
　　the purest water gushed from his insides.

Since Loqmān's wisdom demonstrates this point,
　　what is the wisdom of the Lord of Being?

'*The day on which all secrets are examined*',
　　*something concealed appears from you, unwished
　　for.*

'*Drink scalding water which will rid their bowels*'
　　of all the veils on things that are revolting.

3615　The fire is used to punish unbelievers
　　because the fire is for assaying stones.

So often have we spoken gently to them;
　　those stony-hearted ones would heed no warning.

A vein that's badly cut is healed with pain;
　　the donkey's head ends up a meal for dogs.

'*For unclean women, unclean men*', says wisdom,
　　and ugly is a proper mate for ugly.

So go and mate with anything you like,
　　and be absorbed in it, its form and features.

3620　If light is what you want, be worthy of it!
　　If you'd be far away, be vain and distant!

And if you would escape this ruined gaol,
  don't spurn the Friend, '*bow down and come
  towards Him.*'

The Rest of the Story of the Reply of the Prophet (Peace Be Upon Him)

These words are endless. Be upstanding, Zayd;
  tie up Borāq, the steed of rational speech.

As speech reveals the error of your ways,
  it's tearing down the veil of what is hidden,

And God requires concealment for a time.
  Drive off this drummer-boy; close off the road!

Don't gallop; draw the reins. Restraint is better;   3625
  it's better all are happy in their views.

God wishes those who have no hope in Him
  to not avert their faces from His worship.

While there's still hope, they've still nobility.
  A day or two they run beside His stirrups.

He would prefer His mercy shone on all,
  on good and bad, in universal mercy.

God wishes every prince and every pauper
  was full of hope and fearful and was cautious.

This fear and caution are within a veil,   3630
  so that behind the veil they are protected.

Where's fear, where's caution, when the veil is torn?
  The awesomeness of unseen worlds is shown!

Thought struck a youth upon a river-bank:
'That fisherman of ours is Solomon!

If that's him, why's he on his own, disguised;
if not, then why the look of Solomon?'

He was in two minds, thinking thoughts like this,
till Solomon returned as king and sovereign.

3635   The demon fled the throne and left the kingdom;
the sword of fortune spilled that demon's blood.

And when he put the ring upon his finger,
the hordes of sprites and demons gathered round.

And men came too to see what they could see –
among them was the youth who'd had the vision.

And when he saw the ring upon his finger,
his wonderings and worries went at once.

Suspicion's at its height when something's hidden;
investigation chases what's unseen.

3640   Imagining the absent one inflamed him;
when he appeared, imagining dispersed.

If shining heaven is not devoid of rain,
nor is dark earth devoid of verdant growth.

Because I need the sense '*they trust the unseen*,'
I've closed the window of this worldly mansion.

If I cleave heaven apart for all to see,
how could I say, '*Can you see cracks in it?*'

So in this darkness they investigate;
each person turns his face in some direction.

Awhile the world's affairs are upside down,   3645
   the thief will take the governor to the gallows.

And many a sovereign prince and noble soul
   becomes his servant's servant for a while.

In absence, good and beautiful is service;
   recalling absent ones in service pleases.

The one who stands before the king to praise him
   is what, compared to him who's meekly absent?

The governor who is at the empire's outposts,
   far from the sultan and the royal shadow,

Defends the fortress from the enemy –   3650
   he'll not forsake the fortress for a fortune.

Remote from court and in outlandish outposts,
   he keeps his loyalty like one who's present.

And for the king he's better than the rest
   who serve him there and sacrifice their lives.

The smallest scrap of duty's care in absence
   is worth a hundred thousand in his presence.

Obedience and faith are precious now,
   but after death, when all is clear, they're surplus.

Since absence, absent one and veil are best,   3655
   then close your lips: a quiet mouth is best.

O brother, steal yourself away from words
   for God Himself reveals inspired knowledge.

The sun's face is the witness of the sun.
   'What is the greatest testimony? – God.'

No, I shall speak, for God and all the angels
　　and learned men agree in explanation:

'God and the angels and the learned witness:
　　there is no lord except the Lord abiding,'

3660　Since God has testified who are the angels,
　　that they are partners in His testimony.

It is because weak hearts and eyes can't bear
　　the beams of light and presence of the sun.

It's like a bat that's given up all hope
　　because it cannot tolerate the sunlight.

Be sure, the angels help as we are helpers,
　　reflectors of the sun in highest heaven.

We say we've gained this splendour from a sun;
　　we've shone upon the weak as did the caliph.

3665　And like a moon that's new or half or full,
　　each angel has perfection, light and power.

By rank each angel has from that effulgence
　　a three- or fourfold set of wings of light,

Just like the wings of human intellects,
　　among which there is so much variation.

The partner of each human, good or evil,
　　is just that angel which resembles it.

The bleary-eyed who cannot bear the sun –
　　the star is meant for him to find his way.

The Prophet (Peace Be Upon Him) Said to Zayd, 'Do Not Tell this Secret More Plainly than This, and Keep Watch over Your Obedience'

The Prophet said, 'My followers are stars,   3670
    a lamp for travellers, and for Satan stoning.'

If every person had the eye and strength
    to take the light of the celestial sun,

Who would have need of stars, O wretched man,
    to give an indication of the sun?

The moon declares to earth and cloud and
      shades,
    'I was a mortal "but it is revealed . . ."'

And in my nature I was dark, like you.
    The sun revealed to me a light like this.

Compared with suns, I have a darkness in me,   3675
    but I have light for darkness of the souls.

I'm fainter so that you can bear my truth,
    for you are not a man of brilliant suns.

I'm blended in like vinegar and honey,
    so I can reach the sickness in the liver.

O addict, when you've shaken off your illness,
    leave off the vinegar and feed on honey.

The throne, which is the heart set free from lust –
    now see 'the Merciful sits on the throne.'

3680   Thereafter God controls the heart directly,
            for now the heart has found the true relation.

        These words go on forever – where is Zayd
            that I may warn him not to seek disgrace?

                Returning to the Story of Zayd

        You'll not find Zayd, for he has disappeared:
            he's fled the shoe rack, and he's dropped his shoes.

        And who are you? Zayd could not find himself;
            he's like the star on which the sun has shone.

        You'll find there is no sign nor signal of him;
            you'll find no clue along the Milky Way.

3685   The sense and speech of our forefathers are
            suffused within the light of our king's wisdom.

        Their senses and intelligences lost
            in wave on wave of *'be arraigned before us'*.

        When morning comes it is the time of burden;
            the stars that had been hidden go to work.

        God gives sensation to the senseless ones,
            to rings of them, with rings upon their ears.

        They dance and wave their hands about in praise,
            rejoicing with *'O Lord You have revived us.'*

3690   Their scattered skin and dislocated bones
            turned into horsemen churning up the dust,

        On Resurrection Day the grateful and
            ungrateful change to being from non-being.

Why snatch away your head? Do you not see?
  Did you not turn it first in non-existence?

Your feet were planted firm in non-existence.
  You asked, 'Who will uproot me from my place?'

Do you not see the action of your Lord?
  He is the One who takes you by the forelock.

And so He draws you to all sorts of states   3695
  of which you had no inkling or conception.

Non-being is eternally his servant.
  To work, O demons! Solomon's alive!

The demon fashions bowls '*like water-troughs*'.
  He does not dare refuse or answer back.

See how you are atremble out of fear;
  be sure non-being's also ever-trembling.

And if you're striving after high position,
  it's just the fear your spirit is in turmoil.

For all except the love of God most fair   3700
  is turmoil, even if it's sugar-coated.

So what is turmoil? Going towards death,
  not having plunged into the living water.

The people's eyes are cast on earth and death;
  they doubt life's water with a hundred doubts.

Strive to reduce your hundred doubts to ninety;
  be gone by night or, if you sleep, night goes.

By night's obscurity seek out that day
  and find that darkness-burning intellect.

3705   In evil-coloured night there is much goodness;
            the living water is the bride of darkness.

        Yet who can lift his head up out of sleep
            and sow these hundred seeds of inattention?

        The deadly sleep and deadly food befriend you.
            The master slept; the night thief went to work.

        Do you not recognize your enemies?
            The fiery ones are foes of those of earth.

        Fire is the foe of water and her children
            as water is the rival of his spirit.

3710   The water will extinguish fire because
            it is the enemy of water's children.

        And so the fire's the fire of human lust
            in which there lies the root of sin and error.

        The outer fire may be put out with water;
            the fire of lust will take you down to hell.

        The fire of lust is not appeased by water,
            because it has hell's nature in tormenting.

        What is the cure for lust? The light of faith:
            'Your light will quench the fire of unbelievers.'

3715   What kills this fire? The light of God Almighty,
            so make the light of Abraham your teacher,

        So that your body like a timber frame
            escapes your fire of self, which is like Nimrod.

        This fiery lust does not abate with practice,
            but only by abstaining does it lessen.

So long as you lay firewood on a fire,
  how will the fire die down by stoking it?

When you deprive the fire of wood it dies,
  so fear of God pours water on the fire.

How can the fire besmirch the lovely face   3720
  whose cheeks are rouged with 'reverence of
    their hearts'?

A Fire Breaks Out in Medina in the Days of Omar (May God be Pleased With Him)

A fire broke out back in the days of Omar;
  it was consuming stones like kindling wood.

It fell on buildings and on dwelling houses,
  and even caught the wings and nests of birds.

And half the city went up in the flames,
  and water boiled in shock in fear of them.

And those who had their wits about them threw
  their water-skins and vinegar on the fire.

The fire was growing stronger in its rage;   3725
  the source that fuelled it was infinite.

The people flocked in haste to Omar's side:
  'We cannot put the fire out with water!'

He said, 'Indeed that fire's a sign of God –
  a flame out of your fire of stinginess.

What's water? What is vinegar? Give bread!
  Bypass your meanness if you are my people!'

The people said, 'We've opened wide our doors;
   we have been liberal and bountiful.'

3730   'You've given out of habit and by custom.
   You have not opened up your hands for God

But all for glory, showing-off and pride,
   not piety and fear and dedication.

Wealth is a seed, don't sow in barren soil;
   don't put a sword in every brigand's hand!

And know the faithful from the hateful ones;
   seek out companions of the truth and join them!

Each person shows a liking for their own.
   A fool alone then thinks he's done good deeds.'

HOW AN ENEMY SPAT IN THE FACE OF THE COMMANDER OF THE FAITHFUL ALI (MAY GOD BESTOW HONOUR ON HIS PERSON) AND HOW ALI THREW HIS SWORD FROM HIS HAND

Learn purity of action from Ali;
    know how the lion of God was free from fault.   3735

He'd overcome a warrior in battle;
    he'd quickly drawn his sword to see him off.

He spat at Ali's face – Ali, who was
    the pride of every Friend of God and prophet.

He spat upon the cheek to which the moon
    bows low her face towards the place of worship.

Ali threw down his sword immediately
    and drew back in the struggle of the conflict.

The warrior was astonished at this action   3740
    of unexpected mercy and forgiveness.

He said, 'You raised your sharp sword over me.
    Why have you thrown it down and pitied me?

What did you see as better than my slaughter,
    so that you slackened in despatching me?

What did you see that settled so your anger,
    that such a flash appeared and disappeared?

What did you see that, when I saw its image,
    a flame appeared inside my heart and soul?

3745 What did you see beyond all being and space,
    worth more than life, and then you gave me life?

You are the lion of God in bravery,
    and who can understand your manliness?

In manliness you're Moses' desert cloud
    from which came trays and food beyond compare.

The clouds gave wheat, which by their own exertion
    mankind prepared and made as sweet as honey.

But Moses' cloud spread open wings of mercy
    and gave forth bread and sweetness without effort.

3750 For those who ate the generous trays of manna,
    His mercy raised a banner for the world.

For forty years that gift and that allowance
    did not for one day fail the Israelites

Till they rose up in avariciousness
    and asked for leeks and vegetables and herbs.

O people of Mohammed, who are noble,
    that food shall last you till the Resurrection.

When *"with my Lord I pass the night"* was spoken,
    "He gives me food and drink" was seen as food.

3755 Accept these things without interpretation
    so that you swallow them like milk and honey.

Interpretation is to spurn the gift,
    When one regards the truth of it as false.

Regarding it as false is mental weakness:
   great mind is kernel; partial mind is shell.

Interpret your own self, and not tradition!
   Pick your own brains, not gardens laid with roses!

Ali, O you who are all mind and vision,
   give us the savour of what you have seen.

The sword of your endurance tore our soul;   3760
   the water of your knowledge cleansed our earth.

Declare it as I know these are His secrets.
   His method is to slay without the sword.

The Worker without instruments or limbs,
   the Giver of these advantageous gifts,

He gives the mind a hundred thousand wines
   to taste, to which the eyes and ears are shut.

O heavenly falcon of good hunting, tell
   what you have lately seen of the Creator!

Your eye has learnt the sight of hidden things;   3765
   the eyes of those who stand and stare are
      stitched.'

One man will see a moon in all its fullness,
   another sees the world obscured in darkness,

And yet another sees three moons together –
   these three men sit in one position, yes!

All three have open eyes and hearing sharp;
   they're fixed on you and they're in flight from me.

Is this strange, hidden grace some trick of sight?
    To you a wolf's form comes, to me a Joseph.

3770 Though there be more than eighteen thousand worlds,
    not every eye will catch these eighteen thousand.

'Reveal the secret, O Ali, approved one,
    "O *happy fortune after evil fortune!*"

Declare the things your intellect has grasped,
    or I shall mention what has shone upon me.

It shone on me from you – how could you hide it?
    And like the moon you silently strew light.

But if the moon's disc enters into speech,
    it guides night-travellers on the road the sooner.

3775 From blundering and oblivion they're saved:
    the moon's voice overcomes the ghoulish howl.

See how the moon is guiding without speaking.
    If it should speak, it would be light on light.

Since you're the gateway into wisdom's city,
    and since you are the rays of mercy's sun,

Be open, gate, to him who seeks the gate,
    so that through you the husks are turned to kernels.

Be open evermore, O gate of mercy,
    the court of "*none can be compared to Him.*"'

3780 All space, each single atom, has an aspect –
    when closed, who can discern there is a door?

Unless the watchman opens up the door,
    this notion never stirs within the mind.

When such a door is opened, there's amazement –
  the bird of hope and expectation flies.

A careless man found treasure in the ruin,
  then he was busy searching every ruin.

Until you got the gemstone from one dervish,
  why would you seek one from another dervish?

For years, though thought runs on its own two
      feet,   3785
  it does not reach the end of its own nostrils.

No scent of unseen worlds comes to your nose.
  Do you see anything beyond it, tell me?

The Unbeliever Asks Ali (May God Bestow Honour On His Person), 'When You Were Defeating, Why Did You Throw Your Sword from Your Hand?'

That just-converted Muslim friend now said,
  light-headed and delighted with Ali,

'Tell me, prince of believers, cause my soul
  to move within my body like a foetus.'

O soul, there is a time the seven planets
  make every foetus turn around in service,

And at the time the foetus gains the soul,   3790
  just then the sun becomes defender of it.

The sun will stir this foetus into movement;
  the sun will suddenly give life to it.

From other stars it only took a pattern
   until the sun shone down upon this foetus.

How could it have become dependent on
   the fair-faced sun from deep inside the womb?

In hidden ways, remote from human senses,
   the sun in heaven has many a way like this:

3795   The way that gold gets nourishment from it,
   and how the rocks are turned to gems by it;

The way by which it makes the ruby red,
   and how it makes the horseshoe flash with sparks;

The way it causes fruits to come to ripeness,
   and how it heartens the bewildered soul.

'Speak out, O falcon of the shining wings,
   familiar with the king and with his forearm.

Speak out, you kingly Simorgh-catcher,
   alone, defeating armies with no army.

3800   You're one community, a hundred thousand –
   speak out, O you whose falcon's hunted me.

Why is this mercy standing in for vengeance?
   And whose idea to hand it to the dragon?'

The Commander of the Faithful Answers with the Reason for Throwing His Sword from His Hand in Those Circumstances

He said, 'I wield a sword but for God's sake;
  I am God's slave, not governed by the body.

I am the lion of God, not of desire.
  My actions are the witness to my faith.

In war I am as *"when you threw you threw not."*
  I'm like the sunbeam that the sun is sending.

I've done away with all my goods and chattels;   3805
  the things that are not God I see as void.

I am a shade, the Sun's my overlord.
  I am His valet; I am not His veiler.

I'm like a sword encased with jewels of union;
  I bring men back to life, not death in battle.

Blood does not drench the lustre of my sword.
  How could the winds dispel my clouds of being?

No straw am I, the mount of grace and patience
  and law – how can rough winds bring down the
      mountain?

That which is blown away by wind is trash,   3810
  for truly, the intemperate winds are many.

The winds of wrath and lust and avarice
  swept him away who was not of the prayerful.

My mountain and my being rest on Him;
  if I'm like straw the wind reminds me of Him.

His wind alone can move my inclination.
　　Love of the One alone is my commander.

For kings their anger's king, for me a servant –
　　I have put anger also under harness.

3815　The sword of mercy's severed anger's neck;
　　God's anger has approached me like compassion.

I'm drowned in light although my form is broken,
　　became a garden though I am of dust.

Since accidents have come about in combat,
　　I thought it best to put away my sword,

So that my name becomes *"he loves for God's sake,"*
　　so that my name becomes *"he hates for God's
　　　sake,"*

So that my giving is *"he gives for God's sake,"*
　　so that my being is *"withholds for God's sake"*.

3820　My greed for God, my giving and much more –
　　I'm *all* for God, I am for no one else.

And what I do for God is not pretence,
　　not fantasy nor surmise but for insight.

I am set free from striving and from searching;
　　I've sewn my sleeve onto the skirt of God.

If I should fly, I see my destination;
　　if I revolve, I'm looking at my centre.

I bear a load and know where I must go.
　　I am the moon; my guide the sun's before me.

Beyond this there's no way of telling people;   3825
    there's no room for the ocean in a river.

I speak in hushed tones, up to reason's limits –
    it is not wrong, it was the Prophet's practice.

I'm free of selfhood, hear a freeman's witness.
    The witness of a slave's not worth two figs.

In sacred law the witness of a slave
    has no authority at trial and judgement.

If slaves in thousands stood as witness for you,
    in law their word would not be worth a straw.

But in the sight of God, the slave to lust   3830
    is worse than slaves and hired serving-boys.

The first lives sweetly, dies in bitterness,
    while one word sets the slave free from his
        master.

The slave to lust can never find deliverance,
    save by the grace of God and special favour.

He fell into a pit that has no bottom,
    and that's his sin, not fate or some injustice.

He flung himself into a pit, and I
    can find no rope that reaches to the bottom.

I'll stop, for if this discourse carries on,   3835
    the hardest stones, not only hearts, will bleed.

It's not from hardness if the hearts aren't bleeding;
    it's carelessness, distraction and bad luck.

One day they'll bleed when blood's no good to them,
    so bleed when blood is not to be rejected.

The one who is not slave to ghouls is lawful –
    The testament of slaves is not accepted.

"*We sent you as a witness*" was a warning,
    for he was free of being, free of freedom.

3840   Since I am free, can anger chain me? Come,
    in here are only attributes of God.

Come in! The grace of God has made you free,
    for mercy has prevailed upon His wrath.

Come in now; you are free from any danger.
    The elixir turned your rock into a jewel.

You're free from unbelief and from its thorn-bush.
    Bloom like a rose within His cypress grove.

For You are I and I am You, my shy one –
    you were Ali; how could I kill Ali?

3845   Your sin was better than obedience;
    you travelled all the heavens in an instant.'

So fortunate the sin that man committed –
    do not the leaves of roses grow from thorns?

The sin of Omar – to attack the Prophet –
    did it not take him to acceptance's gateway?

The Pharaoh, by his own magicians' magic,
    did not he draw them in and fortune help them?

Were it not for their magic and disowning,
   who could have drawn them to the wicked
      Pharaoh?

How would they see the miracles and staff?   3850
   O sinful people, sin became obedience.

For God has struck the neck of hopelessness
   since sin has come to be like piety.

For He is now transforming evil deeds;
   he makes them piety despite the liars.

And so accursed Satan gets a stoning:
   he blasts with envy and is split in half.

He tries to propagate the sinfulness,
   and by that sin he brings us to a pit.

But when he sees that sin is turned to service,   3855
   there comes for him an inauspicious time.

'Come in, I'm opening the door for you.
   You spat, and I present you with a gift.

I give such things to him who is oppressive
   for this is how I turn the other cheek.

Imagine what I give the blessed faithful –
   the treasures and the kingdoms everlasting.

The Prophet (Peace Be Upon Him) Said into the Ear of the Groom of Ali (May God Bestow Honour On His Person), 'Prince of Believers, I Told You That the Murder of Ali Would Be by Your Hand'

'I am the kind of man whose nature's sweetness
   did not turn sour in vengeance for his slayer.

3860   The Prophet whispered in his servant's ear,
   "One day the servant will cut off my head."

The Prophet, by God's revelation, told him,
   "My death will finally be by his hand."

And he replies, "Kill me before that happens,
   that I shall not commit this dreadful crime."

I answer, "Since my death will come from you,
   how can I seek to cheat my destiny?"

He is prostrate before me: "Gracious one,
   for God's sake, cut me into equal halves

3865   That such an evil end may not befall me
   and my soul burn in grief for its beloved."

I say, "Be gone; the ink of fate is dry.
   How many have come to grief upon this pen!

There is no malice in my soul for you
   because I do not see it as your doing.

You are God's tool; the agent is God's hand.
   How could I blame or beat God's instrument?"'

He said, 'Then, what's retaliation for?'
  'It is from God; it is a hidden secret.

If He should cause displeasure by His action,   3870
  from that displeasure He makes gardens grow.

Displeasure comes to Him from His own action,
  for He is one in vengeance and in grace.

In this ephemeral city He is prince.
  He is the overseer of all the kingdoms.

And if He were to break His instrument,
  He would repair that thing which had been
    broken.'

Sir, see how '*any verse We abrogate . . .*'
  is followed by '*We bring a better one.*'

If God has contradicted any law,   3875
  He's taken grass and substituted roses.

The night abolishes the work of daytime.
  See how the mindless state enlightens minds.

Again, night is abolished by the daylight,
  so mindlessness is burnt up by that phoenix.

Though slumber and light sleep are found in
    darkness,
  is not life's water there within the darkness?

Is not the mind made new again in darkness?
  A silence gives the voice a source of power.

From opposites the opposites appear: 3880
  light was created in the heart of darkness.

The Prophet's battles were the source of peace;
   the peace of future times was from his battles.

That ravisher of hearts cut countless heads off
   to save the heads of all humanity.

The gardener will cut off the withered branch
   so that the date-palm gains in height and
      goodness.

The wise man pulls the weeds out of his garden
   so that his fruits and flowers look delightful.

3885   The doctor will pull out the rotten tooth
   to spare the patient any pain or sickness.

Thus many forms of goodness lie in faults.
   For martyrs, life is to be found in death.

The throat that swallows daily bread, when severed
   may savour 'being sustained and their exulting'.

The throat of beasts that's severed lawfully
   grows as a human throat and is improved.

So when the human throat is cut, consider
   what will ensue? Comparing this with that,

3890   A third throat is produced, and for its care
   there is God's drink and His illumination.

The severed throat will drink the drink, but only
   the throat that's free from 'No' and dead in 'Yes'.

Enough, ungrateful, stubby-fingered one;
   how long will your soul's life be based on bread?

You have no fruit from it, just like the willow;
   for white bread you discredited yourself.

If sensual nature can't resist this bread,
   try alchemy. Change copper into gold!

You there, you wish to have your clothes washed,   3895
     do you?
   Don't turn your face from where they wash the
     clothes!

Though bread has broken up the fast for you,
   rise up and cling to Him who mends what's
     broken,

For since His hand can mend what has been broken,
   His breaking, then, is really a repairing.

If you should break it, He will say, 'Come on!
   Repair it!' You do not have any means.

And so He has the right to break, for He
   is able to repair what has been broken.

She who can sew knows how to tear apart.   3900
   She who can sell knows better how to buy.

From top to bottom He destroys the house,
   then in an instant makes it more delightful.

If He should cut one head off from a body,
   He puts a hundred thousand on at once.

Had He not caused the sinners retribution
   or not said there is life 'in retribution',

Who would have been so bold that of himself
   he'd use a sword on one condemned by God's law?

3905　　For anyone whose eyes are opened knows
　　　　　the slayer was compelled by fate to slay.

　　　　And he upon whose head that verdict came
　　　　　must use his sword on even his own child.

　　　　Be gone, be fearful; do not curse the wicked.
　　　　　Before the snare of law, know your own weakness.

How Adam (Peace Be Upon Him) Was Astonished at Eblis the Accursed's Going Astray, and Became Haughty

　　　　When Adam cast his eye on wretched Eblis,
　　　　　he looked at him contemptuously, with scorn.

　　　　Puffed up with arrogance and vanity,
　　　　　he ridiculed accursed Eblis' state.

3910　　The majesty of God cried out, 'My friend,
　　　　　you do not understand the hidden secrets.

　　　　If He were to reveal His other aspect,
　　　　　He'd smash the mountain peaks to their
　　　　　　foundations.'

　　　　Just then He'd have disowned a hundred Adams
　　　　　and made as many Muslims out of Eblis.

　　　　And Adam said, 'I do repent this look.
　　　　　I'll not think so presumptuously again.'

　　　　'Helper of those who beg for help, guide us!
　　　　　There is no pride in knowledge or in riches.

3915　　*Let not a heart led by Your grace be lost;*
　　　　　ward off the evil which the Pen has written!'

Release our souls from evil pre-ordained;
   do not eradicate us from the pure ones!

For nothing is more bitter than Your absence –
   without Your shelter, nothing but distress!

Our worldly riches steal our heavenly riches;
   our bodies tear the clothing of our souls.

And since our hand will likely spite our foot,
   how can we save our souls without Your care?

And if you save your soul from these great   3920
      dangers,
   you'll have amassed defeats and piles of fear.

For when the soul's not one with the Beloved,
   it's blind and blue forever on its own.

When You exclude the soul that's saved itself,
   regard as dead the soul that lives without You.

If You are heaping insults on Your servants,
   it is Your privilege, Auspicious One.

If You should say the moon and sun are flotsam,
   if You should call the lofty cypress crooked,

If You should call the vault of heaven low,   3925
   if You should call the mines and oceans needy,

By contrast with Your perfect state it's true:
   Your power is to perfect the mortal things.

For You are free from risk and non-existence,
   and You give being and sustenance to non-beings.

The cultivator can incinerate
    because the one who rends can also mend.

Each autumn He is withering the garden,
    then grows the rose again to dye the world.

3930   O withered one, come out and be renewed;
    be fair again and famous for your beauty.

He opened up the blind narcissus' eyes;
    He soothed to health the slit reed's severed throat.

We are the fashioned, not the Fashioner;
    we are no more than lowly, humble suppliants.

We all are calling out, 'Save me myself!'
    We all are Ahrimans without Your calling.

For we have been set free from Ahriman
    since You have saved our souls from sightlessness.

3935   You are the guide for all who are alive.
    Without his guide and staff, where is the blind man?

Apart from You, all pleasant things and painful
    scorch humankind and are of fiery essence.

All who take fire as refuge and protection
    become a Magian and a Zarathushtra.

'*All things except for God are vanity;*
    God's grace is like a rain cloud overflowing.'

Returning to the Story of Ali (May God Bestow Honour On His Person) and His Leniency towards His Murderer

Let us return to Ali and his killer,
   the grace and magnanimity he showed him.

He said, 'I cast my eye upon the foe.   3940
   I have no anger for him night or day.

For death is sweet as honey-dew to me;
   my death has got its grip on Resurrection.

The deathless death will be allowed to us;
   the ration without rationing will be ours.

Its outside's death and inside it is life,
   outside cut down, inside continuation.

Birth is transition for the unborn foetus,
   to blossom and to flourish in the world.

As I desire the hour of death, the rule   3945
   "Don't die by your own hand" is meant for me.

Because it warns against the sweeter fruit,
   does bitter fruit have any need of warning?

A fruit that's bitter in its flesh and skin
   has warning in its bitterness and sourness.

Death's fruit has turned to something sweet for me;
   For me the verse *"nay, they're alive"* came down.

Kill me, my trusty friends, for I am wretched;
   indeed my death is my eternal life.

3950   *Indeed my life is in my death, young man.*
            How long shall I be severed from my homeland?

        In this my dwelling if there were not severance,
            He would not say, "To Him we are returning."

        He who returns comes back to his own city,
            to unity from his forced separation.

        The Falling of the Groom Each Time before the
        Prince of Believers, Ali (May God Bestow Honour
        On His Person), Saying, 'O Prince of Believers,
        Kill Me and Deliver Me from This Fate'

        'He came back saying, "Ali, kill me quickly
            that I'll not live to see that bitter moment.

        I authorize your spilling of my blood
            that my eyes shall not witness that uprising."

3955   I said, "If every atom were a killer,
            if they assaulted you with dagger drawn,

        They could not cut a single hair of yours
            because the pen has drawn this line on you.

        Don't grieve, for I shall plead for you – I am
            the spirit's master, not the body's slave.

        To me this mortal body is worth nothing.
            I am of noble stock without my body.

        To me the sword and dagger are sweet basil;
            to me my death's a feast, a bed of roses.

3960   Could one who maims his body thus begin
            to lust for princely and imperial power?

Though outwardly he strives for rule and office,
    it is to show the princes how to rule,

To breathe new life into the princely role
    and make the tree of Caliphate bear fruit.'"'

*Explaining That the Aim of Mohammed (Peace Be
Upon Him) in Seeking to Acquire Mecca and Other
Cities Was Not for Love of World Dominion – as He
Has Said, 'The World Is a Corpse' – but That It Was
God's Command That He Do So*

Who could suspect the Prophet's drive for Mecca
    was motivated by a worldly greed?

Whose eyes and heart were shut to treasure vaults
    of seven heavens on the day of testing?

To gaze at him, the houries and the genies   3965
    had filled the tracts of all the seven heavens

And beautified themselves all for his sake –
    how could he feel for any save the Friend?

He was so filled by reverence for God
    that God's own beings had no access to him.

*'We cannot harbour any prophet sent
    nor angel, nor a spirit – understood?'*

We are *'the eye roved not'* but not like *'ravens'*;
    we're drunk on Him that dyes, not on dead
        gardens.

If heavenly beings and treasuries of heaven   3970
    appeared as worthless to the Prophet's eye,

So what are Mecca, Syria and Iraq
  that he should fight campaigns and show ambition?

That thought creates a bad impression of him,
  conceived out of your ignorance and envy.

As when you make a yellow glass a sun-screen,
  the sunlight will appear to you all yellow.

Go smash that glass of yellow and of blue
  that you may know the man behind the dust.

3975   The dust has been stirred up around the horseman –
  you took the dust to be the man of God.

Eblis saw dust and said, 'This man of clay –
  How could the fiery-faced one outstrip me?'

While you regard the glorious ones as evil,
  know that your view's the legacy of Eblis.

If you're not Eblis' child, O wayward one,
  how is it that that dog's bequest is yours?

'No dog am I, truth's lion and devotee.
  The lion of truth is he that's freed from form.

3980   The worldly lion looks for prey and meat;
  the godly lion looks for death and freedom.

He sees in death a hundredfold existence,
  and like the moth he burns his own existence.'

The death-wish was the yoke of truthful men.
  This word was made a trial for the Jews.

It says in the Quran, 'O Jewish people,
  for truthful men death is a boon and treasure.'

Just as there is desire for making gain,
   desire to gain your death is better still.

O Jews, to further men's esteem of you,   3985
   let this request be present on your tongue.

But not one Jew had this much grace to do so,
   when this flag was unfolded by Mohammed.

He said, 'If you could bring yourselves to say this,
   indeed no Jew would tarry in the world.'

And then the Jews paid revenue and tribute:
   'O beacon, do not bring disgrace upon us.'

With all these words there is no end in sight.
   Give me your hand, for you have seen the Friend.

*The Speech of Ali (May God Bestow Honour On
His Person) to His Opponent: 'When You Spat
in My Face, My Lower Self Was Disturbed
and the Equanimity Departed, Which
Prevented Me from Killing You'*

The prince of the believers told the youth,   3990
   'O warrior, at the time of our encounter,

When you spat at my face, my lower self
   was troubled; my composure left in pieces,

Half for the sake of God and half in fury.
   There is no state of compromise in God's work.

You have been hand-drawn by the Lord Himself.
   You are not fashioned by me; you are God's.

And by God's will alone destroy God's image,
 strike the Beloved's stone against His glass.'

3995 The Gabr heard this and a light appeared
 within his heart so that he cut his girdle,

Declaring, 'I was sowing seeds of evil.
 I thought that you were of another kind.

You've been the balance of the One in nature;
 indeed you've been the tongue of every balance.

You've been my roots, foundations and relations;
 you've been the light of my religion's lamp.

I am the slave of that attractive lamp
 from which your lamp received illumination.

4000 Slave of that wave of oceanic light
 which washes up a jewel such as this,

Present to me profession of the faith.
 I see you as the foremost of the age.'

Some fifty people of his kith and kin
 inclined their faces lovingly to faith.

By mercy's sword so many throats were saved;
 he saved so many people from the sword.

For mercy's sword is sharper than the steel
 and more victorious than a hundred armies.

4005 But O, alas, two morsels have been swallowed
 that made the temperature of thought go cold.

A grain of wheat eclipsed the sun of Adam
 just as the dragon hides the full moon's radiance.

Heart's beauty! Yet by one handful of earth
   see how its moon dispels the Pleiades.

When bread was spirit, eating it was wholesome,
   but when it turned to form, it was a nuisance,

Like those green thistles camels eat and get
   a hundred benefits from eating them:

When greenness disappears and they are dry,   4010
   when camels in the desert eat those thorns,

They tear their mouths and lips on them. Alas
   that such a well-trained rose became a sword!

When bread was spirit, it was those green thistles;
   now that it's turned to form, it's dry and coarse.

In former times, as you had been accustomed
   that you would eat this, O delightful one,

With equal hope you're eating this dry stuff,
   when now the spirit is mixed up with earth,

Became mixed up with earth, and dry and barbed.   4015
   Keep well away now, camel, from that plant.

Words are becoming very earth-polluted.
   The water has gone murky; seal the well-head

That God may make it clean and sweet again,
   for He who made it murky purifies it.

And patience brings your heart's desire, not haste,
   be patient, 'God knows what is for the best.'

Appendix

TRANSCRIPTION AND TRANSLATION
OF *MASNAVI* I.1–18: RHYTHM,
STRESS AND RHYME

The opening of the first book of the *Masnavi* is one of the most famous passages in Persian literature. It is presented here in a simplified transcription in order to give the non-Persian reader a rough appreciation of how these couplets sound and also how the rhymes work. The rhymes are in bold type, and the number of syllables of each rhyme is given in the right margin.

The quantity of each of the two eleven-syllable half-lines of the couplet is:

$$- \cup - - / - \cup - - / - \cup -$$

Underlined syllables are stressed. ā is pronounced long as in English 'rather'. ˆ indicates that the preceding syllable is overlength ($- \cup$).

> beshno in nay chun shekāyat mi konad
> az jodā'ihā hekāyat mi konad   6
> – Listen to this reed as it is grieving;
>   it tells the story of our separations.

> kaz nayestān tā marā bobride and
> dar nafiram mard o zan nālide and   3
> 'Since I was severed from the bed of reeds,
>   in my cry men and women have lamented.

sine khwāham sharhe sharhe az farāq
tā beguyam sharh-e dard-e eshtiyāq   1
I need the breast that's torn to shreds by parting
    to give expression to the pain of heartache.

har kasi ke durˆ mānd az asl-e khwish
bāzˆ juyad ruzˆgār-e vasl-e khwish   3
Whoever finds himself left far from home
    looks forward to the day of his reunion.

man be har jam'iati nālān shodam
joft-e badhālān o khwoshhālān shodam   4
I was in grief in every gathering;
    I joined with those of sad and happy state.

har kasi az zenn-e khwod shod yār-e man
az darun-e man najost asrār-e man   3
Each person thought he was my bosom friend,
    but none sought out my secrets from within me.

serr-e man az nāle-ye man durˆ nist
likˆ chashm o gushˆ-rā ān nurˆ nist   2
My secret is not far from my lament,
    but eye and ear have no illumination.

tan ze jān o jān ze tan masturˆ nist
likˆ kas-rā did-e jān dasturˆ nist   3
There's no concealment of the soul and body,
    yet no one has the power to see the soul.

ātesh ast in bāng-e nāy o nistˆ bād
har ke in ātesh nadārad nistˆ bād   2
The reed-flute's sound is fire, not human breath.
    Whoever does not have this fire, be gone!

ātesh-e 'eshq astˆ k-andar nay fetād
jushesh-e 'eshq astˆ k-andar may fetād   9
The fire of love is burning in the reed;
    the turbulence of love is in the wine.

nay harif-e har ke az yāri borid
  pardehā-ash pardehā-ye mā darid   1
The reed is friend to all who are lovelorn;
  its melodies have torn our veils apart.

hamchu nay zahri o teryāqi ke did
  hamchu nay damsāz o mashtāqi ke did   4
Whoever saw a poison and a cure,
  a mate and longing lover like the reed?

nay hadis-e rāh-e porr khun mi konad
  qessehā-ye eshq-e majnun mi konad   4
The reed tells of the road that runs with blood;
  it tells the tales of Majnun's passionate love.

mahram-e in hush^ joz bihush^ nist
  mar zabān-rā moshtari joz gush^ nist   2
This sense is closed to all except the senseless,
  and words are all the ear can ever purchase.

dar gham-e mā ruz^ hā bigāh^ shod
  ruz^ hā bā suz^ hā hamrāh^ shod   2
In all our grief the days turned into nights,
  the days fell into step with searing pains.

ruz^ hā gar raft^ gu rōw bāk^ nist
  tu bemān ay ānke chun tu pāk^ nist   3
If days are gone, say "Go! There is no fear,
  and stay, O You who are uniquely holy."

har ke joz māhi ze ābash sir^ shod
  har ke bi ruzist^ ruzash dir^ shod   3
His flood deluges all except the fish;
  the day is long for him who has no bread.

dar nayābad hāl-e pokhte hich^ khām
  pas sokhan kutāh^ bāyad va 's-salām   1
The raw can't grasp the state of one who's cooked,
  so this discussion must be brief – farewell!

Notes to Dedication

1. In the *Maqālāt* Shamsoddin says, 'Belong to that which is the root and the goal – the root of all roots and the goal of all goals, not that root that one day will become the branch . . .' (William C. Chittick, *Me and Rumi: The Autobiography of Shams-i Tabriz* (Louisville: Fons Vitae, 2004), p. 265).
2. Quran 24.35: 'God is the Light of the heavens and the earth. The likeness of His light is as a niche wherein is a lamp (the lamp in a glass, the glass as it were a glittering star) . . .'
3. Salsabil is the name of a spring in Paradise mentioned in Quran 76.18. In his mentioning the followers of this 'way' (*sabil*), Rumi alludes to a popular explanation of the name as being the Arabic *sal sabilan* 'seek a way', i.e. to union with God.
4. A paraphrase of Quran 25.24: '. . . on that same Day those who are destined for paradise will be graced with the best of abodes and the fairest place of repose.'
5. A reference to the first of the afflictions visited upon the Egyptians by God in Exodus 7:17ff. Reference is made to these trials in Quran 7.130: 'And most certainly did we overwhelm Pharaoh's people with drought and scarcity of fruits . . .'
6. The quotation is from Quran 2.26.
7. A reference to Quran 10.57: 'There has now come unto you an admonition from your Lord, and a cure for all that may be in men's hearts . . .'
8. A quotation from Quran 80.11–16: 'No indeed; it is a Reminder (and whoso wills, shall remember it) upon pages high-honoured, uplifted, purified, by the hands of scribes noble, pious . . .'
9. Quotation from Quran 56.77–9: '. . . this is a glorious Koran, safeguarded in a book which none may touch except the purified; a revelation from the Lord of the Universe'.
10. Quran 41.42.

11. Quoted from Quran 12.64, where Jacob says to Joseph's brothers, 'Am I to trust you with him [Benjamin] as I once trusted you with his brother [Joseph]? But God is the best of guardians: and of all those that show mercy He is the most merciful' [trans. Dawood with author's interpolations].

Notes to *Spiritual Verses*

The Notes are numbered to refer to specific couplets, following the numbering in the margins of the translation.

In Quranic references, the first number is the sura, or chapter, number; the second is the verse number. References follow N. J. Dawood, *The Koran with Parallel Arabic Text* (London: Penguin, 1990; reprint edn 2000). The translations usually follow Dawood and sometimes, where indicated, A. J. Arberry, *The Koran Interpreted* (Oxford: Oxford University Press, 1964), M. Asad, *The Message of the Qur'an* (Dar al-Andalus: E. J. Brill, 1980), and/or the present author.

The following abbreviations are used in the Notes (for full citations, see Further Reading, pp. xxxvi–xxxviii):

NC = Nicholson's *Commentary* to Bk I (Vol. VII of the *Mathnawi* in the Gibb Memorial Series), with page reference
 N = Nicholson's edition and translation of the *Masnavi*, with line reference
 E = Este'lami's edition of Bk I, with page reference and with quotations translated by the present author
EI = *Encyclopaedia Islamica*

1. –: The initial dash indicates a silence of a short beat (∪) before the word *Listen* to translate the imperative verb with which the poem begins. In this way an iambic rhythm is established without the insertion of a 'filler' word.

13. *Majnun's passionate love*: Majnun ('Madman', a romantic epithet of his proper name, Qays) and Layli (or Leylā 'Night') are the archetypal lovers of Persian literary tradition. Their passion is thwarted by the world, but they remain true to each other; in the Sufi tradition they become synonymous with true, as distinct

from superficial, intellectual or base love. They are celebrated most famously in the eponymous twelfth-century poem by Nezāmi.

25. *mountain . . . dancing*: This refers to the epiphany of God to Moses on Mount Sinai in Quran 7.143: '. . . And when his Lord revealed Himself to the Mountain, He levelled it to dust. Moses fell down senseless . . .' Nicholson comments, 'Mystics cannot experience the ecstasy of the Beatific Vision until the "mountain" of their bodily nature has been demolished, i.e. entirely spiritualized by Divine Love' (*NC*, p. 13). Rumi applies a further mystical reading of this theme in I.871–2, and allusions to the story in 1143, 2800 and 3566.

36. *In former . . . was*: The first story of the *Masnavi* is a complex and intensive illustration of the theme of separation and union, which is taken up in the Song of the Reed and is one of the dominant themes of the whole work. According to the divine physician, the cause of the girl's illness is that she is in love with someone from whom she has become separated. This love, as is intimated by the references to towns, streets and neighbourhoods, is a local, common, worldly love. The lovers are reunited, but then the goldsmith is quickly separated from the girl again by sickness and then death. Rumi does not end the story with the king being reunited with his slave-girl, for he has realized that his true love is for the divine. Rather, the story ends with an explanation of why the king acted as he did. Rumi's version is neither a folk tale nor a romance, though it might have started out life as such. As Margaret Mills has shown in A. Banani, R. Hovannisian and G. Sabagh, *Poetry and Mysticism in Islam: The Heritage of Rumi* (Cambridge: Cambridge University Press, 1994), pp. 145ff., Rumi's version is anti-folkloric and anti-romantic, for he subverts the conventional scenario of both genres. He is at pains to urge his readers to look beyond appearances, and he is aware of the difficulty his audience may have with such an apparently brutal tale of murder and deception. But the 'lovers' were neither innocent nor conceived by the poet in innocence: they are signs and ciphers of the deluded love of appearances that is the cause of separation.

50. *'God willing'*: The Arabic phrase *in shā'llāh'*.

53. *oxymel*: A concoction of vinegar and honey, which normally has the effect of soothing biliousness.

54. *myrobalan*: *Terminalia chebula* and *terminalia citrina* are astringent types of plum used as a laxative and restorative tonic.

60. *you ... now*: Quran 40.60: 'Your Lord has said: "Call on me and I will answer you ... " '

80. *feast ... heaven*: Quran 2.57: 'We caused the clouds to draw their shadow over you and sent down for you manna and quails, saying: "Eat of the good things We have given you." ' See also Quran 7.160 and Exodus 16:4. Rumi returns to this story in 3747ff.

81. *Where's the garlic ... lentils*: Quran 2.61 (in which God addresses the Children of Israel): ' "Moses", you said, "we will no longer put up with this monotonous diet. Call on your Lord to give us some of the varied produce of the earth, green herbs and cucumbers, garlic and lentils and onions." ' This element of the story is not in Exodus.

92. *Azāzil*: The name of the former angel Eblis (Satan) before his fall as related in Quran 38.73ff., where he refuses to prostrate himself to newly created humankind. See V.1922.

99. *If You ... will narrow*: From a saying attributed to Ali.

100. *No, if he does not*: See Quran 96.15: 'No indeed; surely if he gives not over, We shall seize him by the forelock, a lying sinful forelock' (trans. Arberry).

116. *sun alone is proof*: This has been related to the saying of Dhu'l Nun of Egypt: 'I know my Lord through my Lord and if not through my Lord I do not know my Lord'; see Quran 3.18: 'God witnesses that there is no god except Him ... '

118. *moon is cloven*: Quran 54, 'The Moon', begins: 'The hour of Doom is drawing near, and the moon is cleft in two,' which is generally interpreted as a reference to the last hour of the resurrection of the dead and the splitting of the moon. The latter was regarded by some as a portent of the Resurrection and by others (including Rumi) as a miracle performed by Mohammed.

123. *highest heaven*: According to Quran 2.29, God created seven heavens.

125. *shirt of Joseph*: Rumi is referring to Quran 12.93–6, in which Joseph gives his brothers his shirt /gown (Arabic *qamīs*) to take from Egypt to their father. When they lay it upon their father's face, he recovers the sight which he had lost in grief for Joseph. Rumi alludes to the enlightening effect of the perfume of Joseph's shirt as an image of his own contact with his beloved, for even the mention of Shamsoddin's name has a wonderful effect on him.

128–9. *Do not ... is illicit*: These two Arabic couplets paraphrase a hadith. In 128a 'dead' translates the Sufi term *fanā* 'passed away, dead to selfhood'.

167. *sweetest Samarqand*: Rumi puns 'Samarqand' with *qand* 'sugar'. Samarqand was the most ancient city in Central Asia and is now in the Republic of Uzbekistan.

194. *He made . . . evil fate*: As Nicholson comments (*NC*, p. 24), this reflects an Arabic proverb: 'He ran with his own feet to shed his own blood.'

195. *Ezrā'il*: The angel of death, one of the four archangels along with Jibril (Gabriel), Mikhā'il (Michael) and Esrāfil.

197. *candle of Terāz*: Terāz was an ancient city in Turkestan, on the site of Dzhambul in modern Kazakhstan, famed for the beauty of its inhabitants. The candle of Terāz is a metaphor for the slave-girl whose beauty will consume the goldsmith as a candle does a moth.

225. *why it . . . boy's throat*: This reflects Quran 18.66ff., the story of Moses and an unnamed sage and servant of God who is identified in Islamic tradition as Khezr (Arabic Khadir).

228. *Lay down . . . before Him*: Quran 37.102ff.; see Genesis 22.

229. *just like . . . the One*: Here, as often elsewhere, Rumi refers to the Prophet Mohammed by the name Ahmed, 'most praise-worthy'. As Nicholson points out, there is a play on words between the name Ahmad and Ahad 'the One', with a mystical significance in the missing 'm', which 'symbolizes the forty grades of Divine emanation from Universal Reason to Man' (*NC*, p. 26).

237. *If Khezr smashed the boat*: Quran 18.79: 'Know that the ship belonged to some poor fisherman. I damaged it because at their rear there was a king who was taking every ship by force.'

264a. *saintly ones*: This phrase translates Persian *abdāl*, the plural of *badal*, which originally meant 'substitute'. These 'substitutes' are the holy men and women who are believed to maintain the order of the cosmos. Their number is fixed, so that when one dies, the place left vacant is immediately replaced by another 'substitute'. See *EI*, 'Badal'.

264b. *'lion' and 'milk'*: In Persian, 'lion' *sher* is written the same as 'milk' *shir* though they are entirely unrelated words.

267. *They say . . . we're human*: In Quran 14.11 the unbelievers say, 'You are indeed but mortals like ourselves', and in Quran 25.7, 'How is it that this apostle eats and walks about the market squares?'

279. *In Moses' day*: Quran 20.56ff.

289. *inhabit different worlds*: Literally '. . . the two are like a man of Ray and a man of Marv together' i.e. inhabitants of distant cities in the far west and east of Iran.

297. *with Him . . . Book*: Direct quotation from Quran 13.39.

298. *barrier . . . breach*: Quran 55.19–20: 'He has let loose the two oceans: they meet one another. Yet between them stands a barrier which they cannot overrun.'

322. *Bu Mosaylem*: Also known as Musailima, a contemporary and rival of the Prophet Mohammed. He is regarded by Islamic tradition as a falsely honoured prophet whose name became synonymous with 'liar'. See *EI*, 'Musailima'.

325ff. *The Story of the Jewish King*: This can be seen as a commentary on Quran 2.135: 'They say: "Accept the Jewish or the Christian faith and you shall be rightly guided." Say: "By no means! We believe in the faith of Abraham, the upright one. He was no idolater."' Also Quran 19.34–9, esp. 19.37: 'Yet are the sects at odds among themselves'; also 43.65 and 2.253.

365. *girdle*: The *zonnār*, a belt or girdle that Christians were obliged (by an edict of 'Umar, the second caliph) to wear in order to distinguish them from Muslims (see A. S. Tritton, *The Caliphs and their Non-Muslim Subjects: A Critical Study of the Covenant of 'Umar* (London: Oxford University Press, 1930), p. 117). As Nicholson notes, the 'girdle' as applied to the early Christians of this story is an anachronism (*NC*, p. 37).

367. *ghoulish soul*: The *nafs-e ghul*, the self that is like a ghoul, namely a spirit that, in particular, waylays travellers on the road just as the *nafs* robs the seeker on the spiritual path.

372. *how habit . . . herd*: My translation is a quotation from Wordsworth's 'Ecclesiastical Sonnets', pt. II, xxviii, 'Reflections. Grant that by this unsparing hurricane'.

376. *Simorgh*: The miraculous Saēna bird (Avestan *saēna meregha* / Pahlavi *sēn murw*) of Iranian mythology. The Simorgh resembles a giant falcon and, according to ancient Zoroastrian texts, perches on the Tree of All Seeds in the middle of the Sea of Vourukasha, scattering the seeds of that tree over the earth. The Simorgh is famous in later tradition (in the Persian national epic *Shāhnāme* 'Book of Kings') for having reared in its nest the foundling hero Zāl, father of Rostam. In Sufi literature, however, it is the symbol of the highest mystical attainment and is most celebrated in Faridoddin Attār's *Manteqottayr* 'Conference of the Birds' as the goal of the birds' spiritual quest (the Persian *si morgh* also means 'thirty birds').

382. *No prayer is done*: A metrical version of the hadith 'There is no prayer without the presence of the heart.'

394. *they were asleep*: The Arabic phrase is a quotation from Quran 18.18: 'You might have thought them awake, though they were sleeping.' This is itself part of the story of the Men of the Cave (Quran 18.13–26). The Persian phrase 'don't flee from this' also reflects Quran 18.18: 'Had you looked upon them, you would have surely turned your back and fled in terror.'

401. *kindler of the dawn*: Quotes Quran 6.96.

403. *Sleep is death's brother*: This hadith is reminiscent of Quran 39.42: 'God takes away men's souls upon their death, and the souls of the living during their sleep. Those that are doomed he keeps with Him, and restores the others for a time ordained.'

428. *Draws out the shadows*: Quran 25.45–7: 'Do you not see how your Lord lengthens the shadows? Had it been His will He could have made them constant. But We made the sun their guide; little by little We shorten them.'

429. *Say like Khalil*: In Quran 4.124 God takes Abraham as *khalil* 'a beloved friend' (i.e. of God), a name by which he is known in Islamic tradition. Abraham says the subsequent words to his father in Quran 6.76, rejecting the idols of stellar, lunar and solar deities;

431. *God's Radiance*: Alludes to Quran 10.5: 'It is He who made the sun a radiance . . .'

432. *Eblis*: Satan, the fallen angel Azāzil.

437. *Purify my temple*: A quotation from Quran 2.125. In 437b 'charm of earth' refers to the human body, which is like a talisman guarding the light of the divine spark and spiritual essence of humankind. See *NC*, p. 43.

442. *cut off their nose and ears*: Equivalent to the English saying 'to cut off your nose to spite your face'; the Persian means literally 'make themselves noseless and earless'.

443. *beloved's quarter*: In Sufi symbolism, Persian *ku* 'street, alley' often signifies the place where the beloved lives, as in 170.

444. *scents . . . gnosis*: There is (also) a pun in the Persian, as *bini* means both 'nose' and 'seeing', i.e. 'vision', 'understanding'.

447. *Do not . . . prayers*: The literal meaning is: 'Do not make your money from highway robbery like the vizier; do not take the people away from their prayers.'

462. *twelve leaders*: Reminiscent of Jesus' twelve disciples but also of Quran 7.159–60: 'Yet among the people of Moses there are

some who preach the truth and act justly. We divided them into twelve tribes, each a whole community . . .'

477. *grace of Hu*: This line is difficult to translate because Rumi uses a specific Sufi term that is misleadingly simple in meaning. The Arabic third-person singular pronoun *hu* means simply 'he', but Sufis use the word to refer to the One who is beyond all duality of self and other, i.e. the unity of God.

485. *take it gladly*: Quran 92.5–7.

492. *its name is 'difficult'*: An allusion to Quran 92.8–11: 'But as for him who is a miser and is self-sufficient, and cries lies to the reward most fair, We shall surely ease him to the Hardship; his wealth shall not avail him when he perishes' (trans. Arberry).

494. *vision*: The holistic vision of the Sufi, which sees beyond appearances, and which is not inherited but which must be worked for.

521. *For me . . . praise*: Rumi holds the mystical truth (*haqiqe*) over and above the partial truths of mundane experience and commonsense. He brings the higher imperative of *haqiqe* to bear not only upon mundane experience but also upon religious and spiritual ideas. This and the following couplet are prime examples of the mystical subversion of conventional religious norms such as 'To praise God is good.'

532. *Jesus' breath*: In Quran 3.49, God announces to Mary that Jesus will say to the Children of Israel, 'I bring you a sign from your Lord. From clay I will make for you the likeness of a bird. I shall breathe into it and, by God's leave, it shall become a living bird.' See also Quran 3.110.

533. *unlettered*: Illiterate. An allusion to Mohammed, as in Islamic tradition he is believed to have received the Quran as a miracle and not as a composition through any poetic competence of his own.

539. *God . . . Venus*: This alludes to one of several stories associated with two angels, Hārut and Mārut (mentioned briefly in Quran 2.102). Hārut and Mārut had boasted of their superiority to humankind, so God sent them down to earth to see if they would, like human beings, give in to temptation. They tried to seduce a beautiful woman, but she resisted until they taught her the word of power that enabled them to ascend to heaven. She then ascended herself, and God transformed her into the planet Venus, while Hārut and Mārut were imprisoned in a pit at Babylon to expiate their sin. See *NC*, p. 52; *EI*, 'Hārūt and Mārūt'. The pair are mentioned again in 3334ff. below.

551. *He nurtures . . . fire*: This line, as elsewhere in the *Masnavi*, is a

poetic elaboration of the Quranic story, in which it is not stated
that Abraham was thrown into the fire but rather that God saved
him from the fire into which idolators wished to cast him. See
Quran 21.68ff., 29.24, 37.97.

552. *burning up of causes*: As Este'lami notes, '. . . the power of God
burns up all causes and effects and He does all that is His will,
and He makes the human condition so perplexed that he despairs
of attaining to reality and like the Sophists he leaves rational
inquiry and discussion to one side. Certainly Mowlana's becom-
ing a Sophist does not involve his becoming lost: the man on the
path of God entrusts himself to God so that divine favour will
bring him to the stage of knowledge' (E, p. 325).

572. *Return*: According to the Quran, on the Day of Judgement the
wicked shall be chastised, but God will say to the righteous
(89.29), 'O serene soul, return to your Lord, joyful, and pleasing
in His sight. Join my servants and enter My Paradise.'

583. *impose . . . do*: Quran 2.286: 'God does not charge a soul with
more than it can bear.'

603–46. *We're like the reed-flute*: After 602 the disciples' speech
seems to change into Rumi's own discourse, which is addressed
to God, not to the vizier of the story.

619. *You did not smite*: Quran 8.17: 'It was not you, but God, who
slew them. It was not you who smote them: God smote them so
that He might richly reward the faithful.' This refers to the
incident during the battle of Badr, when, it is said, the Prophet
threw a handful of gravel at the enemy Quraysh, who then fled.

621. *almightiness . . . lowliness*: In Quran 59.23 God is called *al-
jabbār* 'Almighty'.

634, 638. *You know His power*: This word, translated as 'fate' in
621, is Arabic/Persian *jabr*, a complex theological term denoting
the 'compulsion' – i.e. the almighty power – of God. Those who
assert the primacy of this attribute of God deny the freedom of
the human will. Rumi often reflects (for instance, in 908–1001)
on the intellectual opposition of those who assert free will to
those who favour divine predestination, and finds a spiritual
resolution to the problem.

709. *calamity for them*: Literally 'for their heads'. The walnuts in the
next verse is a reference to their heads.

711. *pomegranates*: Rumi adds 'and apples', but pomegranates are as
much as the English metre can afford.

721. *mercy to all creatures*: This alludes to Quran 21.107, which
addresses the Prophet Mohammed: 'We have sent you only as a

mercy to all creatures' (author's translation). The phrase refers to the universality of the Quran; the word translated as 'all creatures' is literally 'the worlds'.

726. *heart-strong*: I have translated the Persian *sāheb-del* as the opposite of 'headstrong'; *sāheb-del* is literally 'companion/possessor of the heart', i.e. someone perfected in their spiritual nature.

742. *faithful spirit*: As Nicholson notes, in Quran 26.193 this phrase clearly refers to Jibril/Gabriel, the angel of revelation (*NC*, p. 65).

745. *By heaven of the constellations*: Quotes Quran 85.1. Verses 2ff. state: 'Cursed be the diggers of the trench, who lighted the consuming fire and sat around it to watch the faithful being put to the torture. Nor did they torture them for any reason save that they believed in God . . .' Rumi may have supposed, as is part of Muslim tradition, that this was a reference to the sixth-century persecution of the Christians of Najrā by a Jewish king of Yemen.

751. *We have . . . Book*: Quran 35.32–3: 'Then We bequeathed the Book on those of Our servants We chose; but of them some wrong themselves, some of them are lukewarm, and some are outstrippers in good works by the leave of God; that is the great bounty. Gardens of Eden they shall enter; therein they shall be adorned with bracelets of gold and with pearls, and their apparel there shall be of silk' (trans. Arberry).

761. *these stars . . . stoning*: This alludes to Quran 67.5: 'We have adorned the lowest heaven with lamps, missiles to pelt the devils with.' The allusion is explained by Nicholson: 'The radiant soul of the Perfect Man, acting under the direct influence of Divine grace, consumes infidelity in the same way as shooting stars burn the devils who are pelted with them' (*NC*, p. 66f.).

770. *God's dye*: Quran 2.138: 'We take on God's own dye. And who has a better dye than God's? Him will we worship.'

775. *spawned another idol*: Quran 25.43: 'Have you considered the man who has made a god of his own appetite?'.

783. *hell's seven gates*: As Rumi says unequivocally in I.1384, 'This self is hell and hell is like a dragon / that seas cannot extinguish or decrease.' Sāri, the Turkish commentator, explains that the seven ways to hell are pride, cupidity, lust, envy, anger, avarice and hatred (*NC*, p. 68). In VI.4671 Rumi says, 'Hell is a seven-headed fire-dragon, the bait is your desire and Hell's the snare' (N, VI.4657).

786. *Bu Jahl*: A short form of the name Abu Jahl 'Father of Ignorance'. See 1513.

817. *higher knowledge*: This Arabic phrase is literally 'knowledge from us', and is from Quran 18.65: '. . . and We had taught him knowledge proceeding from Us', i.e. from God Himself. In Sufi tradition it is taken as a term for mystical knowledge.

838. *Lord of Judgement*: A version of the Quranic *māliki yawmi 'd-din* 'Lord of the Day of Judgment', one of the names by which God is addressed in the first sura (Quran 1.4).

851. *What is this cause . . . rope*: The first meaning of *sabab* in Arabic is 'rope', which gives rise to its more general meaning 'cause'. As Rumi explains in the next line, the 'rope' is the apparent not the true 'cause' (as in English 'prime mover') of the turning of the wheel in the well of this world.

857–8. *Ād's people . . . Hud*: Reference to the Quranic story of the prophet Hud, who was sent to the idolatrous people of Ād (Quran 7.65–72; 11.50ff.). God destroyed them by sending them a violent wind (Quran 69.6, 51.41), but Hud and those who shared his faith were delivered 'from a horrifying scourge' (Quran 11.58). The Quran is unequivocal: 'Ād denied their Lord. Gone are Ād, the people of Hud' (Quran 11.60). See also l. 3135.

860. *Shaybān*: The eighth-century ascetic Abu Mohammed Shaybān of Damascus, who is renowned in Sufi tradition as having given up his life in the world as an eminent religious scholar to become a shepherd on Mount Lebanon; see *NC*, p. 72f.

867. *Egyptians*: Refers to Quran 26.60–66: 'At sunrise the Egyptians followed them. And when the two multitudes came within sight of each other, Moses' companions said: "We are surely undone!" "No," Moses replied, "my Lord is with me and He will guide me." We bade Moses strike the sea with his staff, and the sea was cleft asunder, each part as high as a massive mountain. In between We made the others follow. We delivered Moses and all who were with him, and drowned the rest' (also 20.77–8 and 2.50; and compare Exodus 14:15ff.).

868. *Qārun*: He was, according to Quran 28:76, one of Moses' people, but he behaved unjustly and exulted in his riches until he was punished by God as in the verse alluded to by Rumi, Quran 28.81: 'We caused the earth to swallow him, together with his dwelling, so that he found none besides God to protect him; nor was he able to defend himself.' Some have seen in Qārun the rebellious Korah of Numbers 16. Arberry and Dawood, for example, translate the name Qārun as Korah.

881. *abyss of hell*: Direct reference to Quran 101:6–9: 'Then he whose good deeds weigh heavy in the scales shall dwell in bliss; but he

whose deeds are light, his mother is an abyss' (my translation) – i.e. his original nature is the abyss of hell; Rumi's mentioning of the child's mother reminded him of this most portentous Quranic phrase. In the Persian line he puns on the rhyme of the words for abyss (*hāviye*) and refuge (*zāviye*).

886. *The perfumes of our words*: A poetic paraphrase in Arabic of the latter part of Quran 35.10: 'To Him good words go up, and the righteous deed – He uplifts it . . .' (trans. Arberry).

899. *Kalila*: This refers to the source of the story that follows, i.e. the Arabic *Kalilah wa-Dimnah*; see François de Blois, *Burzōy's Voyage to India and the Origin of the Book of Kalīlah wa Dimnah* (London: Royal Asiatic Society, 1990).

908. *Zayd and Bakr*: Two common names – like Tom, Dick and Harry – meaning Everyman.

910. *selfhood hiding in myself*: Reminiscent of the hadith 'Your worst enemy is your *nafs* which is between your sides.'

912. *Let caution go*: An Arabic metrical version of a hadith.

915. *Lord of Daybreak*: As Nicholson notes (*NC*, p. 76), 915a alludes to a saying of Sahl ebn 'Abdollāh al-Tostāri: 'The first stage in *tawakkul* ("trust in God") is that one should be in God's hands like a corpse in the hands of the washer . . ." 915b refers to Quran 113.1: 'I take refuge with the Lord of Daybreak' (trans. Arberry).

916. *Prophet's Sunna*: The Sunna of the Prophet comprises the hadith traditions that relate the deeds and utterances of Mohammed as exemplary for Muslim life.

917. *With trust . . . leg*: A Persian version of the advice of the Prophet, 'Tether your camel then trust [in God]'. Nicholson compares it to Cromwell's 'trust in God and keep your powder dry' (*NC*, p. 77).

918. *worker is beloved of God*: Reminiscent of a hadith: 'God loves the man who is gainfully employed.'

930. *Go down*: This phrase is used twice, in Quran 2.36 and 38, by God as he commands Adam and Eve to leave Paradise.

956. *mountain tops be moved*: In Quran 14.46 it is said of wrong-doers: 'They plot, but their plots are known to God, even if their plots could move mountains.'

960. *One morning there arrived*: This story is represented in the manuscript illustration reproduced on the cover of this volume. Note the presence of many birds at Solomon's court (he is said to have learned the language of the birds) as well as animals from the preceding story.

977. *all things are clever*: An unattributed maxim in Arabic.

981. *ever lost . . . faith*: See Quran 2.143: 'God's aim was not to make your faith fruitless. God is compassionate and merciful to men.'

1013–14. *teaching to the bees*: Quran 16.68: 'Your Lord inspired the bee, saying: "Make your homes in the mountains, in the trees, and in the hives which men shall build for you. Feed on every kind of fruit, and follow the trodden paths of your Lord."'

1016. *knowledge*: See Quran 2.31ff.: 'He taught Adam the names of all things and then set them before the angels, saying: "Tell Me the names of these, if what you say be true." "Glory be to You," they replied, "we have no knowledge except that which You have given us. You alone are all-knowing and wise." Then said He: "Adam, tell them their names." And when Adam had named them, He said: "Did I not tell you that I know the secrets of the heavens and the earth, and know all that you reveal and all that you conceal."'

1017. *in spite . . . in doubt*: Azāzil was the angel in question – see 1018.

1018. *six-hundred-thousand-year ascetic*: This is Eblis – the Devil who tempts humankind, the fallen angel Azāzil – and the 'muzzle' is the logical reasoning by which he sought to demonstrate that he was superior to Adam and, as a result, was cursed by God (Quran 38.76ff.). See Nicholson's deliberations (*NC*, p. 82).

1019. *lofty palace*: Such a palace is referred to in Quran 22.45 as one of many things God has often destroyed in order to punish the wicked.

1026. *Companions' dog*: Reference to the Quranic story of the Men, or Companions, of the Cave.

1053. *every secret shared*: A verse in Arabic attributed to Ali; see *NC*, p. 84.

1074. *Like Gabriel . . . burned*: This refers to Quran 53.6ff. and 13ff., where, at the time of Mohammed's ascension to heaven, the angel of revelation, Gabriel, approaches him.

1081. *Borāq*: This name (related to Arabic *barq* 'lightning') is traditionally used for the wondrous horse on which the Prophet Mohammed is supposed to have ridden from Mecca to Jerusalem, on the Night of the Ascension (*me'rāj*), which is alluded to in Quran 17.1 and 53.1–18. In Sufi tradition 'Borāq' became, as here, a symbol of the power of the divine will. See *EI*, 'Burāk'.

1085. *you will . . . asunder*: I.e. you will doubt that Mohammed performed this miracle; see 118 and *NC*, p. 86f.

1114. *for with the hundredth we have ninety-nine*: I.e. he encompasses all the preceding prophets.

1123. *lost his horse*: This image is taken up again in V.1078–9 (N, ll. 1077–8). See also the story of the stray camel in II.2922ff. (N, l. 2911ff.).

1133. *Sohā*: Name of a minor star, which here stands for all the stars.

1143. *Do not see Him*: Quotation from Quran 6.102: 'No mortal eyes can see Him, though He sees all eyes. He is benign and all-knowing.'

1149. *to Him do we return*: Quotation from Quran 2.156 about those who are patient in adversity.

1169. *hare-brained*: The Persian has 'a hare' – the Persian for 'hare', *khargush*, literally means 'ass-ears'.

1196. *river Nile*: Rumi exercises poetic licence here to substitute the Nile for the Red Sea.

1197. *Nimrod*: In later Islamic tradition Nimrod is cursed as the wicked king who suffered a most painful death when God sent a gnat to torment his brain for four hundred years for the crime of consigning Abraham to a fiery furnace (to no avail as God had made the fire cool for Abraham; see also 1852). It is thought that Quran 21.69 and 37.97 allude to Nimrod, though he is not mentioned by name. In Genesis 10:8–10 Nimrod is mentioned as the son of Cush, who was a mighty hunter and ruler of Assyria.

1199. *Hāmān*: Chief counsellor of Pharaoh, mentioned in Quran 40.36 and elsewhere alongside Pharaoh and Qārun.

1210. *birds . . . respects*: See Quran 27.25ff.

1239. *kāfer*: 'Infidel, unbeliever'.

1249. *dragon*: In Quran 7.107 and 20.20 (as in Exodus 4:3–4), when Moses threw his staff to the ground, it turned into a serpent. However, here the *Masnavi* has *ezhdehā* lit. 'dragon', which Rumi used to rhyme with the word for 'staff', *'asā*.

1250. *Omar . . . eternity*: Omar, the second caliph ('successor') of the Prophet had been, prior to his conversion, a fierce opponent of Mohammed and his religious message. 'Eternity' refers to Omar's destiny (as he was to become one of the most pious Muslims of all time) and translates a highly technical Arabic word, *alast*, meaning literally 'Am I not?'. *alast* is taken from Quran 7.172, where God asks the souls of humankind in pre-eternity, i.e. before Creation: 'Am I not your Lord?'. The human souls acknowledged God as Lord, when they replied: 'Yes, We testify' (trans. Arberry) – and thus agreed to a covenant between God and themselves. Hence, this pre-eternal bond is summed up in the term *alastu* and the term is used to refer to the destiny of humankind beyond this world.

1260. *fruit*: In the Quran the 'tree' of which Adam and Eve were forbidden to eat is not specified, and Muslim tradition has it that what they ate was wheat, not fruit.

1263. *O Lord . . . wrong*: The Arabic paraphrases Quran 7.23, where Adam and Eve together confess: 'Lord, we have wronged our souls. Pardon us and have mercy on us or we shall surely be among the lost.'

1276. *the look 'informative'*: Quran 2.273 says of those who are wholly wrapped up in God's cause that 'you can recognize them by their look', i.e. the sign of their outward appearance is informative of their inner state.

1319. *worse for worse*: Quran 42.40: 'Let evil be rewarded with evil. But he that forgives and seeks reconcilement shall be recompensed by God. He does not love the wrongdoers.'

1322. *When . . . God*: Quran 110.1–3: 'When God's help and victory come, and you see men embrace God's faith in multitudes, give glory to your Lord and seek His pardon. He is ever disposed to mercy.'

1323. *elephant*: Refers to Quran 105, 'The Elephant': 'Have you not considered how God dealt with the Army of the Elephant? Did He not confound their stratagem and send against them flocks of birds which pelted them with clay-stones, so that they became like withered stalks of plants which cattle have devoured?' Asad (*The Message*, p. 976) explains: 'This surah alludes to the Abyssinian campaign against Mecca in . . . 570 . . . Abraham, the Christian viceroy of the Yemen (which at that time was ruled by the Abyssinians), erected a great cathedral at San'ā', hoping thus to divert the annual Arabian pilgrimage from the . . . Ka'bah, to the new church. When this hope remained unfulfilled he determined to destroy the Ka'bah; and so he set out against Mecca at the head of a large army, which included a number of war elephants as well, and thus represented something hitherto unknown and utterly astounding to the Arabs: hence the designation of that year . . . as "the Year of the Elephant". Abraham's army was totally destroyed . . .' This defeat, which must have happened just before the birth of the Prophet Mohammed, is traditionally taken as an auspicious omen. Asad explains that 'flying creatures' (his translation) may have been responsible for the spread of the plague that destroyed the enemy forces.

1353–4. *its shoots*: Alludes to Quran 48.49: 'Mohammed is God's apostle. Those who follow him are ruthless to the unbelievers but merciful to one another. You see them worshipping on their knees, seeking the grace of God and His good will. Their marks are on their faces, the traces of their prostrations. Thus they are ... like the seed which puts forth its shoot and strengthens it, so that it rises stout and firm upon its stem, delighting the sowers...' See the two brief parables of Mark 4:26–9 and 30–32.

1380. *eternal kings ... Sāqi*: The 'kings' are perfect Sufis who have transcended this world; the Sāqi is the cupbearer, God, who pours out everlasting wine to those who renounce this world and its intoxications.

1382. preceding heading. *Commentary ... Jehād*: As Nicholson explains (*NC*, p. 103), 'So the Prophet is reported to have said, on returning from an expedition against the infidels. "The greater *jihād*" is the struggle with the flesh...'

1388–9. *Are you full up*: 1388 translates a question God asks on the Day of Judgement (Quran 50.30): 'On that day We shall ask Hell: "Are you now full?"' Rumi quotes Hell's answer in Arabic in 1389.

1390. *Be and it was*: From beyond the realm of being, God silences Hell with his original declaration of his creation, paraphrasing Quran 16.40: 'When We decree a thing, We need only say: "Be", and it is.' See also 2.117. As Nicholson notes, there are several traditions which say that when Hell asks for more, God will plant His foot on it, and Hell will cry "Enough! Enough". Nicholson refers to a line from VI: 'For this reason, O sincere man, Hell is enfeebled and extinguished by the fire of love' (N, l. 4608; E, p. 4622).

1395. *outer combat*: In this and the following three lines, Rumi returns to the tradition (alluded to in 1382) that the inner struggle against selfishness is more difficult than the struggle against infidels.

1397. *with just a needle*: Alludes to a saying in Persian and Arabic that it is easier (for a human being) to remove mountains with needles than to eradicate self-conceit. Qāf is a mythical mountain that surrounds the world.

1400. *to Omar from the Caesar*: In other words this story purports to be about 'Umar Ibn al-Khattāb (r. 634–44 CE) and the envoy of the Byzantine emperor Flavius Heraclius Augustus (r. 610–41). As Nicholson says, however, '... the episode is almost devoid of incidents, and the whole of it may well have been invented by the poet' (*NC*, p. 104).

1407–8. *There is God's face*: Quoted from Quran 2.115.

1414. *They hide . . . garments*: This refers to Quran 71.6–9, in which Noah reports to God: 'Lord . . . night and day I have pleaded with my people, but my pleas have only aggravated their aversion. Each time I call on them to seek Your pardon, they thrust their fingers into their ears and draw their cloaks over their heads, persisting in sin and bearing themselves with insolent pride . . .'

1435. *jinn*: According to Quran 55.15, God 'created man from potter's clay, and the jinn from smokeless fire' – they are intelligent, imperceptible and salvable creatures to whom the prophet Mohammed was sent as well as to humankind, and who will go both to the garden of Paradise and to the fire of hell; see *EI*, 'Djinn'.

1437. *greeting then the meeting*: This translates the Arabic hadith into Persian.

1438. *Also with you*: It is obligatory for a Muslim to reply thus to the traditional greeting from another Muslim.

1439. *Be not afraid*: Allusion to Quran 41.30: 'As for those who say: "Our Lord is God", and take the straight path to Him, the angels will descend to them, saying: "Have no fear, and do not grieve. Rejoice in the Paradise you have been promised."'

1445, 1448. *Hāl . . . maqām*: Both are Sufi terms. *Hāl* is a 'state' in a succession of psychological states through which the Sufi must progress on the way to God; *maqām* is a higher 'stage' or 'station' of perfection of the adept who is no longer subject to changing conditions.

1475. *headstrong*: The Arabic word *ammāra* 'commanding' (i.e. to evil) is a quotation from Quran 12.53, which refers to the soul that inclines to evil, when Joseph says: 'Not that I claim to be free from sin: man's soul is prone to evil.'

1485. *Salsabil*: Fountain in Paradise whose waters are mentioned in Quran 76.18 as a reward for the righteous: 'They shall be served on silver dishes, and beakers large as goblets; silver goblets which they themselves shall measure; and cups brim-full with ginger flavoured water from a fount called Salsabil.'

1488. *power*: Human power is as nothing compared to divine power: Rumi quotes the Quran in a paraphrase to make sense of a famous trope, already mentioned (see 118).

1490. *preceding heading. You Have Led Me into Sin*: First quotes from Quran 7.23, where Adam and Eve admit to having been seduced by Satan into eating from the forbidden tree: 'They replied: "We have wronged our souls. Pardon us and have mercy on us, or we shall surely be among the lost."' By contrast, in the second quotation, from Quran 7.16 and 15.39, Satan blames God for having been led astray.

1505. *good women . . . good men*: See Quran 24.26.

1513. *Omar . . . Bu'l Hakam*: Refers to Abu 'l-Hakam, the influential Meccan merchant, contemporary and bitter opponent of the Prophet Muhammad, whom Islamic tradition has since referred to as Abu Jahl, 'Father of Ignorance' (Bu Jahl is a shortened form); this inverts his proper name, which is derived from the Arabic root denoting wisdom. He was the uncle of Omar, i.e. 'Umar ibn al-Khattāb, the second caliph of Islam, who had been fiercely opposed to the Prophet's mission until his own conversion.

1519. preceding heading. *And He . . . You Are*: Quotes from Quran 57.4.

1539. preceding heading. *Whoever Wants . . . God*: This unattributed Arabic verse reflects a familiar theme in Sufi literature; see *NC*, p. 111.

1553. *spirit*: As Nicholson notes, here *din* is opposed to *donyā* 'the world' and should be translated as 'the spirit', not 'the religion'. In the next line Rumi puns with *bedin*, meaning 'thus', i.e. again not 'religion'.

1575. *harm . . . strife*: Compare 244. The lover's perverse delight in the cruelty of the beloved is a common theme in Rumi and other Sufi poets, as discussed in the Introduction.

1588. *Here I am*: This quotes from a hadith, 'When the slave says "*Yā Rabb*" ["O Lord"], God says "*Labbayka*" ["I am here]", O my slave! Ask and it will be given unto thee.' Prayer is answered by God as it is spoken by human lips.

1593. *the four streams*: See Quran 47.15: 'Such is the Paradise which the righteous have been promised: therein shall flow rivers of water undefiled, and rivers of milk for ever fresh; rivers of wine delectable to those that drink it, and rivers of clarified honey . . . Are they to be compared to those who shall abide in Hell for ever, and drink scalding water which will tear their bowels?'

1625. preceding heading. *Will . . . Staff*: A Persian translation of a question asked by Pharaoh's magicians in Quran 7.104ff.: 'Moses said: "Pharaoh, I am an apostle from the Lord of the Universe and may tell nothing of God but what is true. I bring you a clear sign from your Lord. Let the Children of Israel depart with me." He answered: "If you have brought a sign, show it to us if what you say be true." Moses threw down his staff, and thereupon it changed to a veritable serpent.' The version in Exodus 7:11–13 is different. See also Quran 20.62–76.

1632. *Listen silently*: See Quran 7.204.

1638. *And enter . . . doors*: This is a metaphorical use of a phrase in Quran 2.189: 'Righteousness does not consist in entering your dwellings from the back. The righteous man is he that fears God. Enter your dwellings by their doors and fear God, so that you may prosper.'

1681. *and does . . . and meat*: A proverb meaning 'so that no harm will be done to either party', which Rumi uses again in a slightly different, perhaps more correct, form in the heading to VI.286: '. . . neither the spit will be burnt nor the meat be left raw' (N, l. 284).

1683. *abrogate a verse*: See Quran 2.106.

1684–7. *they wiped My memory from you*: Quran 23.109 ff.: 'Among my servants there were those who said: "Lord, we believe in You. Forgive us and have mercy on us: You are the best of those that show mercy." But you derided them until they caused you to forget My warning; and you laughed at them. Today I shall reward them for their fortitude, for it is they who have triumphed.' As Nicholson notes, in this passage the 'servants' who are scorned by sinners are the true believers or Companions of the Prophet, but 'Rumi is, of course, speaking of the Sufi saints' (*NC*, p. 117).

1690. *I shall . . . of this*: As often in the *Masnavi*, Rumi holds back from explaining more, here by reference to the spiritual masters of the Sufi tradition who, as perfected beings, are the centre of the universe and guardians of the stability of the cosmos.

1719. *I do . . . in affliction*: See Quran 90.1–4: 'I swear by this city (and you [Mohammed] are a resident of this city) by the begetter [Adam] and all whom he begot: We created Man to try him with afflictions.'

1751. *thirsty may seek water*: Compare III.4401–2 (N, ll. 4398–9).

1769. *except*: The reference is to the Muslim profession of faith, *lā ilāha illa 'llāh* 'There is no god except God.'

1773. *preceding heading. Sa'd*: Sa'd Ibn 'Ubāda was a Companion of the Prophet who is remembered by tradition for having a jealous character.

1775. *certain in his prayerful focus*: I.e. though faith is laudable, once the eye of certainty is opened, the return to mere faith is a retrograde step. Here begins an ecstatic spiritual discourse.

1791. *I am lamenting*: This harks back to the first line of the *Masnavi*: there, *shekāyat* 'lamenting' is used, rhyming with *hekāyat* 'story, telling'. Here Rumi uses the word with another rhyme, *revāyat*, which means 'a telling, an account'.

1797. *Nard*: Backgammon. This line is expressive of the Sufi understanding and transformation of a Quranic verse such as 51.56 – 'I created the *jinn* and mankind only that they might worship Me' – in so far as God is, from the non-dualistic position of the Sufi, both the worshipper and the object of worship.

1799. *O word of Being*: Literally 'the command "Be"' of Quran 16.40; see 1. 1390.

1816. *and God inherits*: See Quran 15.23: 'It is surely We who ordain life and death. We are the Heir of all things.'

1819. *Hallāj's wine*: Hallāj is the Sufi martyr Hosayn ebn Mansur al-Hallāj (c. 860–922 CE), who is celebrated as the epitome of ecstatic self-sacrifice. He was executed, according to Sufi tradition, for having said, 'I am the Truth.' In Sufi poetry, wine generally symbolizes the vision that induces selfless ecstasy, and Hallāj's wine is of the very best vintage. See also 3949–50.

1831. *Each day . . . labour*: See Quran 55.29: 'Whatsoever is in the heavens and the earth implore Him; each day He is upon some labour' (trans. Arberry). This is also quoted at 3084.

1834. *all eyes and ears attending*: See Quran 10.65: 'And do not let their saying grieve thee; the glory belongs altogether to God; He is the All-hearing, the All-knowing' (trans. Arberry).

1853. *the Baptist*: As Nicholson notes (*NC*, p. 127), this refers to a legend that when John the Baptist was fleeing from the Jews, who wished to kill him, a mountain opened up and received him into its interior. III.1018 also mentions the Baptist in a passage that, as here, mentions Abraham and Moses.

1926. *Like Esrāfil*: Esrāfil is the archangel who is the 'kindler of the dawn' of the Resurrection (mentioned in 401), when he will blow the last trumpet.

1928. *hundred-year-old corpses*: See Quran 39.68–9: 'The Trumpet shall be blown, and all who are in the heavens and on earth shall fall down fainting, except those that shall be spared by God. Then the Trumpet will be blown again and they shall rise and gaze around them. The earth will shine with the light of her Lord, and the Book will be laid open . . . none shall be wronged.' See also Quran 36.51.

1934. *If you . . . through*: See Quran 55.33.

1944a. *veiled or unveiled*: Recalls Quran 42.51: 'It is not vouchsafed to any mortal that God should speak to him except by revelation, or from behind a veil, or through a messenger sent and authorized by Him to make known His will. Exalted is He, and wise.'

1944b. *what He gave to Mary*: See Quran 21.91: 'And she who guarded her virginity, so We breathed into her of Our spirit, and appointed her and her son a sign to all beings' (trans. Arberry). See also Quran 66.12.

1948a. *By me you hear and see*: A phrase from a hadith beloved of the Sufis: 'God said: "My servant does not draw near to Me by any means that pleases Me better than performance of the obligatory duties of worship which I have laid upon him; and My servant does not cease to draw near to Me by voluntary works of devotion until I love Him, and when I love him, I am his ear, so that he hears by Me, and his eye, so that he sees by Me, and his tongue, so that he speaks by Me, and his hand, so that he takes by Me."'

1948b. *secret*: Nicholson (*NC*, p. 131) cites two hadiths: 'Man is a secret among secrets' and 'Man is my secret and I am his secret.'

1949. *In fondness . . . for him*: As Nicholson says (*NC*, p. 131), the mystical interpretation of the hadith of which this verse is a quotation is that he who gives himself up entirely to God in *fanā* ('passing away' from the self) is united with Him in *baqā* ('remaining' in God).

1956. *What joy for him*: This is a metricized version of a hadith.

1961. preceding heading. *Indeed . . . Breaths*: Refers in Arabic and in the Persian couplet to part of a hadith. See further *NC*, p. 132.

1967. *Prophet's heavenly tree*: Refers to a tree, called Tubā, which, according to tradition, grows in the Prophet Mohammed's house in Paradise and whose branches reach over all the houses there and produce all the fruit that is required. For Rumi this tree is a symbol of God's unfailing provision for the righteous.

1969. *but they refused to carry it*: See Quran 33.72: 'We offered Our trust to the heavens, to the earth, and to the mountains, but they refused the burden and were afraid to receive it. Man undertook to bear it, but he has proved a sinner and a fool.' The Quranic verse recognizes humankind's valour in undertaking to act as God's vice-gerent at the same time as it reaffirms humankind's innate fallibility.

1972. *Loqmān*: Triggered by the mention of *loqme* '(piece of) food' in 1971b, here Rumi twice puns on the similarity of the name of the legendary pre-Islamic sage Loqmān, sometimes identified with Aesop. Loqmān's name is given to Sura 31 of the Quran and also features in a short story below (3598 ff.). See further *EI*, 'Lukmān'.

1984. *Homayrā*: The Prophet is said to have called his wife, Ā'isha, by the affectionate name Homayrā 'rosy, fair coloured' (a diminutive of *hamrā'* 'red'). By association with the name, Rumi refers to a Persian saying recalling a belief that if one inscribes the name of a person on a horseshoe and casts it into the fire, that person's heart will be inflamed with love.

1997. *Belāl*: A Companion of the Prophet who had once been an Abyssinian slave. His voice was so powerful that he was chosen by the Prophet to be the first muezzin.

2000. *night of halting*: Refers to a story that the victorious Muslims halted for the night after the battle of Khaybar (628 CE) and did not awake until after the dawn prayer.

2002. *halting . . . bride*: As Nicholson explains, there is a subtle meaning hidden in an etymological connection in Arabic between the words for 'halting' (*ta'ris*) and 'bride' (*'arus*) – i.e. here Rumi is alluding to the spiritual marriage of the loving soul with the Beloved, God. Characteristically, Rumi reveals that he has alluded to a spiritual secret in the explanations of the lines that follow.

2008. *unbelief is wisdom*: As W. Björkman notes in the article on Kāfir 'unbeliever' in *EI*, '*kāfir* and *kufr* ("unbelief") underwent a special development of meaning in the terminology of mysticism. Compare, for example, the well-known verse of Abu Sa'id: "So long as belief and unbelief are not perfectly equal, no man can be a true Muslim" with the various explanations given in Muhammad A'lā, *Dict. of Technical Terms . . .* according to one of which *kufr* is just the equivalent of *imān-i haqiqi* '(essentially) true faith.'

2013. *Nard*: Nicholson (*NC*, p. 137) suggests that this reference might be to 'an imaginary and merely nominal addition which is sometimes made to the numbers thrown by the dice' in backgammon.

2015. *salt . . . refined*: There is a pun here that I have all but lost in translation. Rumi uses the Persian word for salt (*namak*) but juxtaposes it with the Arabic word I translate as 'more refined' (*amlah*), from a root meaning both 'to be salty' and 'to be comely, elegant, beautiful'. Behind this line, as Rumi states in the second half of the couplet, is the hadith 'I am more lovely [*amlahu*] than my brother Joseph, though Joseph is more beautiful [*ajmalu*] than I.'

2017–19. *where is the 'front'*: These lines are remarkably close to an important didactic theme in the Middle English mystical treatise *The Cloud of Unknowing*: 'Make sure that you are in no way within yourself; and, to be brief, I do not want you to be outside yourself, or above, or behind, or one side or the other. "Where shall I be, then?" you ask. "Nowhere, by what you tell me!" Now truly, you are right: that is where I would have you, because nowhere in the body is everywhere in the spirit . . .' (A. C. Spearing, trans., *The Cloud of Unknowing* (London: Penguin, 2001), chap. 68, p. 93).

2037. *no eye's really there*: See Quran 7.179: 'We have predestined for Hell numerous jinn and men. They have hearts they cannot comprehend with; they have eyes they cannot see with; and they have ears they cannot hear with. They are like beasts – indeed, they are more misguided. Such are the heedless.'

2038. *Seddiqe*: 'Faithful witness of the truth', an affectionate name given to Ā'isha, the wife of Mohammed and daughter of Abu Bakr, his successor as first caliph. Seddiq, the masculine form of the name, was her father's surname.

2046. preceding heading. *Verse of Hakim*: Quotes two verses said to be from the *Hadiqe al-Haqiqe* of Hakim Sanā'i of Ghazna. The heading interrupts the metaphor Rumi has just started to develop and is evidence of the later interpolation of the headings in the text.

2047. *in doubt as to the new creation*: Quotes Quran 50.15, in which God declares, referring to those who disbelieved God's prophets, 'Were we worn out by the First Creation? Yet they are in doubt about a new creation.' In the Quran this latter phrase refers to the Resurrection, but Rumi is referring to the regeneration of life in the garden of the soul of the spiritual aspirant.

2053. *saints*: Approximately translates *abdāl*; see 264a.

2103. *heavenly flowers*: These are tulips – in Persian (*lāle*) a flower endowed with a mystical mythology that is remote from the common tulip of modern European acquaintance. To take just one aspect of its symbolism, the *lāle* with its long, spiked, overhanging scarlet petals is reminiscent of the blood-stained garments of the martyred holy men and women of Islam.

2107–8. *fount of Job*: Compare Quran 38.41 ff.: '. . . Our servant Job . . . called out to his Lord, saying: "Satan has afflicted me with sorrow and misfortune." We said: "Stamp your feet upon the earth, and a cool spring will gush forth. Wash and refresh yourself." '

2124. preceding heading. *Answers ... the Pillar*: In order to illustrate the point that even apparently inanimate creation is responsive to God, Rumi recalls the traditional story that a pillar of the mosque at Medina, which was formed out of a palm-tree trunk, complained when the Prophet ceased to lean against it, as he had been accustomed to do when he preached. The pillar began to moan like a child being hushed. When at last it became quiet, the Prophet said, 'It was made to cry by the verses of the Quran that it used to hear me reciting' (see N, I.141).

2137. *conjectures*: On conjecture as opposed to truth, Quran 10.36 says of idolators: 'Most of them follow nothing but mere conjecture. But conjecture is in no way a substitute for truth. God is cognizant of all their actions.'

2140. *Pole*: Translates an important Sufi term, *qotb*, 'axis, pivot, chief', which denotes the supreme head of the spiritual élite of *abdāl*, the holy 'substitutes'. See 264.

2151. *He gave the staff to you*: Rumi puns on the Arabic words for 'staff' and 'disobey', which are homophones, with reference to the fall of Adam in Quran 20.121: 'Thus did Adam disobey his Lord and stray from the right path.'

2154. *if this perception ... absurd*: This may be compared with the phrase of the Christian Church Father Tertullian *credibile est quia ineptum* 'It is credible because it is absurd.'

2163–4. *Their ... them*: These lines are reminiscent of the fate of the sons of Adam who followed Satan in Quran 36.66: 'On that Day [of Judgement] We shall seal their mouths. Their hands will speak to us, and their very feet will testify to their misdeeds. Had it been Our will, We could have put out their eyes: yet even then they would have rushed headlong upon their wonted path. For how could they have seen their error.'

2169. *Shahādat*: The Muslim profession of faith, which Rumi puts into verse in the next couplet.

2204. *zirafgand*: Literally 'dejected', one of the twelve modes (*maqām*) of Iranian classical music. Each mode is associated with a particular natural constitution, or humour: as a minor mode, the *zirafgand* is associated with moistness – hence the pathos of the musician's lament that even though he played in this mode, the seed of his heart withered.

2205. *two dozen modes*: Each of the twelve scales can be major or minor; hence the musician speaks of twenty-four modes.

2207. *from Him ... than me*: Quran 50.16: 'We created man. We know the promptings of his soul, and are closer to him than his jugular vein.'

2234. preceding heading. *O God, Give Every Greedy One*: This hadith is reminiscent of Quran 2.264: 'Believers, do not mar your almsgiving with taunts and mischief-making, like those who spend their wealth for the sake of ostentation and believe nether in God nor in the Last Day ...'

2240. *In the Quran*: Quran 8.36: 'The unbelievers expend their riches in debarring others from the path of God. Thus they dissipate their wealth, but they shall rue it, and in the end be overthrown. The unbelievers shall be driven into Hell.'

2245. *Direct us on the righteous path*: See Quran 1.6, 6.161 etc.

2247. *You'll earn your bread*: See Quran 6.160: 'He that does a good deed shall be repaid tenfold; but he that does evil shall be rewarded only with evil.'

2269. *Sāmeri*: Reference to someone called as-Sāmeri ('of the Sāmeri clan', Samaritan?) in Quran 20.85. This person is said to have led the Children of Israel astray by forging a golden calf idol for them. On discovering what Sāmeri had done, Moses declared him to be an outcast (20.97).

2275. preceding heading. *How Novices Are Deceived*: The fact that this heading occurs in the middle of the wife's speech indicates that the headings are a later addition to the composition of the *Masnavi* and not original.

2286. *Bāyazid*: Abu Yazid of Bestām, the early Sufi (d. 874 CE) associated with the 'intoxicated' form of Sufism and renowned for his ecstatic utterances (*shatahāt*), the most famous of which is 'Glory be to Me! How great is My majesty.' Far from being self-glorifications, such statements are understood by Sufis to be the ultimate expression of extinction of the self and absorption in God (see *EI*, 'Al-Bistāmī').

2299. *It's mostly gone*: After the first verse of the speech, Rumi interjects a passage of reflection, and the speech does not begin again until 2316, when he has asked to return to the story.

2315. *Tamar*: Understood by Nicholson as a feminine proper name referring here to the Bedouin's wife (*NC*, pp. 150, 372). Este'lami takes it to be a diminutive of the masculine name Timur, the name of a male scribe to whom Rumi calls to get back to the story (p. 446).

2326. preceding heading. *Why Do You Say What You Do Not?*: Quotes Quran 61.2-3.

2353, 2368. *I'm poor and proud*: According to tradition the Prophet said, 'Poverty is my pride and I boast of it.'

2374. *up in the pear tree*: Being 'up the pear tree' is a metaphor for being in a state of illusion. Rumi includes a story that illustrates the metaphor: an adulterous wife who wishes to embrace her lover in front of her husband resorts to the trick of climbing a pear tree from which she accuses her husband of embracing another man. He accuses her of being confused because she is up a tree. She comes down and sends him up the tree instead. She then embraces her lover and, when the husband protests, replies that the pear tree has turned his head (IV.3545–58 (N, ll. 3544–57)). Nicholson, who translated the bawdier lines of this story into Latin, notes (*NC*, p. 153) that Boccaccio has a similar story in the *Decameron* (Seventh Day, Novel 9).

2379. *You've spoken truly, dear one*: A deep irony is to be found in that the Bedouin's speech includes this brief cameo of a dialogue between Mohammed and his wife, the ideal married couple. At 2382 the Bedouin husband returns to address his own wife.

2405. preceding heading. *The Wife . . . Said*: Nicholson (*NC*, p. 154) thinks this is an allegory of the self-reproaching soul (*an-nafsu 'l-lawwāma*) mentioned in Quran 75.2, which by undergoing ascetic discipline is transformed into the soul at peace with God (*an-nafsu 'l-mutma'innah*) of Quran 89.27.

2436. *To men alluring*: Compare Quran 3.14: 'Alluring unto man is the enjoyment of worldly desires through women and children and heaped up treasures of gold and silver . . .'

2437. *he might . . . in her*: See Quran 7.189.

2438. *Rostam*: The ancient Iranian warrior-king and hero of Ferdowsi's *Shāhnāme* 'The Book of Kings' (early eleventh century). Hamze is Hamzah ibn 'abd al-Muttalib, uncle of the Prophet Mohammed and also renowned as a warrior.

2458. *Both Moses and the Pharaoh*: See Quran 10.90: 'And We brought the Children of Israel over the sea; and Pharaoh and his hosts followed them insolently and impetuously till, when the drowning overtook him, he said, "I believe that there is no god but He in whom the Children of Israel believe; I am of those that surrender"' (trans. Arberry).

2464. *they beat the pans*: An allusion to the traditional practice of beating metal bowls during a lunar eclipse in order that the dragon believed to be covering the moon with its tail or devouring it might be scared away by the noise. A similar practice is recorded as being found among the ancient Romans by writers including Plutarch, Statius, Livy and Tacitus.

2466. *Exalted Lord*: In Quran 79.24 Pharaoh had summoned his people and declared, 'I am your exalted Lord.' The Quran continues: 'God smote him with the scourge of the hereafter, and of this life. Surely in this there is a lesson for the God-fearing.'

2477. *bats of the creative word*: Of the polo-field, here a metaphor of the divine command of God's creative word 'Be', which impels everything into existence.

2478. *colour-free is prisoner of colour*: Colours are metaphors for the multiplicity of the created world as contrasted with the pure, colourless light of the absolute unity of the divine world, just as pure, unrefracted light is the source of colour. In this line the purity of the divine world is said to be imprisoned by the colours of phenomenal existence. But whereas in the scriptural accounts, Moses is in conflict with Pharaoh, Rumi here asserts that the absolute unity underlying existence being what it is, it is more accurate to say that the conflict of phenomena and divine essence resembles a conflict between Moses and himself. As the next line indicates, such conflict is resolved when 'colour' (i.e. the separateness we imagine ourselves to have as discreet 'selves') is relinquished.

2493. *The shoes . . . good man*: Nicholson (*NC*, p. 158) cites a Persian verse of the nineteenth-century poet Qā'āni to explain the origin and the meaning of this image: 'To make them lose track of your horse's hooves, / reverse the horseshoes' order, Turcoman!' (my translation).

2494. preceding heading: *He Loses . . . to Come*: Compare Quran 22.11.

2504. *They have the amber*: I.e. because of its magnetic force, amber is a symbol of divine attraction.

2508. *Say, my servants*: Quran 39.54: 'Say: Servants of God, you that have sinned against your souls, do not despair of God's mercy, for God forgives all sins.' Though the Quranic text (and Rumi's Persian) says 'my servants', some translators avoid the implication that Mohammed is referring to his own servants (e.g. Dawood 'Servants of God', Arberry 'O my people'). As Nicholson remarks (*NC*, p.160), 'Mohammed's mystical union is such that he becomes the mouthpiece of God.'

2521. preceding heading. *so that God . . . Done*: A quotation from Quran 8.44, which passage is said to refer to the battle of Badr.

2521. *As Sāleh's camel*: This story of the prophet Sāleh and his people, the tribe of Thamud, is told in Quran 7.73–9. Sāleh told the people of Thamud to worship God alone and, as a token of their fidelity, to leave a she-camel, belonging to God, alone to pasture on God's earth. But in their arrogance they slaughtered the she-camel and repudiated Sāleh, daring him to bring down punishment on them. They were subsequently destroyed in an earthquake for not following Sāleh's advice. See also Quran 26.141–59. Some strands of the story in this passage of the *Masnavi* are based upon a traditional elaboration of the Quranic account.

2523. *God's female camel drank*: Compare Quran 26.155–8: ' "Here is this she-camel", he [Sāleh] said. "She shall have her share of water as you have yours, each drinking on an appointed day." '

2525. *Let God's she-camel drink*: See Quran 91.13.

2551a. *Gabriel*: Literally 'the faithful Gabriel', as he is called 'the faithful spirit' in Quran 26.193.

2551b. *fallen prostrate*: This Arabic phrase quotes from Quran 7.78, where the people of Thamud are punished.

2570. *How should . . . people?*: Rumi has quoted the Quranic text (7.92–3) in a form modified for metrical purposes. The Quranic prophet Sho'ayb addresses the people of Midian after they have been punished by an earthquake for disobeying the commands of God. As Nicholson says (*NC*, p. 163), the phrase 'don't misread' probably signifies that although the cited passage refers to the prophet Sho'ayb, it can be applied to Sāleh, whose people suffered a similar fate.

2582. preceding heading. *Between Them . . . Breach*: See Quran 55.19f.

2608. *And call it . . . mere words*: See Quran 29.63: 'If you ask them who it is that sends down water from the sky and thus resurrects the earth after its death, they will surely reply: "God." Say "Praise, then be to God!" But most of them are senseless.'

2615. preceding heading. *that God . . . Future Sins*: See Quran 48.2.

2616, 2618. *Lord, give me*: Quran 38.30–35: 'We gave Solomon to David; and he was a good and faithful servant. When, one evening, his prancing steeds were ranged before him, he said: "My love for good things has distracted me from the remembrance of my Lord; for now the sun has vanished behind the veil of darkness. Bring back my chargers!" And with this he fell to hacking their legs and necks. We put Solomon to the proof and placed a body upon his throne, so that he at length repented. He said: "Forgive me, Lord, bestow on me such power as shall belong to none after me. You are the Bountiful Giver." '

2646. *is seeing by God's light*: Paraphrase from a hadith: 'Beware of the keen eye of the believer for indeed he sees by the light of God.'

2657. *love makes blind and* deaf: Refers to a hadith.

2665–7. *I am . . . low*: Paraphrases the following hadith: 'Neither My heaven nor My earth contains Me, but the heart of My servant who believes, who is god-fearing, pure and pious contains Me.'

2668. *Come in among My servants*: See Quran 89.27–30; see also 1. 572.

2671. *Until this moment*: This speech reflects a passage in Quran 2.30–34 in which God announces that he will place Adam on earth as ruler and God's deputy. At first the angels dispute with God: 'Will You put there one that will do evil and shed blood, when we have so long sung Your praises and sanctified Your name.' But when commanded to 'Prostrate yourselves before Adam', they all do so except Azāzil (Eblis, Satan).

2684. *My mercy . . . wrathfulness*: Translates a hadith.

2690. *And by the froth*: The Bedouin husband is addressing his wife.

2706. *Say, Come*: See Quran 6.151, also 3.61.

2721. *God has purchased*: See Quran 9.111.

2726. *Cast . . . worldliness*: Paraphrases Quran 24.30: 'Enjoin believing men to turn their eyes away from temptation and to restrain their carnal desires. This will make their lives purer. God has knowledge of all their actions.'

2730. *beneath which rivers flow*: See Quran 2.25.

2759. *sura of The Forenoon*: 'Forenoon' refers to the name of Sura 93, which contains the words '. . . and as for the beggar, scold him not . . .' (trans. Arberry).

2770. *was not begotten*: See Quran 112. This sura is a definitive Muslim denial of the Christian notion of incarnation.

2790. *Ja'far's gold*: As Nicholson notes (*NC*, p. 173), this is a reference to the Shi'ite Imam Ja'far Al-Sādeq, the reputed author of many works on alchemy.

2799. *in Joseph's face . . . water*: See Quran 12.19: 'And a caravan passed by, who sent their water-bearer to the well. And when he had let down his pail, he cried: "Rejoice! A boy!" ' Thus Joseph, who had been thrown down a well by his brothers, was rescued.

2800. *fire that rescued him from fire*: Refers to the divine fire Moses saw, which rescued him and his people, as in Quran 28.29: 'And when he . . . was journeying with his folk, Moses noticed a fire on the mountain-side. He said to his people: "Stay here, for I can see a fire. Perhaps I can bring you news, or a lighted torch to warm yourselves with." When he came near, a voice called out to him from a bush in a blessed spot on the right side of the valley, saying: "Moses, I am God, Lord of the Universe. Throw down your staff." '

2801. *which took him to the fourth estate of heaven*: Refers to the Muslim belief, alluded to in the Quran (4.158), that Jesus was not crucified, but 'God lifted him up to Himself.'

2813. preceding heading. *They Shall Be Barred*: Quotation from Quran 34.51ff.

2817. preceding heading. *If You Commit Fornication*: Nicholson (*NC*, p. 175) gives a learned reference to the source of this proverb and adds that 'The Arabic adage resembles Luther's *pecca fortiter* ("sin bravely"), but here . . . its moral is "aim high: love none but the spiritually free, i.e. the saints who have sunk their individuality in the Whole." ' II.1432–3 (N, ll. 1428–9) has:

> Go steal the spirit's pearl, you, worthless dog,
> from *in*side, from the inside of the gnostics.
> Since you are stealing, let it be a fine pearl;
> since you are bearing, bear a noble load.

2875. *hidden treasure*: Immediately evocative of the hadith 'I was a hidden treasure and I desired to be known and so I created the creation in order that I might be known.'

2915. *at variance and perverted from it*: Quotes Quran 51.7ff., which chastises the wicked.

2919. *flower's beauty*: I.e. the flowers have a beauty that is expressed in the poetic image of the archetypal rose, just as the turtle-dove's song is like that of the archetypal nightingale's.

2947. preceding heading. *Pir*: The Persian *pir*, like the Arabic *sheykh*, means simply 'old' as in 'senior', and in Sufi terminology always refers to the spiritual authority who acts as guide to the disciple.

2949. *lamp and glass*: These two words suffice to evoke Quran 24.35ff., the Light sura, so often is it alluded to in Sufi literature. I quote Arberry's translation, as he sets it out:

> God is the Light of the heavens and the earth;
> the likeness of His Light is as a niche
> wherein is a lamp
> (the lamp in a glass,

the glass as it were a glittering star)
kindled from a Blessed Tree,
an olive that is neither of the East nor of the West
whose oil well nigh would shine, even if no fire touched it;
Light upon Light;
(God guides to His Light whom He will.)

2955. wine that is of God: An evocation of the words by which God describes divine knowledge in Quran 18.65: 'Then they found one of Our servants unto whom We had given mercy from Us, and We had taught him knowledge proceeding from Us' (trans. Arberry). Rumi substitutes the symbol of wine for knowledge.

2969. Consult them: In the hadith from which this is a quotation, 'them' refers to women, but as we see in the next line, Rumi is referring to the carnal nature of the human *nafs*.

2970. they will divert you: A quotation from Quran 38.26, in which God warns David: '. . . behold, We have appointed thee a viceroy in the earth; therefore judge between men justly, and follow not caprice, lest it lead thee astray from the way of God. Surely those who go astray from the way of God – there awaits them a terrible chastisement, for that they have forgotten the Day of Reckoning' (trans. Arberry).

2972. preceding heading. *When Everyone . . . Draw Close*: As Nicholson explains (*NC*, p. 181f.), this heading paraphrases a hadith related by Ali, cousin and son-in-law of Mohammed, in which the latter counsels Ali to draw near to God by means of qualities of the intellect – i.e. wisdom – rather than by piety alone.

2983. This is the parting: Paraphrases Quran 18.78, where the (unnamed) Khezr announces, 'Now has the time arrived when we must part.'

2985. God's hand is above their hands: As Nicholson notes (*NC*, p. 182), this refers to the oath of allegiance received by the Prophet from his followers at Hudaybiya; see Quran 48.10.

3019. inclining . . . towards the right: Partial quotation from Quran 18.17, in which it is said that God protected the Companions of the Cave: 'And thou mightest have seen the sun, when it rose, inclining from their Cave towards the right, and, when it set, passing them by on the left, while they were in a broad fissure of the Cave. This was one of God's signs . . .' (trans. Arberry). God is said to have protected the Sleepers from the glare of the rising and setting sun by facing the cave's opening of the cave to the north. The cave is taken as a metaphor of Paradise, which is thought of as a place of shade – a concept perhaps more attractive to those who live perpetually in strong sunshine than to inhabitants of colder climes.

3030. *community's a mercy*: Quotation from a hadith: 'Community is a mercy, disunity is a punishment'. Here the meaning is 'It is good to have company.'

3032. *Counsel them*: In Quran 3.159, the Prophet is advised that he should consult his followers: 'It was thanks to God's mercy that you dealt so leniently with them. Had you been cruel or hard hearted, they would have surely deserted you. Therefore pardon them and implore God to forgive them. Take counsel with them in the conduct of affairs; and when you are resolved, put your trust in God.'

3050. *And those who harbour evil thoughts*: Quotes Quran 48.6.

3065–8. *All things are perishing*: Quotes Quran 28.88. The significance of Rumi's next three lines is that all who die to themselves and submit to God participate in real being and are not in fact annihilated, but those who cling to selfhood are refused eternal life.

3070. *there's no room for the raw*: This is reminiscent of 18.

3078. *needle's eye*: Quran 7.40: 'Those that cry lies to Our signs and wax proud against them – the gates of heaven shall not be opened to them, nor shall they enter Paradise until the camel passes through the eye of the needle' (trans. Arberry); compare Matthew 19:24, Mark 10:25 and Luke 18:25.

3080. *Be and it was*: Quotes Quran 2.117, 16.40. In the Quran the tense is present, but Rumi has emended this for metrical purposes.

3082. *The Dear Lord's word*: Refers to the Prophet Jesus. Quran 3.51 states: 'He will say: "... By God's leave I shall heal the blind man and the leper, and raise the dead to life."'

3084. *Each day He ... labour*: See 1831.

3091. *The 'B' and 'E'*: This line poses a problem for a translator. I have tried to solve it with a pun, since the double-letter word *Be* sounds like the letter 'B'. Rumi is referring to the Arabic letters *Kef* (k) and *Nun* (n); together they form the word '*Be!*', which God is said to utter in order to create (see 1390, 1831, 2477, 3080). Nicholson's explanation of the next lines is worth quoting: 'Although the Creative word *KuN* consists of two letters, yet essentially it is one, and its effect, i.e. its bringing the whole contingent universe into being, is single; it may be compared to a noose which, though double in form, has but one meaning and object, namely, to draw the world, hidden in the knowledge of God, from potential into actual existence . . .' (*NC*, p. 187).

3105. *that place*: Here translates *maqām*: compare 1445.

3116. *So we took vengeance on them*: A phrase that occurs several times in the Quran: see 7.136 (of the Egyptians), 15.79 (of the Midianites) and 43.25 (generally of those who reject God's prophets).

3133. *people who've . . . shown them*: I.e. Muslims, according to a hadith (cited in *NC*, p. 188) and following the logic that true Muslims are said to be those who have heeded the warnings given them in the Quran, unlike those of whom the Quran speaks as having denied God's prophets.

3135. *fates of Ād and Pharaoh*: See 857–8 and 2466.

3169. *reverence of their hearts*: Quotes Quran 22.31–2.

3170. *the sincere one*: 'Sincere, true one' is the epithet of Joseph in Quran 12.41.

3177. *seed-pearl*: In the traditional medicine of Iran, seed-pearls were pounded, mixed with powdered antimony (collyrium) and put into the eye. This was thought to have the effect of strengthening the eyesight, and so it was called 'precious antimony'.

3186. *Alone and you have come to Us*: Quran 6.93–4 describes the wretched state of sinners on the Day of Judgement: '. . . Could you but see the wrongdoers when death overwhelms them! With hands outstretched, the angels will say: "Yield up your souls. You shall be rewarded with the scourge of shame this day, for you have said of God what is untrue and scorned His revelations. And now you have returned to Us, alone as We created you at first, leaving behind all that We bestowed on you."'

3192. *those who asked forgiveness*: An Arabic paraphrase of Quran 51.15–18: 'Surely the god-fearing shall be among gardens and fountains taking whatsoever their Lord has given them; they were good-doers before that. Little of the night would they slumber, and in the mornings they would ask for forgiveness' (trans. Arberry).

3195. *God's earth is vast*: Quotes Quran 39.10.

3200–3202. *The Friends . . . the Cave . . .*: An allegorical interpretation of Quran 18.18, where God says: 'You might have thought them awake, though they were sleeping. We turned them about to right and left, while their dog lay at the cave's entrance with legs outstretched.' See also 3019.

3207. *Arabian Sea*: Literally 'Oman', for the Gulf of Oman, actually the north-western part of the Arabian Sea.

3208. *caraway to Kermān*: This is a Persian proverb. Persian *zire* is 'cumin' (green or white *zire*); *zire-ye kermāni* is 'caraway' from the central south-eastern province and city of Kermān – hence this is like 'taking coals to Newcastle'.

3229. *I am better*: Quotes Quran 7.12.

3241. preceding heading. *Scribe of Revelation*: Identified as 'Abdullah ibn Sa'd ibn Abi Sarh, a foster-brother of (the future caliph) 'Uthmān (mentioned in the Persian pronunciation as Osmān in 3241). The story here, which runs to 3252, reflects the tradition that this scribe apostatized and was executed when Mohammed entered Mecca in triumph. Other accounts have it that Osmān procured his pardon. See *NC*, pp. 192–3.

3243. *and he . . . in himself*: The story has in mind the theme of Quran 6.93: 'Who is more wicked than the man who invents a falsehood about God, or says: "This was revealed to me," when nothing was revealed to him? Or the man who says: "I can reveal the like of what God has revealed." ' See also Quran 10.15–17.

3255–6. *chains . . . are raised*: Compare Quran 36.8–9: 'Surely We have put on their necks chains up to the chin, so their heads are raised; and We have put before them a barrier and behind them a barrier; and We have covered them, so they do not see' (trans. Arberry). These are the heedless who persist in disbelief despite warnings from God's prophets.

3257. *Fate*: I.e. divinely intended fate, as announced in Quran 36.8–9.

3271. *from the Faith*: Literally 'from the community (of faith)', reminiscent of Quran 10.20: 'There was a time when mankind were but one community. Then they disagreed among themselves: and but for a Word from your Lord, long since decreed, their differences would have been firmly resolved.' Commentators explain that this passage implies it was God's decree ('Word') that men should differ in their intellectual approach to the problems touched upon by the divine revelation; see Asad, *The Message*, p. 292, n. 29.

3289–90. *on Judgement Day*: Quotes Quran 99.1–5.

3311. preceding heading. *Bal'am*: A false prophet in Muslim tradition, identified with the unnamed figure referred to in Quran 7.175–6: 'Tell them of the man to whom We vouchsafed Our signs and who turned away from them: how Satan pursued him and he was led astray. Had it been Our will, We would have exalted him through Our signs: but he clung to this earthly life and succumbed to his desires. He was like the dog which pants if you chase it away but pants still if you leave it alone. Such are those who deny Our revelations.' Compare the story of the soothsayer Balaam, son of Beor, in Numbers 22–4; see also *NC*, p. 195.

3317. *dragged by the forelock*: See Quran 55.41 and 96.9–15.

3321. *These signs . . . rational self*: As Rumi warns in 3318, humankind is beloved of God but must not stray like the people of Ād (see 857–8) and Thamud (see 2521), who rejected their prophets Hud and Sāleh, more beloved of God (see 3319). The 'signs' of the present verse are such warnings from God. Rumi goes on to explain that humankind's 'rational soul' (*nafs-e nāteqe*, lit. 'articulate, speaking self') must itself be sacrificed for the sake of reason (Persian *hush* in 3322b). Reason is part of the Universal Mind of Reason (3323) and is therefore divine. Nicholson thought that the *nafs-e nāteqe* referred to the soul of the prophet or saint who is the organ of Universal Reason (*NC*, p. 196), but in the larger context of this passage, this does not seem likely.

3327. *frightened asses fleeing*: Quran 74.48–51 says of sinners on the Day of Judgement, 'No intercessor's plea shall save them. Why do they turn away from this reminder, like frightened asses fleeing from a lion?'

3334. preceding heading. *Hārut and Mārut*: Two fallen angels who suffer eternal punishment for their transgression: see 539.

3348. *it makes the 'j' or 'h' or 'd'*: The first half of the couplet spells out the word *jehād* 'struggle', which is completed by its synonym *jodāl* in the second half.

3352. *Religion's leader . . . the Worlds*: It would seem that the Sheikh of Faith is Shamsoddin of Tabriz himself. In the *Maqālāt* (see Introduction), Shamsoddin is reported to have said 'Meaning is God' in reply to one Shaykh Muhammad, who may in fact have been Ibn al-Arabi (see William C. Chittick, *Me and Rumi* (Louisville: Fons Vitae, 2004), p. 73, n. 319). Nicholson, following early commentators, thinks this line probably refers to Sadroddin of Konya, a contemporary and intimate friend of Rumi who had been a celebrated pupil of Ibn al-Arabi (*NC*, p. 197). The epithet 'the sea of meanings of the Lord of Worlds' is an allusion to a phrase in the first, 'opening' (*Fātiha*) sura of the Quran.

3393. *To curb your anger*: A reference to Quran 3.133–4: 'Vie with each other to earn the forgiveness of your Lord and a Paradise as vast as the heavens and the earth, prepared for the righteous:

those who give alms alike in prosperity and in adversity; who curb their anger and forgive their fellow men . . .'

3403. *Beware . . . ignited*: Nicholson thinks this Arabic verse is reminiscent of a hadith that is quoted in an Arabic version in 382: '*No prayer is done without the heart's attention*' (see *NC*, p. 199).

3405. *Guide us*: This phrase occurs in the *Fātiha*, which is repeated in every section of the ritual prayer.

3406. *with prayers . . . stray*: This phrase is from the last verse of the *Fātiha*.

3413. *There shall be "no relations"*: Recalls Quran 23.101: 'And when the Trumpet is sounded, on that day their ties of kindred shall be broken, nor shall they ask help of one another.'

3416. *Bu Jahl*: Abu Jahl ('Father of Ignorance') was an enemy of the Prophet. His son 'Ikrimah was condemned to death by the Prophet but escaped to Yemen. He was subsequently pardoned by the Prophet. An unnamed son of Noah, by contrast, would not board the Ark with his father, sought refuge in the mountains to escape the flood and was drowned (Quran 11.42–3). In III.1309ff. (N, ll. 1308ff.), Rumi tells a story of this son of Noah, naming him Kan'ān in accordance with exegetical tradition.

3424. *speech of birds*: See Quran 27.16: 'And Solomon was David's heir, and he said, "Men, we have been taught the speech of the birds, and we have been given of everything; surely this is indeed the manifest bounty"' (trans. Arberry). Thereafter, as in the title of Attar's mystical poem 'The Speech of the Birds', the phrase was used for the language of divine inspiration. So 'God's bird' (3421) refers to a person inspired by God.

3429. *we're ranged*: Quotes Quran 37.165, in which God's true servants declare, 'We each have our appointed place. We are ranged in adoration and give glory to Him.'

3445. *This world's a play and a diversion*: Translates Quran 57.20. See also 29.64.

3451. *Doldol*: Name of a white mule ridden by the Prophet and/or Ali. On Borāq, see 1081.

3454. *The spirit will ascend*: An Arabic verse inspired by Quran 70.3–7: 'He is the Lord of the Ladders, by which the angels and the Spirit will ascend to Him in one day, a day whose space is fifty thousand years. Therefore conduct yourself with becoming patience. They think the Day of Judgement is far off: but We see it near at hand.'

3456. *surmise does not avail*: Quotes Quran 10.36. See also 53.28.

3457. *You may prefer . . . shining*: Nicholson explains this Arabic verse as follows: '. . . to mystics the vanity of the world and all exoteric knowledge is clear as noonday. The same words are used in hadith to express the same idea in reference to vision of God at the Resurrection' (*NC*, p. 201).

3462. *like the ass*: Compare Quran 62.5: 'The likeness of those who have been loaded with the Torah, then they have not carried it, is as the likeness of an ass carrying books (trans. Arberry).

3479. *a Kurd by night . . . morning*: Alludes to an Arabic verse that Rumi quotes in his dedication: 'In the evening I was a Kurd and in the morning an Arab.' He attributes the verse to an ancestor of Hosāmoddin, but though it is associated with a number of poets, this attribution is otherwise unattested.

3500. *from the heart's mirror on Moses' breast*: The text of Este'lami's edition differs slightly from Nicholson's in this densely packed line. The word translated 'breast' occurs only in Quran 27.7ff. and 28.32 among the five scriptural passages to which the line alludes. The relevant passage of 27.7ff. is: 'Tell of Moses, who said to his people: "I can descry a fire. I will go and bring you news and a lighted torch to warm yourselves with." And when he came near, a voice called out to him: "Blessed be He who is in the fire and all around it! . . . Moses, I am God, the Mighty, the Wise One. Throw your staff." And when he saw it slithering like a serpent, he turned and fled, without a backward glance. "Moses, do not be alarmed," said He. "My apostles are never afraid in My presence. As for those who sin and then do good after evil, I am forgiving and merciful to them. Thrust your hand into your bosom and it will come out white although unharmed. This is but one of the nine signs for Pharaoh and his people; surely they are wicked men." But when Our visible signs were shown to them, they said: "This is plain sorcery"' (trans. Arberry). Thus Rumi's allusion is to the hand illuminated by the light of God in Moses' breast.

3507. *certainty*: The Arabic phrase '*ayn al-yaqin* is literally 'the eye of certainty', as in Quran 102.7. As Nicholson notes (*NC*, p. 204), this phrase is used by Sufis as a technical term denoting the second of a triad of ascending states of spiritual experience: the knowledge of certainty, the eye of certainty and the truth of certainty.

3513. *Sure Abode*: See Quran 54.55 (Arberry's translation).

3514. *Zayd*: Zayd Ibn Hāritha, a freed slave and adopted son of the Prophet Mohammed, mentioned in Quran 33.37. Nicholson (*NC*, pp. 204–5) translates the hadith that was the basis of

Rumi's narrative (I have modernized): 'One morning the Prophet said to Zayd: "How are you this morning, Zayd?" He answered, "O Prophet of God, this morning I am a true believer." The Prophet said, "Indeed, everything has an essence: what is the essence of your faith?" Zayd answered, "I have separated myself from the world: I have passed my days in thirst and my nights in wakefulness, and I seem to see the Throne of my Lord before my eyes and the people of Paradise enjoying their pleasures and delights, and the people of Hell-fire howling at one another like dogs (*or* 'being tormented')." The Prophet said, "You have attained (to real faith): hold it fast."'

3525. *the day ... white*: This quotation from Quran 3.106 (with changes for metrical purposes) is about the assembly of all humankind on the Day of Judgement: 'Be not as those who scattered and fell into variance after the clear signs came to them; those there awaits a mighty chastisement, the day when some faces are blackened, and some faces whitened' (trans. Arberry).

3526. *womb*: A metaphor for the human body, which contains and fosters the soul during life in the world.

3527a. *The damned*: This quotes from a hadith: 'The blessed is he who is blessed in his mother's womb, and the damned is he who is damned in his mother's womb.'

3527b. *their state ... body*: Refers to Quran 55.41: 'The sinners shall be known by their mark, and they shall be seized by their forelocks and their feet' (trans. Arberry).

3536. *the fairest stature*: Quotes Quran 95.4–6.

3538. *their faces ... white*: a repetition of 3525b. By now it will seem that Rumi was following a traditional medieval stereotype of white and black races, but, as we know from everything else in his writings, he always looked beyond surface appearances, and these words too are mixed with irony.

3546a. *Companions of the left*: Quran 56.41 uses this phrase to refer to sinners, while the righteous are 'companions of the right'. This metaphor originates in the opening to this sura: 'When that which is coming comes ... some shall be abased and others exalted. When the earth shakes and quivers, and the mountains crumble away and scatter abroad into fine dust, you shall be divided into three multitudes: those on the right (blessed shall be those on the right); those on the left (damned shall be those on the left); and those to the fore (foremost shall be those).'

3546b. *deceitful*: The Persian word *āl*, which I have translated 'deceitful', means 'stain, dye, treachery, deceit' etc. It is also an Arabic word meaning 'people, family'. Hence Nicholson first translated the line as 'I will show forth the colour of infidelity and the colour of the (Prophet's) folk' but later revised his interpretation to 'the colour of deceit' (*NC*, p. 206).

3547. *seven holes of their deception*: Nicholson identifies these with the seven vices of the carnal soul: pride, lust greed, envy, anger, avarice and malice (*NC*, p. 206). Quran 15.44 refers to Hell's seven gates.

3558. *God is not ashamed*: Quotes Quran 33.53.

3566. *made your heart a Sinai*: I.e. 'You are too excited and vulnerable.' Rumi puns on *sinā* 'Sinai' and *sine* 'heart, bosom'; see 25–6.

3568. *underhand and underarm*: Rumi puns *daghal* 'deceitful, villainous' with *baghal* 'armpit' – a difficult pun to match in English.

3572. *ocean subject to mankind*: Alludes to Quran 16.14: 'It is He who has subdued the ocean, so that you may eat of its fresh fish and bring up from its depths ornaments to wear.'

3573. *Salsabil and Zanjabil*: Two of the four rivers that flow in Paradise. Salsabil is mentioned in Quran 76.15; see also l. 1593.

3598. preceding heading. *How Servants and Staff*: The story announced in this heading is intended to explain the previous line. On Loqmān see 1972.

3613. *day ... examined*: A slight elaboration on a phrase in Quran 86.5–9.

3614. *Drink scalding water*: Quotation from Quran 47.15 (3614b is an elaboration on the same): 'Such is the Paradise which the righteous have been promised: therein shall flow rivers of water undefiled, and rivers of milk for ever fresh; rivers of wine delectable to those that drink it, and rivers of clarified honey. There shall they eat of every fruit, and receive forgiveness from their Lord. Are they to be compared to those who shall abide in Hell for ever, and drink scalding water which shall tear their bowels.'

3615. *fire is for assaying stones*: The hearts of sinners are said in Quran 2.73–4 to be harder than stones: '... God brings to life the dead, and He shows you His signs, that you may have understanding. Then your hearts become hardened thereafter and are like stones, or yet even harder; for there are stones from which rivers come gushing, and others split, so that water issues from them, and others crash down in the fear of God' (trans. Arberry).

3616. *So often have we*: God's prophets in the Quran.

3621. *bow down and come towards Him*: The last line of Quran

96, which enjoins the believer to ignore those who would deny religion and to approach God.

3629. *God wishes*: If sinners were deprived of hope, as would happen if Zayd were able to declare the reality of the unseen world, then faith in God would disappear.

3632–8. *Thought struck . . . at once*: These lines are an example of Rumi's use of a story that is so well known that he does not have to tell it but instead can merely allude to it, in order to illuminate the meaning of 3631: the truth is present, even though it may be hidden to us temporarily. In the traditional story, an evil spirit steals Solomon's ring so that he loses his throne for forty days and has to become a fisherman to survive. He catches a fish, cuts it open and finds his ring inside. Solomon then recovers his kingdom (see *NC*, p. 209).

3641. *If shining . . . growth*: The rain of heaven (a symbol of divine mercy) is set in parallel to the earthly verdant growth of life in response to that mercy.

3642. *they trust the unseen*: Quoted from Quran 2.2–3: 'This is the Book, wherein is no doubt, a guidance to the god-fearing who believe in the Unseen, and perform the prayer, and expend of that We have provided them' (trans. Arberry).

3643. *Can you see cracks in it*: Quotes Quran 67.3.

3658a. *sun's face*: This is reminiscent of 116ff.

3658b. *What is the greatest testimony? – God*: Quotes Quran 6.19.

3660. *God and the angels*: A metrical Arabic paraphrase of Quran 3.18: 'God bears witness that there is no god but Him, and so do the angels and the sages.'

3666. *By rank each angel*: Paraphrase of Quran 35.1: 'Praise belongs to God, Originator of the heavens and earth, who appointed the angels to be messengers having wings two, three and four, increasing creation as He wills' (trans. Arberry).

3670a. *My followers are stars*: An allusion to the hadith 'My companions are like the stars: whichever of them you follow, you will be led in the right way.'

3670b. *a lamp . . . stoning*: A reference to Quran 67.5: 'And We adorned the lower heaven with lamps, and made them things to stone Satans . . .' (trans. Arberry).

3673. *but it is revealed*: God says to Mohammed in Quran 18.110, 'Say: "I am but a mortal like yourselves. It is revealed to me that your God is one God. Let him that hopes to meet his Lord do what is right and worship none besides his Lord."' See also 41.6.

3679. *Merciful sits on the throne*: See Quran 20.5. This line echoes the hadith 'The heart of the believer is the Throne of God.'

3686. *be arraigned before us*: See Quran 36.32: 'What, have they not seen how many generations We have destroyed before them, and that it is not unto them that they return? They shall every one of them be arraigned before us' (trans. Arberry).

3689. *You have revived us*: Quotes Quran 40.11.

3694. *He ... forelock*: A metaphor of God's governance and alludes to Quran 11.56: 'Truly I put my trust in God, my Lord and your Lord; there is no creature that crawls, but He takes it by the forelock ...' (trans. Arberry).

3696–7. *To work ... back*: These lines allude to Quran 34:12–13, where Solomon is allowed by God to set the *jinn* (demons) to work for him: 'We made the Fount of Molten Brass to flow for him. And of the *jinn* some worked before him ... fashioning ... whatsoever he would: shrines and statues, basins like water-troughs and anchored cooking-pots' (trans. Arberry).

3721. *fire*: This story seems to have been stimulated by Rumi's mention of fire in every one of the thirteen previous lines.

3735. *Learn purity ... fault*: Here begins a story that is only finished at the very end of this book, at 4003. The word Rumi uses for Ali's opponent is the Iranian *pahlavān* 'champion, brave warrior, hero' (3736, 3990). He is also called an 'unbeliever' (*kāfer*) and 'new Muslim convert' (3787) and turns out to have been a Zoroastrian – see 3995. Nicholson relates a summary of the traditional story of Ali and the warrior thus: 'Ali, having overthrown a man in combat, sat down on his breast in order to behead him. The man spat in his face. Ali immediately rose and left him. On being asked why he had spared the life of his enemy, he replied, "When he spat in my face I was angered by him, and I feared that if I killed him my anger would have some part in killing him. I did not wish to kill him save for God's sake alone"' (*NC*, p. 213).

3752. *asked for leeks and ... herbs*: See l. 81 and Quran 2.61.

3754. *He gives me food and drink*: This alludes to a hadith which relates that when the Prophet Mohammed was asked why he forbade his followers to fast without interruption as he did himself, he said, 'I am not as you are: my Lord gives me food and drink' (*NC*, p. 214). As the following lines indicate, Rumi advises against the over-intellectualized interpretation of such a story.

3758. *Interpret your own self*: Compare 1088b, which is almost identical to 3758a.

3766–70. *One man ... thousand*: This passage seems to be a reflection on inner vision and the power of insight into mystical truths, not part of the warrior's speech (but Nicholson is unsure and regards the passage as perplexing; see *NC*, p. 215).

3769. *To you ... Joseph*: Refers to Quran 12, the story of Joseph, where his brothers lie to their father that he has been taken by a wolf (a wild beast in Genesis 37:33), when in fact they have thrown him down a well.

3777. *Since you're ... city*: Paraphrases in Persian from a hadith that states that the Prophet said, 'I am the city of knowledge, and Ali is the gate.'

3779. *none can be compared to Him*: Paraphrases Quran 112.4: '... and equal to Him is not any one' (trans. Arberry).

3804. *when you threw you threw not*: See Quran 8.17 and l. 619.

3818–19. *he loves ... he hates for God's sake*: These lines quote a hadith.

3839. *We sent you as a witness*: Quotes Quran 33.45.

3852. *He is now transforming*: Alludes to Quran 25.63ff.

3859. preceding heading. *The Prophet ... by Your Hand*: The interruption of Ali's speech strongly suggests that the heading is a later addition.

3874. *any verse ... better one*: Compare Quran 2.106 and see l. 1683.

3876–7. *night ... daytime*: This evokes Quran 17.12: 'We have appointed the night and the day as two signs; then We have blotted out the sign of the night and made the sign of the day to see ...' (trans. Arberry).

3878. *Though slumber ... in darkness*: This evokes Quran 25.47: 'It is He who appointed the night for you to be a garment and sleep for a rest, and day He appointed for a rising' (trans. Arberry); see also 78.10.

3887. *being sustained and their exulting*: Paraphrases Quran 3.69–70: '... well-provided for by their Lord ... rejoicing in God's grace and bounty'.

3888–91. *throat of beasts ... Yes*: Refers to the idea of the evolution of life through death and rebirth in the next life, most articulately stated in a famous passage in IV.3638ff. (N, l. 3637); see also *NC*, pp. 220–21.

3891. *free from 'No' and dead in 'Yes'*: Alludes to Quran 7.172; see also l. 1250.

3903. *in retribution*: I have used this translation for metrical reasons where most translators have 'retaliation' in Quran 2.178: 'In retaliation there is life for you, men possessed of minds; haply you will be god-fearing' (trans. Arberry).

3915. *Let not . . . be lost*: Paraphrases Quran 3.8: 'Lord, do not cause our hearts to go astray after You have guided us. Grant us mercy through Your own grace; You are the munificent Giver.'

3933. *Save me . . . Ahrimans*: Nicholson (*NC*, p. 222) relates a hadith that on the Day of Judgement, when the followers of every prophet will beseech him to intercede for them, Mohammed will turn to God and cry *'ummati ummat'* ('Save my people, save my people!'); all other prophets will cry *'nafsi, nafsi'* ('save me myself, save me myself'). Ahriman is the 'Hostile Spirit', the Devil, of the Zoroastrian religion.

3938. *All things . . . vanity*: Quotation from an Arabic poem by the pre-Islamic poet Labid ibn Rabi'ah.

3945–7. *don't die . . . hand*: Paraphrases Quran 2.195: 'And expend in the way of God and cast not yourselves by your own hands into destruction, but be good-doers; God loves the good-doers' (trans. Arberry). Rumi goes on to say that though there are some, like Ali, who see death as sweet and are cautioned by the Quranic verse, for most the prospect of death is bitter enough, and no warning is necessary.

3948. *nay, they're alive*: This alludes to Quran 2.154: 'Do not say that those slain in the cause of God are dead. They are alive, but you are not aware of them.'

3949–50. *Kill me . . . homeland*: Rumi writes two lines of homage in Arabic to one of the greatest martyrs of the Sufi tradition, Hallāj, by imitating the opening lines of one of his most famous odes: 'Kill me, my trustworthy friends, for indeed in my perishing is my life, and my dying is in my living and my living in my dying.' Rumi provides his own link line in Arabic in l. 3951 before quoting Quran 2.156: 'We belong to God, and to Him we shall return.' With the mention of 'severance', Rumi himself returns to the theme with which he began the *Masnavi* some 4,000 couplets ago, namely the severance from our true home in God.

3952. *comes back to his own city*: Rumi gives one of the most articulate expressions of this theme in a famous passage from IV.3629–57 (N, ll. 3628–56).

3958. *of noble stock*: An attempt to translate a complex phrase that refers to the ethical, social and spiritual ideal of *futuwwah*, 'chivalry', 'young-manliness'. See *EI*, 'Futuwwa'.

3959. *To me . . . roses*: This is, as Nicholson points out, adapted from an Arabic couplet attributed to Ali: 'The sword and dagger are our sweet basil: fie on the narcissus and myrtle!' (*NC*, p. 224). My 'bed of roses' is poetic licence for the unmetrical 'bed of narcissi'.

3963. preceding heading. *The World Is a Corpse*: Quotes from a hadith: 'The world is a corpse and those who seek it are dogs.' Nicholson quotes another tradition, attributed to Ali: 'Worldly wealth is a carcase: if anyone desire aught thereof, let him not complain of having to mix with dogs' (*NC*, p. 224).

3966–9. *And beautified ... his sake*: Refers to the Prophet Mohammed's experience of ascension alluded to in Quran 53.1–18 and the night journey of 17.1 from the Holy Mosque (at Mecca) to the Further Mosque (at Jerusalem) in which he was shown ultimate truths of heaven.

3968. *We cannot ... sent*: Paraphrases a hadith: 'I have with God a moment in which none of the archangels and prophets that have been sent can rival me.' In Rumi's version, the pronoun *We* denotes the state of mystical union with God already attained.

3969. *eye roved ... ravens*: Refers to Quran 53.17: 'Indeed he saw him another time by the Lote-Tree if the Boundary nigh which is the Garden of the Refuge, where there covered the Lote-Tree that which covered; his eye swerved not, nor swept astray. Indeed he saw one of the greatest signs of his Lord' (trans. Arberry). 'Ravens' refers to those who, like carrion birds, pick at the corpse of the world referred to in the heading to this section: this is part of a complex word-play in the couplet which justifies the slight pun in the translation. God is the divine dyer whose colours (attributes) suffuse all creation.

3975. *dust ... horseman*: See 799. Rumi used the imagery of the horseman raising the dust about him in 3690, and develops it more fully in II.1284ff. (N, l. 1280ff.), which may be summarized as follows: The world of phenomena is like dust raised by the wind, the horse is the sensuous eye, and the rider is the light of God, who must train the horse to cure it of its habit to search for grass instead of finding its way through the dust of this world to the truth of the unseen world.

3983–8. *O Jewish people*: Alludes to Quran 62.6–8, where God tells the Prophet Mohammed to remind the Jews that they have betrayed God by denying his revelations in the Torah. Quran 2.94 also says: 'Say: "If God's Abode of the Hereafter is for yourselves alone, to the exclusion of all others, then wish for death if your claim be true!" But they will never wish for death, because of what they did; for God knows the evil-doers. Indeed

you will find they love this life more than other men: more than
the pagans do. Each one of them would love to live a thousand
years. But even if their lives were indeed prolonged, that will
surely not save them from the scourge.'

3988. *Jews paid revenue and tribute*: The implication is that instead
of listening to Mohammed and being true believers, the Jews
rejected chose to be *dhimmis* – i.e. payers of the *jizya* (poll-tax)
and *kharāj* (land-tax) – and accept inferior status as a separate,
tolerated religious community.

3995. *Gabr*: An insulting Muslim name for a Zoroastrian. The 'girdle'
refers to the sacred thread worn around the waist of every faithful
Zoroastrian. Rumi uses the Arabic word *zonnār*, a general term
for a belt or girdle that Christians and Jews are said to have
worn. This disclosure that the 'warrior' was a Zoroastrian gives
the light imagery of 3998–4000 a special significance.

4005. *two morsels have been swallowed*: As Nicholson suggests (*NC*,
p. 225), this is a figurative way of saying that the flow of the
poet's inspiration has temporarily ceased. There was to be a long
interruption (of more than a year) before Rumi composed the
second book of the *Masnavi*.

Index

Numbers refer to specific verses of the translation. Frequently occurring words, e.g. death, God, soul, spirit, are not included.

THE STORY OF PENGUIN CLASSICS

Before 1946 ...'Classics' are mainly the domain of academics and students, without readable editions for everyone else. This all changes when a little-known classicist, E. V. Rieu, presents Penguin founder Allen Lane with the translation of Homer's *Odyssey* that he has been working on and reading to his wife Nelly in his spare time.

1946 *The Odyssey* becomes the first Penguin Classic published, and promptly sells three million copies. Suddenly, classic books are no longer for the privileged few.

1950s Rieu, now series editor, turns to professional writers for the best modern, readable translations, including Dorothy L. Sayers's *Inferno* and Robert Graves's *The Twelve Caesars*, which revives the salacious original.

1960s The Classics are given the distinctive black jackets that have remained a constant throughout the series's various looks. Rieu retires in 1964, hailing the Penguin Classics list as 'the greatest educative force of the 20th century'.

1970s A new generation of translators arrives to swell the Penguin Classics ranks, and the list grows to encompass more philosophy, religion, science, history and politics.

1980s The Penguin American Library joins the Classics stable, with titles such as *The Last of the Mohicans* safeguarded. Penguin Classics now offers the most comprehensive library of world literature available.

1990s The launch of Penguin Audiobooks brings the classics to a listening audience for the first time, and in 1999 the launch of the Penguin Classics website takes them online to a larger global readership than ever before.

The 21st Century Penguin Classics are rejacketed for the first time in nearly twenty years. This world famous series now consists of more than 1300 titles, making the widest range of the best books ever written available to millions – and constantly redefining the meaning of what makes a 'classic'.

The Odyssey continues ...

The best books ever written

PENGUIN ⟨🐧⟩ CLASSICS

SINCE 1946

Find out more at www.penguinclassics.com